More praise for
<u>Intuitive Astrology</u>

"Elizabeth Rose Campbell has done something that I have not seen done before: She has taken the art and science of astrology and wrapped it in a user-friendly gift of intelligence, accessibility, and depth. She has humanized astrology. This beautifully written book reads like a story but teaches anyone a new and contemporary way to use the ancient tool of astrology to help us creatively navigate our way through life."

—ELIZABETH LESSER
Cofounder of Omega Institute and author of *The Seeker's Guide*

"Elizabeth Rose Campbell is a poetic, skilled, and compassionate astrologer, and in *Intuitive Astrology*, she weaves her deep sense of the planetary symbolism into a warmhearted series of stories and images."

—STEVEN FORREST
Author of *The Inner Sky*, *The Changing Sky*, and other astrology books

"Elizabeth Rose Campbell brings the intuitive language of the heavens down to earth for all of us to understand. I loved *Intuitive Astrology*."

—MONA LISA SCHULZ, M.D., PH.D.
Author of *Awakening Intuition*

"An inspiration for anybody who desires to live life to the fullest . . . [*Intuitive Astrology*] is filled with exercises that help readers not only learn the craft of astrology, but also importantly teach them how to apply astrology in their own lives by using the astrology chart as a guide. As an introductory book, *Intuitive Astrology* is a welcome and valuable addition."

—Amanda Owen
President of the Philadelphia Astrology Society
Author of *Lucky Stars*

"Elizabeth Rose Campbell provides the key to a new intimacy with the constellations that accompany us on our journey through time and space. Reading *Intuitive Astrology* we come to know the planets as a benevolent family who instruct, nurture, and advise. This book is a gentle, yet concise tool that will assist each reader with self-understanding and self-compassion. It will also foster a wondrous new sense of *belonging* to the universe."

—Ione
Psychotherapist and author of *Pride of Family,
Four Generations of American Women of Color*, and
This Is a Dream!: A Handbook for Deep Dreamers

"*Intuitive Astrology* is the first book about astrology that truly helped me to understand the basics of astrological chart reading. *Intuitive Astrology* walks the reader through the concepts of the planets, signs, and houses step by careful step."

—Annie Berthold-Bond
Author of *Better Basics for the Home*

Intuitive Astrology

Intuitive
Astrology

Follow Your Best Instincts
to Become Who You Always Intended to Be

Elizabeth Rose Campbell

Ballantine Books ✳ New York

A Ballantine Book
Published by The Random House Ballantine Publishing Group
Copyright © 2003 by Elizabeth Rose Campbell

Grateful acknowledgment is made to the following for permission to reprint previously published material:

Astrolabe, Inc.: Solar font and charts from Solar Fire 5. Reprinted by permission of Astrolabe, Inc.

Christian McEwen: "Homeground" © 2000 by Christian McEwen. Reprinted by permission of the author.

Pantheon Books: excerpt from *Dancing Naked in the Mind Field* by Kary Mullis. Copyright © 1998 by Kary Mullis. Used by permission of Pantheon Books, a division of Random House, Inc.

Charles E. Tuttle Co., Inc.: excerpt from *Rhythm of Compassion* by Gail Straub. Reprinted by permission of Charles E. Tuttle Co., Inc., Boston, Massachusetts, and Tokyo, Japan.

University of North Carolina Press: excerpt from *Mama Dip's Kitchen* by Mildred Council. Copyright © 1999 by the University of North Carolina Press. Used by permission of the publisher and author.

www.ballantinebooks.com

Library of Congress Cataloging-in-Publication Data
Campbell, Elizabeth Rose.
    Intuitive astrology : follow your best instincts to become who you always
intended to be / Elizabeth Rose Campbell.— 1st ed.
        p.   cm.
    1. Astrology.   2. Self-actualization (Psychology)—Miscellanea.
3. Intuition—Miscellanea.   I. Title.
BF1729.S38 C35 2003
133.5—dc21
                                                                          2002034465

ISBN 0-345-43710-1

Book design by Jaime Putorti

Cover design by Beck Stvan
Cover photograph © Reza Estakhrian/Getty Images

Manufactured in the United States of America

First Edition: June 2003

10 9 8 7 6 5 4 3 2 1

This book is dedicated to my mother and father,
who grew good things.

Contents

Intuitive Astrology

Your Birthchart:
Catalyst to Creativity

D o you want to explore your creative potential? For seventeen years, I have been using astrology to encourage people to do just that, employing their birthchart as a catalyst to creativity. With this book, I would like to share what I've learned as an astrologer who loves people more than astrology. I believe using the human heart—your own—is the fastest way to learn the symbol system of astrology.

Intuition and heart are deeply related—they both require being receptive to what cannot be proven. I would like to invite you on an adventure into that territory, exploring the symbolism of the planets in your birthchart as they pose certain questions to you. *Who are you? Where are you going?* There are no right or wrong answers to these questions, but I believe each of us is capable of intuiting the best answers for ourselves.

This book is designed to encourage you to appreciate your unique talents through the lens of astrology, with the goal of sharing those talents and enriching the community around you. I will directly assist you in the development of your intuitive skills, in order to explore your story from within, as well as give you sound information about the basic symbolism of planets, signs, and houses—the three components of astrology.

I've grounded that information in true stories and true voices—people like you who speak for themselves about their life paths. Empathizing with these stories will allow you to intuitively connect with the ways in which each of us expresses a planet and its purpose through our own life. The common denominator among these people is that they are living lives of passion and meaning, at times consulting astrology as a cross-referencing tool to enhance their inner voice of guidance. They are all good gardeners, in a sense, growing good things, which they inevitably want to share with their communities, large and small.

The question I want to ask you as you read this book is: *What am I meant to grow?* The journal exercises in each chapter are designed to help you explore that question in a personal and meaningful way.

But before we embark on that adventure, I would like to describe my own beginnings, so that you can understand the ground from which I grew and how I came to be a practitioner of intuitive astrology.

The Ground from Which I Grew

My introduction to the creative life was through food. *Who made this?* I wanted to know, as the plump sweetness of a perfectly ripened strawberry exploded in my mouth at the age of two. Had it come from my father, who planted the garden? Or from the earth, the sun, the rain? There was no clear answer to these questions, but at that early age I decided we were all here to grow things, and the earth itself—nature—was the master teacher.

My broader introduction to the creative life was through my family, all of whom, like the earth, grew things. They were colorful characters at the heart of a village filled with people who, like us, were second- or third-generation villagers.

There were twelve square blocks in our southern town, four churches, and one synagogue. Church was both entertainment and glue for the community. The community cared for its own, and this lifestyle had gone on for generations, a bedrock beneath us; it was also creative, as love in motion, responding when you lost your health, spouse, money, or laugh. Our town was the center of the universe, a solar system unto itself, a careful structure of checks and balances, cohesive and whole.

Extended-family households were more common than not, with several generations often living in one home. In our case, my grandparents' house was separated from ours by a few thousand feet. From my bedroom, if the window was open, I could hear my grandmother sneeze on her back porch.

Everyone grew something he was called to create. My grandfather grew vegetables, fruit trees, pecan trees, figs, pomegranates, and grapes. My grandmother grew roses, moonflowers, irises, gardenias, and camellias. My father grew compost, piles and piles of compost, for his own roses and our vegetable garden. My mother grew stories; she memorized who said what to whom and why. She grew photograph albums, which celebrated every chapter of our lives, every visitor and occasion. My sister grew networks of people. She joined clubs or grew new clubs—church clubs, school clubs, exchange-group clubs.

I grew things too: raised dogs as if they were my children; cared for my horse. And, like my mother, I grew stories—but, unlike her, I didn't speak them; I wrote them down in my journal, which was always hidden. It was my means of digesting life and had been since I was eight, a private conversation in which I described everything that happened, including the best of family stories told around the dining-room table after Sunday dinner— tall tales, silly stories, sad stories, poignant and true stories. The power of storytelling was real and yet taken for granted in their conversations. I was a deep listener, and in my journal I would record what they had said and my response to it.

Through journaling, I began to explore the power of perception, to understand that we each have a story uniquely our own. Each of us writes the script for our potential, by virtue of the way we describe our stories to ourselves.

In 1961, at the age of nine, I thought that I would grow up to live, perhaps, on the next hill over, growing my own garden and family. I would not have believed then that by the age of thirty-three I would have married and divorced, moved north, and become a storyteller for a somewhat larger family: the solar system itself.

I'd never heard of an astrologer and I'd never been north. Yankees were people who drove too fast and crashed their cars on the bypass; astrology was something on the cartoon page of the newspaper that uneducated people read—astrology thumbed its nose in the face of God.

Although there was no reason to leave home, I loved travel. With every trip away from the center of my known universe— whether on my horse, exploring nearby farmlands, or later, when I went to college—my journal exploded with growth. The stories came thicker and faster, and through them I reinvented the script of possibility and my own language.

I loved inner travel as much as outer. I remembered my dreams in detail every night and was compelled to write them down. Symbolic language thus introduced itself to me naturally. As a consequence, symbols seemed sacred, yet practical, by link-

ing my inner and outer worlds. I realized there was a unity between my dreams of flying far from home and the faith I felt in
consciousness—a living universe that was everywhere.

It was my father who first pointed to a starlit sky, one night
when we were lying in the hammock together, long before I left
home, and said, "How can you look at the stars and not *know*
there is a divine plan?"

And it was my father's unexpected departure that became
the catalyst for leaving the deep roots of my beginnings. The
summer day he left us, he was fifty-eight and I was nineteen, and
had been sitting with him, my mother, and my sister, enjoying a
leisurely lunch. When his soup spoon suddenly clattered to the
floor, we looked up from our bowls to see that his head had
dropped, as if he had fallen into a deep sleep at the table. The
heart attack was a gentle death for him; for the rest of us—my
mother, my sister, and me—it was like being blasted out of a can-
non into a new chapter none of us expected. In an instant, as
he died, I turned into someone else. My father's death was a major loss, as if an anchor were gone. Yet none of us drifted. We
expanded.

After college and travels in Europe, I went to work for a small
magazine in Chapel Hill, North Carolina, where I found my voice
as a writer. My sense of belonging had shifted from a sleepy turn-
of-the-century village to a more cosmopolitan culture. My interest in the sacred had grown too, and I voraciously read every
esoteric tradition I could find, as well as a mass of contemporary
literature, from poetry to fiction.

Yet six years after my father's death, I needed a new way to
make sense of it—or, more accurately, of my relationships with
men. I wanted help. Someone suggested a reading with astrologer
Steve Forrest and I made an appointment.

A First Step into Astrology

The experience of that first reading was like waking from a trance. Twenty years of journal keeping and two years of therapy had not done that. I recognized myself, and my best instincts, in the story he told of my potential. That potential is laid out in a birthchart, a map of the planetary positions at the precise time you were born. These planets embody particular instincts that, taken together, outline a life script—an assignment to explore a meaningful life through particular purposes. The birthchart is an index to those purposes. An astrologer can describe our assignment, but it is up to each of us to develop that potential in our own unique way.

I began to study with Forrest and learned that there are two types of astrology: *evolutionary astrology* and *predictive astrology*. Predictive astrology emphasizes predestination and fate, rather than free will; it assumes certain outcomes. If one asks, "When will I meet the person I will marry?" a predictive astrologer will venture a definitive answer.

Evolutionary astrology presumes that we are not preprogrammed for a specific fate or destiny but that the planets in our birthchart outline questions we will spend a lifetime answering so it is helpful to clarify the questions and consider our choices in answering them. For this reason, evolutionary astrology is also often called "choice-centered astrology." Astrologers help clarify the questions and consider choices in responding to them. Evolutionary astrology can be predictive but only in an archetypal sense, with the birthchart as a blueprint of open-ended potential.

What predictive and evolutionary astrology have in common is some agreement about what the symbols suggest, as well as the mathematics of astrology (which is precise data, involving careful calculations of where the planets are when you are born or at any point in time). What one does with that information is a different story. A predictive astrologer might say, "You are going to become a teacher of great renown." An evolutionary astrologer might ask, "What kind of role model would you most like to be?" Both predictive and evolutionary astrology can make good suggestions about *timing* life changes to optimize a certain outcome, but the evolutionary approach affirms that the actual moves needed to create that outcome are yours alone to make. Predictive astrology sees the planets and the symbolism around them as static and separate somehow from the spirit that animates each of us.

Evolutionary astrology places responsibility on the individual, acknowledging the vast creativity within each of us to respond to the questions the birthchart poses. It suggests that we are able to partner with the unknown and dance with it, welcoming life experience as meaningful and symbolic—whether we get what we want or not. The planets help clarify our life questions; with our responses, we script our lives.

In my classes, I studied not only my own chart but the charts of the people I knew best. In every case the reality of their lives dovetailed with the planetary symbolisms in their charts. Even a quick glance at the Sun sign would show that its qualities matched the qualities of the people I knew: My father was a Cancer and was extremely nurturing; my mother was a Scorpio and threw herself at life with a passion. As I studied the charts of family members, my compassion for them grew; I could see both the beauty and the struggle of their lives based on their birthcharts. It was much easier to trust their paths and let go of expectations that they be more like me. That was liberating.

The planets of our solar system were a family too, I realized—the larger family with thousands of years of symbolism and story, from every civilization and culture, wrapped around each body.

As I began to study planetary configurations, I had the distinct impression that each planet was talking to me. Each was a story-teller that spoke with a slightly different accent and tone in each birthchart. Each person was a filter for a cosmic play, bringing that play to Earth in a fresh way, to ground it in a new time. These voices of the planets (described in chapter 2) were able to transport me to inner and outer places, much as the stories of my parents and grandparents had. Story had mysteriously crossed the lines of first family to cosmic family. And the planets, just like the villagers in my hometown, were purposeful characters with a private side but always connected to the larger community, part of the universal story.

I began to suspect that the planets carried the same be-nevolent intentions that the church of my childhood did in its efforts to care for the community. If the birthchart suggested that one area of life would be difficult, other planets in the chart seemed to create strategies of support and balance. This was a master plan, a careful system of checks and balances, cohesive and whole, on an extraordinary scale. I began to see the stars as an insurance policy given to us by Divinity: If you lose your way, look up. The map is there.

By 1980, my immersion in evolutionary astrology was total. By 1985, I'd started a private practice. By 1988, it was my sole source of income and I had a waiting list for new clients. But while at-tracting clients was not difficult, publicly claiming the role of astrologer was.

Again and again I had to explain, no, I did not write horo-scopes for the newspaper. Those columns are a superficial use of the most obvious symbol in astrology, the Sun. Horoscopes are good for entertainment value but a chart cast for date, time, and location of birth describes the gift of individuality and perceives *every* planet as informative. I would go on to explain that astrology at its best is an open-ended symbol system, capable of encompassing every experience yet shifting like a kaleidoscope in terms of what it reveals as the interpreter grows more skilled at seeing the patterns within the whole design and the beauty of the larger image.

Of course, there is a danger of identifying too heavily with a map, any map, as if it were the source of experience. To acknowledge that danger, I have always reminded every client that the deepest level of identity is mysterious and sacred; some call it the soul. That same unique spark or spirit that enters the body at birth also slips into the life script represented by the birthchart and begins to bring it to life, in a way unique to you.

Your birthchart is no definition of identity but rather an index to your identity. For example, if six people were born simultaneously in the same place, on the same date, at the same time, they would have identical charts, but their lives would be as different as six people who buy the same model new car and drive off in six different directions. The car is the same; the driver is different. That is why *no astrologer can tell you who you are.* Astrologers can only offer an interpretation of your life at the level of their own understanding, and in readings may inadvertently be talking about themselves through your story, thereby distorting it. *You* will animate the script much more skillfully, because it is yours and matches your nature.

Intuitive astrology stands on the shoulders of evolutionary astrology and shares the same assumptions but aligns choice with a specific skill: intuition. This book evolved out of my studies and practice of evolutionary astrology and my development of intuitive methods for exploring our life scripts. The foundations of intuitive astrology can be described as follows:

Basic Tenets of Intuitive Astrology

1. The question we each bring to astrology is *Who am I?* Intuitive astrology assumes that the deepest source of identity is spirit. This spirit is sacred and operates day-to-day through intuition.

2. The birthchart is a map of the planets at the precise time you were born, and these planets embody particular instincts.

3. The planetary instincts reflected in a birthchart synthesize into a life script—an assignment to explore a meaningful life through specific roles.

4. Intuition is your best ally in exploring the fulfillment of your life script.

However, you do not need to learn astrology in order to thrive and grow into your gifts. The planets are in perfect synchronization with your own best instincts. Your intuitive guidance system and instincts are always in place, independent of any symbol system. Then why learn astrology?

Reasons to Explore Your Birthchart

1. Your birthchart will be an affirmation of who you already know yourself to be. It is an opportunity to deepen self-trust.

2. Knowing your birthchart provides the synchronistic connection between yourself and the larger world—the cosmos. As you explore this connection, it becomes easier to take responsibility for your actions while simultaneously ac-

knowledging that you cannot control the cosmos. You learn not to take unexpected or difficult events so personally, as there are forces beyond your control within the unfolding archetypal story we all share.

3. No astrologer can interpret your birthchart for you as accurately as you can (though they can skillfully point the way). For that reason alone, learning your birthchart is well worth the time involved. As you study it, your intuition will take over, using the information in your chart to point out possibilities in your life. The symbols are alive and grow with you; they are not static.

4. Learning your birthchart gives you access to a cosmic database—a wellspring of creativity encouraging you to trust your potential completely and to love who you are in the present as well.

Many people practice intuitive astrology without calling it that. They may know a little astrology or a lot, but they use their birthcharts as a mirror rather than a crystal ball. As their self-awareness grows, the chart reveals new information. They understand that the future changes with every thought they think and every attitude of the heart they hold. They understand both their own role in manifesting their dreams and their partnership with the unknown. They recognize that their life stories mirror the themes of their birthcharts, affirming a marvelous and mysterious exchange between inner space and outer space.

Nearly twenty years of close work with such people gives me a deeper appreciation of the word *archetype* and how it originates in the personal. In my childhood dreams, I often found myself with a group of dreamers and we all knew the same thing at the same time: *We were having a dream together as one.* In them I was aware of being both the small "I" and part of a gigantic "we."

In the tedious world of time, I believe I am living out the minutiae of many of these group dreams through work with my clients. Many of their best creative ideas are part of an archetypal dream that first surfaced on the dream level. As their ally, I realize the trick is to encourage them to let go of expecting the dream to manifest perfectly. I am to support them to give that dream their best shot, on a scale practical to their resources and energy.

More specifically, I am able to support them with information about optimal times to move forward in manifesting their dreams, by translating current astrological cycles as they interface with that person's birthchart.

Knowing your cosmic clock—which seasons and cycles you occupy at any point in time—is a dramatically powerful decision-making tool. These cycles are invitations to grow in new ways, exploring an evolving identity. Though one's response to the invitation is open-ended, what is certain is the timing of the cosmic clock. Planetary orbits, called *transits*, can be calculated by computer down to the minute and second. In these transits certain instincts rise to the fore and invite you to grow. As you respond, you play a vital role in shaping your own future. What transpires is always a natural, organic extension of your life and choices. This topic is deserving of a second book all its own (see the resources guide for recommended texts).

Supporting the archetypal projects of my clients requires an exploration of unfolding events as relevant and meaningful, no matter what happens. Whether the event is welcome or not, I noticed it *always* matches in some way the symbolism of the chart and its cycles. My task is to strengthen faith in the unity of inner and outer events, deepen appreciation for the remarkable synchronicity at play, and strengthen the creativity and self-trust of the player involved.

This is what I hope *Intuitive Astrology* will do for you: help you locate the dreams you are carrying, as well as provide a natural strategy for building the launching pad for those dreams. Where is the discipline to do it? Your birthchart can remind you where and how. Once you are upon that path, I can guarantee you that a rich and expansive story will be whispered in your ear: *When you follow your best instincts, you follow the stars, that want you to grow.*

How to Use This Book as Catalyst to Your Own Creativity

First of all, engage a sense of fun. Creativity is love in motion, life in motion. You are about to explore your inner community of selves in charge of both life and love, congratulate them if they are awake and active, and jog them into service if they are not.

Get a copy of your birthchart. You can get one within minutes at no charge from a variety of Web sites (see resources guide). If you do not have access to the Internet, you can order a chart by phone for a few dollars and get it the same day from any of dozens of astrological services (see the resources guide). In either case, you will need to provide your time of birth, the city of birth, and, of course, the date. [Note: If you do not know the exact time you were born, simply provide the date. When you get the chart, explore the planets in signs but ignore the houses, which are dependent upon knowing the birth time; chapter 3 will explain why.] Even without your birthchart in hand, you can still read this book as preparation for study or for sheer entertainment.

A journal will be invaluable in helping you remember the images and associations that come up as you read about yourself through the symbols. There is a witness within you, with deep memories and intuitive ability—active or latent. That witness will be your best friend in utilizing this book.

The exercises at the end of most chapters will help your witness connect—planet by planet, sign by sign, house by house—with the richness of the story you live. These exercises are optional but will serve you well, focusing the content your astrological mirror can reveal.

If you become overworked or overwhelmed by the new information, please remember that the exercises are optional. You may even want to skip ahead to chapter 6, to enjoy the life stories of the twelve people who serve as illustrations for this book. In their stories, they unknowingly voice their birthcharts and demonstrate in a rich and enjoyable way how astrology works in real life. If you are a beginner in astrology, you might use these stories as an accessible and entertaining introduction before going back to earlier chapters to polish your technical knowledge.

If you are an expert in astrology, these stories will enrich your understanding of the surprising ways in which each individual can bring an astrological script to life, often belying the formula that predictive astrologers would offer.

We could call many of these people practical mystics—people with dreams who have found the practical skills to manifest them. They have agreed to participate in this book to celebrate the synchronicity between their life paths and their astrological mirrors and to encourage you to explore your own.

You will begin to do that by first owning your intuitive skills. I encourage you in chapter 1, "Source: The Sea of Intuition," by describing the evolution of my life as an intuitive, suggesting that the source of intuition comes from a flow of wisdom larger than any one person or purpose. The chapter ends with suggestions on how to identify and develop your own intuitive skills.

Chapter 2, "The Planets: Your Best Instincts," introduces planets as individual "instincts"—servants or channels to this great flow of intuition. Journal exercises will help you identify your instincts through your planets.

Chapter 3, "How to Read Your Birthchart," will help you understand what signs and houses are and how to begin to visually identify planets in relationship to signs and houses in your birthchart.

Chapters 4 and 5 will deepen your understanding of the planets as they operate in signs and houses. You will begin to understand how a planet in a sign and house can play out in the lives of real people who reveal themselves in this section of the book. With your birthchart in hand, you can use the exercises at the end of these chapters to begin to immediately recognize your life script and its deeper dimensions. Every planet in every sign and house is translated briefly to help you along.

Chapter 6, "Twelve People Who Have Followed Their Best Instincts," powerfully synthesizes into a whole most of the people you have glimpsed in previous chapters. Formerly, you met them in truncated fashion, planet by planet, sign by sign, house by house. Now, in their own words, each person tells you his or her own story, expressing a symphony of purposes. You will meet twelve radically different people, from a human rights activist who negotiates the release of political prisoners to a pioneer publisher who has popularized herbal medicine globally, as well as many others. These five men and seven women range in age from forty-five to eighty-eight. Most are Americans, though you'll meet a German-born composer, a Scottish writer, and a Dutch scientist. Some are married, others are single or divorced; some are straight, some are gay. What they have in common is the ability to patiently manifest a vision and, as a consequence, to enrich their communities.

Their birthcharts appear with a shorthand translation of each planet in their charts, to further illustrate what you have learned thus far—and, more important, the larger unifying spirit that brings each birthchart to life in a unique way.

Chapter 7, "The Aspects: Basic Syntax in the Language of Astrology" will help you understand the symbolic meaning behind the actual angles the planets form to one another in a birthchart, how that translates through the lives of the twelve people you just met, and how it might translate through your own chart.

Chapter 8, "Putting It All Together to Ground Your Dreams," encourages you to make the reality of your life the foreground and astrology the background, as you identify your dream, from the power of the present. Twelve short exercises are given to support your manifestation of that dream, as you befriend time, to patiently manifest a vision—to grow something good.

As your guide, I have only one wish—that you recognize you are part of a larger plan. Your best instincts are always based in truth. Nature embodies that truth, and the solar system is nature in motion, carrying that truth. Knowing your birthchart is a catalyst to creativity, encouraging you to become who you always intended to be.

CHAPTER 1

Source:
The Sea of Intuition

The sacred is the emotional force
which connects the parts to the whole.

—AUTHOR UNKNOWN

So profoundly does the ocean affect those who live near it that
it follows them forever. I couldn't have been more than a few
years old the first time I saw the ocean and went crazy with ecstasy, racing back and forth on the beach, splashing in the shal-
lows. That ecstasy arrived every summer with our return to the
ocean, to the same stretch of beach along the South Carolina
coast, the town where great-grandparents were buried and their
offspring still lived. It was a homecoming for my grandparents,
but as I got older I began to understand it more clearly as a different sort of homecoming all my own. When I swam in the ocean, a
strange thing happened: My sense of self dissolved and then
resurfaced, bigger and emptier, but definitely better. I let go of
who I thought I was and then remembered who I really was. It
was as simple as that.

This phenomenon came into focus completely the summer I

was ten. It was June, and though the sun was hot, the water was cold. I got used to the temperature of the water, moving farther and farther into the breakers. Beyond the breakers, with the water up to my chest, and my feet resting lightly on the ocean floor, my arms floated on either side; I turned my face to the sun and out to sea.

As I did this, I forgot my life story—age, gender, family, everything. As it evaporated, a deep happiness came over me and I lost gravity slightly, the salt water making my body buoyant and lighter, part of the sea. A self returned that knew its own nature, something without boundaries but focused in me. I was both empty and full.

I turned back to watch my grandfather and father fishing down the strand from where I floated in the sea. I could see the bucket of bait and my grandfather's black Labrador sitting on her haunches next to him. I watched my mother and grandmother and sister and cousins in their folding chairs on the beach, reading and laughing. A straw sun hat caught in the wind and blew down the beach. I watched them all and knew we belonged to one another, but for all the pull and strength of that belonging, I belonged even more to this larger self, this knowing, this inner atmosphere, which felt like an invisible companion with answers to questions I had not yet asked. It did not require that I do anything at all but witness it. As I did, it grew stronger, as if to say: Call upon me, anytime.

These spells of knowing that began in the sea informed me of my own deeper nature in a way nothing else could. They taught me about being in the flow. Eventually, I could find this knowing, this flow, anywhere, but it came most easily when I was around a body of water, whether a small creek or a filled bathtub. Water triggered this ability to forget myself and to return to some essential state that was both empty and full. That space allowed me to understand interrelationship, the exchange of energies between everything. And though I could not know enough to predict the outcome of these exchanges, I could feel their potential, as if they were part of my sea. It was like an extra natural sense, in addition to smell and taste. Much later, I would learn that there was a word for this: *intuition*.

This extra sense, this intuition, was an inner eye capable of accurately relating parts to a whole. Intuition originated in the heart, not the head. It offered no guarantees, no certain facts, but rather a knowing whose confidence was based upon its capacity to flow—flowing along a pathway with no falsehood in it at all.

Everyone is intuitive. Each of us has his or her own flow, depending on our focus. You may pick up totally different worlds of information from what your spouse or best friend may tune in to.

Each of us has a different method of letting go of who we think we are and remember ourselves as being. Music was my grandfather's sea of self-forgetting. Stravinsky or Strauss did for him what the ocean did for me. He'd listen to "The Blue Danube" and fall into a light sleep after dinner, and when he woke up, he'd often announce an intention: "Think I better cover those young tomatoes, we could have a cold snap tonight." His intuition and hunches were about planting and pruning and weather.

By my teens, I felt at least two rivers of intuition operating for me. The first was personal and based on what I cared most deeply about: my horse, my dogs, my family, my friends. The second was impersonal, as if my personal resonance had merged with a larger one and, as a consequence, I received impressions I hadn't asked for but were simply there. Both rivers of intuition required that I occupy a soft uncertainty—*a not knowing*—through which the knowing could come. Sometimes it arrived spontaneously, out of nowhere, when I was far from any thought related to the information that came.

For example, as I woke up one morning around age thirteen, I suddenly knew that my dog was down the hill behind our home barking at a poisonous snake that would bite her if I did not intervene. I didn't even put on shoes or stop to wonder if the impression was right. I leapt from my bed, raced down the hill barefoot in my pajamas, and there was my little terrier, barking fiercely at a snake coiled to strike. I called her to me in my most commanding voice, my heart pounding as she snapped at the snake. She didn't come, and I grabbed her from behind and carried her back up the hill to the house, leaving the snake to retreat on its own.

Most instances of intuitive flow around my personal life were far less dramatic but instead involved impressions about the soul of things, what was going on emotionally with this person or that. I also began to play with the idea of asking myself—or this deeper self—questions that could be answered yes or no. I found, however, that the intuitive force didn't care so much about mundanities, like whether I should go to the movies with my friends or stay home, but surged with knowing when I asked about deeper assumptions. Is there more than physical reality? *Yes.* Am I right that spirit is everywhere? *Yes.* Will I ever be comfortable being visible to other people in my full sensitivity? *Yes.* Will I ever find a way to thrive in the world, using my sensitivity as my strength? *Yes.*

Some intuitive promptings seemed impersonal, beyond the range of my own experience. These seemed to provide friendly guidance, drawing me, for instance, to a book or a movie—the two great doorways for me into the larger world during the 1960s—without explanation. It was as if someone had placed a cue card there for me—encouragement to step into an archetypal schoolroom that was connected to a larger story.

For example, when I was eleven I went to a yard sale and for no apparent reason, opened the bottom drawer of a desk that was for sale. In it I found a book about Edgar Cayce, someone I'd never heard of. He was in fact famous as the "sleeping prophet," whose extraordinary intuitions enabled him to diagnose diseases and offer detailed information about healing foods and treatments for people who came to consult him. His method of letting go of who he thought he was, was literally to fall asleep—during which time a deeper self surfaced from his psyche. I found Cayce's life story at a pivotal time, for it reinforced my own intuition that these inner knowings come through recognizing a resonance, a sense of connection to something. Intuition can guide you to make choices.

I began to recognize two styles of flow: One was this larger sea that required dissolving identity, being totally empty. Intuition originated there. From that flow came a second: specific urges or instincts to explore, to act, to do. These instincts were servants to intuition. *They directed the intuitive flow; gave it focus and form.*

The Twelve Instincts

Life experience develops one's instincts. We act on the knowing through our instincts—we become a living story. And each individual story includes these twelve instincts:

1. The instinct to shine in your life, from a true center
2. The instinct to have a home
3. The instinct to communicate
4. The instinct to love
5. The instinct to act

6. The instinct to philosophize, to sum it all up

7. The instinct to commit

8. The instinct to heal

9. The instinct to express truth

10. The instinct to express soul

11. The instinct to express power

12. The instinct to gaze at your past and your future

As an astrologer, I saw these same instincts beautifully embodied in the planets. We will explore them in the next chapter.

To Encourage the Intuitive Flow in You...

The following exercise will strengthen your intuitive flow. Keep in mind that it is through your beliefs that you create the open doorway through which experience comes. If you do not believe you are intuitive, it is difficult for the flow to give you guidance. It's like having the radio on with the volume turned off. Use the following exercise to help you turn the volume up.

Prepare: Set aside at least ten minutes to sit in a quiet room where you will not be disturbed. Sit comfortably and breathe deeply for a few moments. Think of your responsibilities and visualize them as a hat you are wearing. Now remove the hat. If you feel you are wearing a mask, that you have to be someone in particular—someone who answers the phone when it rings, or someone who must make dinner later, or someone who must be in control of what comes next—just take off the mask. Set it aside. Take a deep breath.

Imagine: You are at a scene, past or present, in which you are relaxed and aware. There are no obstacles, no sorrows in this moment. It is a scene in which a deep happiness prevails that is not dependent upon anyone or anything. Float there with an open heart for several minutes.

Invite: After a few minutes of floating, ask yourself the following series of questions, to deepen your receptivity to the flow. Consider that you are inviting the flow, the source of this sea of intuition, to come near you, to engage with you, every time you open your heart and voice a yes. Even a few yeses will open the way to your own sea of intuition.

Can I imagine a flow of life that is infinite?

Do I believe that this flow is benevolent?

Do I believe that this flow moves through me?

As I feel this flow, does it accept me, just as I am?

Can I accept me, just as I am, in this moment?

As I do, am I able to flow more fully with this sea?

Will this sea take me to my purpose, even though I cannot fully see that purpose?

Am I willing to take off my mask, my hat of responsibility, once or twice a day to occupy this sea?

As a consequence, will I be happier? Healthier? More creative?

Does stepping into this flow benefit not only me but all life?

Accept: The sea of intuition asks that you do nothing but occupy it. This sea communicates knowing through feeling. Here, your sensitivity is your strength.

CHAPTER 2

The Planets:
Your Best Instincts

It is the day of your birth—square one—the true beginning of your life on Earth. You emerge from your mother, draw your first breath, and all of the presences in the room bombard your senses—from family members to the midwife, doctor, or nurse who helped bring you into this world. You engage immediately with the reality of being here. Sounds, smells, sensations surround you.

Welcome to Earth: A Brief
Introduction to the Planets

Your infant body was sensitive not only to the atmosphere of the room, but to the ultimate life giver: the Sun. Imagine the energy of the Sun as it travels at the speed of light, crossing 93 million miles to reach you. Somehow you receive its signature, as well as those of all the planets in the solar system. You have inherited a life code and a cosmic clock from the larger family of the solar system. Like the genetic code you inherited from your family of origin, this code encourages particular styles of growth and instinctual exploration.

Meanwhile, your cosmic clock, following the rhythms of the planets, encourages you to grow, slow down, or speed up at particular times over the rest of your life. The content of what you grow is entirely up to you. Your cosmic family supports that growth through your planetary instincts.

This chapter's purpose is to familiarize you with the symbolic content of the planets, but you can also begin to become visually familiar with the planetary glyphs through the birthchart below. Take a moment, if you like, to look at each planet's glyph and then find it in the sample birthchart shown here (or your own birthchart, if available). With each glyph is a brief introduction to the instinct of the planet it represents. The planets will

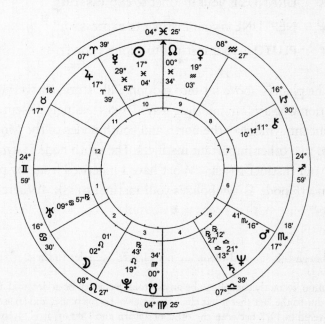

speak their purposes at more length through the rest of this chapter.

⊙ **The SUN** is your instinct to shine from the center of your life story.*

☽ **The MOON** is your instinct to have a home.*

☿ **MERCURY** is your instinct to communicate.

♀ **VENUS** is your instinct to love.

♂ **MARS** is your instinct to act.

♃ **JUPITER** is your instinct to philosophize, to sum it all up.

♄ **SATURN** is your instinct to commit.

⚷ **CHIRON** is your instinct to heal.**

♅ **URANUS** is your instinct to express truth.

♆ **NEPTUNE** is your instinct to express soul.

♇ **PLUTO** is your instinct to express power.

The planets above set into motion a life story, answering the question *Who am I?* in multiple ways. Two seemingly obscure but significant symbols—the north and south nodes of the Moon—reveal two other important instincts. The south node ☋ symbolizes your instinct to ask, "What have I inherited from my past?" The north node ☊ symbolizes your instinct to ask, "Where am I going?"

---

* Although the Sun and Moon are not planets, we refer to them as such in astrology.
** Chiron, formerly thought to be an asteroid, has since been declared a planetoid due to the fact that it has characteristics of both a planet and an asteroid. Discovered in 1977 between the orbit of Saturn and Uranus, it is given equal weight to the planets as an influence by astrologers who study it.

☉ THE SUN:
The instinct to shine from the center of your life story

When you took on the signature of the Sun at the moment of birth, you became an emissary of that Sun. Just as the Sun is the center of the solar system, the Sun's placement in your birthchart symbolizes *the optimal expression of your true center*. It is the guiding light of your story. Visualize a wheel with spokes that meet at the center. Within your inner family, the Sun is the "I" in charge of the entire wheel—the gravitational center of self. As you step outside the privacy of your inner family into your village, the Sun is the shaft of light at the center of the town square where everyone instinctively gathers—a central force pulling everyone together as a community, creating the unique identity of that town.

The Sun's purpose is to convince you that this is the only life you're ever going to have and so you better occupy it fully, play director. No one else can occupy your director's chair for you. The Sun is the functional ego. When you wake from a deep sleep, that conscious waking state you enter every day of your life is your Sun—the constant presence of the "I."

Find the Sun ☉ at work in your life by completing this sentence:

Above all else, I want to _____.

Intuitive assignment:

Now let's explore the same question with the heart, not the head, to encourage the intuitive voice of the Sun to speak to you about how it operates in your life. Take a moment to relax and let go of the shoulds that may enter your mind about what you "should" want. Then imagine the following and note your experiences in your journal.

I am at the center of a wheel with many spokes. At that center, I am the "I" that is my constant waking companion, the "I" that oversees my entire day. Occupying the center of the wheel, I remember the constancy of the Sun, at the center of the solar system. I feel the warmth of that Sun as it encourages me to grow a true center, a true identity to which I can be loyal, as a life path.

Dialogue with this center, as you occupy it, asking: "What is my central purpose today? What is my central purpose on most days?"

Imagine your answer to these questions as a constant fire, the flame at your core. Stand close to the light of the fire. It says to you: *You have a right to exist. You have a right to survive, and thrive. You have a purpose.*

The Sun advises you: Celebrate your center, the precious chord only you can play.

Now ask yourself again:

Above all else, I want to _____.

Your Sun knows the answer to this question.

☽ THE MOON:
The instinct to have a home

The Moon within your inner family is the mother. Just as you grew in your mother's womb before you were born, you continue to survive and thrive throughout your life as a consequence of nourishment; of having a bed to sleep in; food on the table; a family perhaps; a house; a home. Within your cosmic village, the Moon is the cook in your favorite café, the masseuse with healing hands, the therapist who listens and understands.

The Moon's placement in the chart by house, and by sign, will reflect your optimal path of self-nourishment. It may also reflect your approach to mothering yourself, as well as your approach to forming emotional bonds.

When you were still inside your mother, you heard her heartbeat every day for nine months, like a great drum, anchoring you within the rhythm of this world from the inside out. The Moon reflects your heartbeat of happiness—where you are most likely to enjoy emotional richness. Like the emotional rudder of the boat of happiness, the Moon steers you toward experiences that give you easy access to happiness.

The Moon may also be related to unconscious patterns inherited through your family line—the desires and dreams of generations of people, passed on through the heartbeat of the mother. These unconscious patterns simply *are*; they need no judgment unless they sabotage the Sun, the true center of your life path. The purest instinct of the Moon is to know through feeling, to intuit the inner space. The Moon is your instinct to understand and be understood. Home is where you are understood.

Find the Moon ☽ at Work in your life by completing this sentence:

My mood always improves when I (describe an activity): _____.

Intuitive assignment:

Explore the following questions with your heart:

> What activities make me happy on a daily basis?
> If home is where I am understood, who understands me deeply?
> What activities make me happy?
> I see umbilical cords running from me to other people who feel like family, whether they are coworkers, friends, or blood family. What do I have in common with them that

keeps those umbilical cords in place? How do we nourish each other?

The Moon knows your answers to these questions.

☿ MERCURY:
The instinct to communicate

Mercury is your desire to capture and transmit information: It's the messenger, the tape recorder, the camera, the database builder of your life story. Within your inner family, Mercury is the story-teller; within your village, Mercury might be your friendly librarian, aware of your interests, setting aside particular books for you to read. Mercury works through your eyes; your ears; the bottom of your feet; your fingertips; and very much your throat, your tongue, your lips—your ability to speak. Mercury is the synapse between the brain and the tongue. How will you translate your reality? What words will you use?

Mercury is intelligence on a constant reconnaissance mission. For example, imagine 150 people sitting in church all facing the front, listening to the same sermon. The lady in the first row is noticing the color in the stained-glass windows. She is an artist, and her eyes naturally gravitate to nuances of color and light. The man in the second row is watching the lady in the first row and having a sexual fantasy about her. His Mercury tends to sexualize whatever he is focused upon—sex is his favorite story. The preacher is looking at the congregation and seeing people in spiritual need of Jesus, for whom he speaks. He sees everything through the eyes of his Christian training. Each person can see the same scene but focuses quite differently.

Mercury is the intelligent eye, the intelligent ear, focused upon something in particular. Mercury is also communicative touch, communicative cadences—through voice, song, or dancing feet, dancing out a story. Mercury is the messenger.

Find Mercury ☿ at work in your life by completing this sentence:

I naturally communicate perspectives, a point of view about _____.

To further define your Mercury, answer these questions:

What page do I turn to first in the newspaper?

If words are my favored form of communication, what outlet do those words generally take (personal letters, creative writing, conversation, teaching, singing)? Does my Mercury seem more dedicated to a particular topic or focus than any other? (For clues, look at the books and magazines by your bedstand.)

If I frequent libraries, which section do I gravitate toward?

If I am a visual artist, what style do I work in most frequently? Realism? Surrealism? Abstract expressionism? What perceptions within me inspire this style?

If I am a dancer, what rhythm do I most readily move to? What is the message of that rhythm?

If I am a cinematographer, why do I use a particular lens on the camera to trigger the imagination of the viewer? What is it I want them to see?

If I am a masseuse, what strokes create my language of touch? What message do I give through my touch?

Intuitive assignment:

Imagine yourself free to communicate in any way you like—through words, telepathy, touch, images. How would you do it?

Imagine the thought, idea, or emotion that you would most want to communicate—to share with others. What is it?

Your Mercury knows the answers to these questions.

♀ VENUS:
The instinct to love

Venus is the instinct to love as well as the instinct to create beauty, art, and healing. Within your inner family, Venus is where you fall in love with yourself. Then, as a consequence of being in love with yourself, others—the people in your village—fall in love with you too. Venus is where you are a perennial flower—where you will bloom again and again if you express this part of yourself. As a consequence, love flows easily and so do love relationships with other people. Your creative life thrives through Venus. Venus also blesses your health.

Venus is Eros, the very basic recognition that love and creativity are deeply wedded to pleasure. Venus is the feminine principle of pleasure, saying: *Kiss me!* Venus is female fertility. Whether you are male or female, Venus embodies your ability to be gracefully abundant (including financially). Venus's placement in your chart reflects where you are making love to life.

Find Venus ♀ at work in your life by completing this sentence:

I fall in love with life again and again when I _____.

Intuitive assignment:

Imagine yourself saying, "I am in touch with the grace and beauty that flows through me (and this is what it is like). I know that, with ease, the best of me can rise to any occasion (and this is what it is like). I remember the first time I fell in love (and this is what it was like).

"Thinking of someone I love now, who also loves me, I feel the deep pleasure and recognition that we share this love (and this is what it is like).

"I see a scene of great natural beauty—a rose garden, the ocean, a mountain range. I see my presence growing equally beautiful (and this is what it is like).

"I am beauty, grace, and love finding new form (and the form looks like this). This part of me, when given expression, softens the hard edges of even the roughest day."

Venus, your love affair with life, inspires each of these scenes.

♂ MARS:
The instinct to act

Mars says: Claim your courage to act. Mars promotes a clear yes or no. Mars is the sword of the will, the arrow of intention that seeks to carry out a particular plan that will give you energy if you fulfill the plan, and drain your energy if you do not. The purest instinct of Mars is to do. Whereas Venus fertilizes, Mars forges.

Within your inner family, Mars is the high testosterone leader, choosing activities that will give you energy, get-up-and-go. As you live in your village, Mars is the policeman directing traffic with firm gestures at the intersection, signaling stop, turn, and go. Mars is the neighborhood bully who needs to dominate, as well as the skater skillfully weaving around a crowd of people, a clear destination in his mind.

Mars is also in charge of your survival as you discover your wholehearted no. If someone steps on your foot, you say, "Stop!" Without your instinct for self-defense, you cannot survive. Mars rules anger and, as a consequence, your ability to be assertive, to say, "Don't ever do that to me again!"

Mars is the warrior designed to protect and defend your center—your Sun. But Mars is also your wholehearted *yes*, as you recognize what you want and the need to ask for it.

Mars at its most elegant is about living fully and thriving. Mars reflects your will to follow through on your deepest intentions and achieve your goals.

Mars is also directly connected to your libido; what turns you on. This planet's energy gets you quickly to *yes!* Considered to be yang (outer-directed), the glyph for Mars looks much like a phallus; indeed, Mars reflects where you are fertile and ready to seed something in a proactive way.

Mars is will in motion.

Find Mars ♂ *at work in your life by completing this sentence:*

I always have energy to _____.

To further define your Mars, answer these questions:

What drives me?

What turns me on, makes me love life, brings a clear *yes* to my lips?

When I am attracted to someone, what is my strategy of approach? Do I contact this person? Wait to be contacted? Default on the desire? Plant a seed mentally that I will have an opportunity to get to know him or her better?

What makes me mad, brings a clear *no* to my lips? What is my style of combat when I am angry? Am I passive/aggressive? Direct? Explosive? What trips my trigger in anger?

When my energetic gas tank runs low, the thought of doing what particular activity instantly gives me energy?

When my energy is running low, the thought of doing what particular activity exhausts me even more?

Intuitive assignment:

Imagine yourself before birth as an arrow in a bow, about to be launched. With your birth this arrow is released. You soar, you fly, you do not fall. You are free will, and as that free will you are on a mission. What is your target? Your bull's-eye? How does it feel to trust your free will to explore something in particular?

Your Mars knows the answers to these questions.

♃ JUPITER:
The instinct to philosophize, to sum it all up

Jupiter is the ultimate optimist, aware that everything is interconnected. Within your inner family, Jupiter is the student of life in search of the Big Picture. As Jupiter finds it, he sums it all up into a cosmology that becomes an inner map of permission, a formula for renewing faith because you believe.

As you move out into your village, Jupiter is the generous professor eager to share his large library with you. Jupiter is the expansive, funny woman who is wiser than you yet treats you like a peer. She leads trips around the world, has made a lot of contacts, is about to go again, and says "Come on! You come, too! Enjoy my connections with me!"

Jupiter may also be the venture capitalist in your community, the risk-taker making wise bets that produce abundance and the desire to reinvest in that abundance. For that reason, Jupiter is considered to be the ruling planet of capitalism and perpetual economic growth. Jupiter is the biggest, most gravitationally influential planet in the solar system.

Spiritually, Jupiter is the generous *eureka!* experience, an insight that provides the larger context in which to understand your life. This can mean, simply, space in which to grow and contemplate who and where you are. Whenever you look up on a clear day and recognize the ease with which you can think, you are merging with your Jupiter. Details take on a different perspective under that blue sky. We could call this Blue Sky Mind. With Blue Sky Mind, you let details take care of themselves as you recognize the larger context in which they have meaning.

Jupiter also illuminates where the universe supports your growth—not 100 percent, but 200 percent. You may in turn become an expansive coach, helping others grow similarly: a benevolent power, capable of improving the human lot, making the world a better place.

Jupiter's purest instinct is to discover quality rather than quantity while embodying new options and inclusive truth rather than elitist energies. Jupiter is a magnifier of what you've created (both positive and negative), giving you an opportunity to learn lessons, see the obvious, sum it all up, and take risks while the winds are with you.

Find Jupiter ♃ at work in your life by completing this sentence:

I love exploring this area of my life because it gives me a larger perspective on things: _____.

To further define your Jupiter, answer these questions:

What activities have I found that consistently give me appreciation for how much more there is to know—and the joy of discovering each step?

Where do I discover Blue Sky Mind—the ability to remember the larger truths I trust, that do not judge but encourage me to begin again, exactly where I am, with enthusiasm?

Where do I enjoy being the generous educator and ambassador to new possibilities for others?

Intuitive assignment:

Imagine yourself in the company of someone you respect, who sees your potential and beams it back at you in an act of wholehearted faith. How does this feel?

Your Jupiter knows the answers to this question.

♄ SATURN:
The instinct to commit

Saturn is the instinct to commit to growth. Saturn shows up before you are even born, as your skeletal system, the first thing to form in a fetus. The skeletal system gives you the physical support to move around the earth upright. It gives you spine. Likewise, Saturn teaches, step by step, maturity, self-responsibility, the capacity to commit, to develop a support system for yourself. Within your inner family, Saturn is the father figure, the teacher and authority to whom you look for steady, certain support. In your village, Saturn is the 200-year-old tree in the center of the field, complete unto itself. Saturn is the mentor, the grandparent, seasoned with the wisdom of years.

Saturn is in charge of your ability to recognize which decisions no one else can make for you, including where your boundaries are. It is Saturn that teaches you to build boundaries by informing others, *Ask, don't assume (that I am available, that I am who you think*

I am, etc.). Saturn teaches you how to give reality checks to your-self and others.

Saturn also shows up within your inner family as the crippling critic. It tenses at the possibility of imperfection. Saturn in this role can exhaust you and others with its judgments. Yet the same Saturn is capable of being discerning without being judg-mental. Saturn can identify what is off *and* describe how it could be more on—without charging the situation with negative judg-ment. This is Saturn as kind and patient teacher who honors er-rors as learning experiences. Saturn asks: *Did you finish what you started, even if it wasn't perfect?* Goethe spoke for Saturn when he said, "The master first reveals himself in limitation." Saturn is your weakest link, but it is capable of becoming your greatest strength.

Saturn loves clear form; clean boundaries; the ability to define small, realistic steps, one after the other, until the job is done. Wherever Saturn is in the birthchart, it reflects the vow that was upon your lips when you were born: "if I do nothing else, I will make my best effort at *this.*"

Saturn is ultimately the ticktock of the clock saying: *You weren't born to die, but you were born with a deadline.* So get on with it: Build the backbone of a life story that supports you to become who you always intended to be.

Find Saturn ♄ at work in your life by completing this sentence:

I want to mature over time in order to build: _____.

To further define your Saturn, answer these questions:

Where do I excel when I have total control and work hard?
What do I most enjoy organizing in order to "get to work"?

When I look at the stepping-stones of successes and failures in my life, do I see a tradition of trying? In what life arena do those stepping-stones lie? What is the next step on that path, in which I make my best effort and commit to finishing what I start?

Around what area of my life am I most self-critical, most likely to keep a constant scorecard on myself? In what area of life have I been most easily influenced by external authority figures or role models, whether they were benevolent or forbidding?

In what life arena did either of my parents seek to "make their mark" but left the path unfulfilled, silently asking me to fulfill it for them?

In what area of my life do I begin to feel guilty if I don't pay regular attention?

In what area of my life do I have trouble saying no, because I feel indebted to the inner perfectionist who could always do more?

Intuitive assignment:

Imagine that you can make a phone call to an older, wiser version of yourself, one that is the result of you making the best choices all along your life path. This more seasoned self can give you important information about how to learn all you can from where you are in your limitation and struggle. Speak with this self now. What good advice do you hear?

Your Saturn knows the answers to this question.

⚷ CHIRON:
The instinct to heal

Chiron is the instinct to heal, to shift out of wounding assumptions and partial insight into wisdom. Within your inner family, Chiron is the healer who sees what is possible if you are given the room to explore it with no constraints. Within your village, Chiron is the doctor, the medicine man or woman who understands the difference between being a healer and being a rescuer.

The shadow side of Chiron is the rescuer who sabotages true healing by imposing a cure on someone without knowing what he or she really needs, acting out of his own need to "fix." This rescuer aspect of Chiron's shadow may also take on the wounds of the person he tried to rescue.

The healer Chiron has the ability to link the physical dimension (including the health of the body) with the metaphysical (where miracles can occur in the twinkling of an eye). This link cannot occur on command but by invoking, inviting, and allowing it the possibility to form. Chiron's position in your birthchart can indicate where you have a God-given gift or magic touch. This might not be in an area of healing. Chiron helps you discover your gift for turning things around when facing challenges of all kinds. It could be the ingenious solution to repairing a greasy motor that refused to work before.

Frequently called "the key of connection," the gifts of Chiron come when you give up and stop looking for the key. Notice that the glyph for Chiron looks very much like the key to a door. A key is a very small thing, yet it unlocks a door and allows passage through the wall. Keys are easily lost, too, though walls tend to stay put and continue blocking the way. The wounded side of Chiron can indeed be much like a wall. Chiron symbolizes both the wall *and* the key.

Chiron works well when you adopt an attitude of allowing the blockage or limited area of your life to inform you before it heals so that you *can* heal, rather than simply eliminating the symptom. In this way it is much like homeopathic medicine, presuming the inner healer will ultimately know what to do. It is more inclined to withhold its healing gifts if you rush to fix, repair, or rescue at all costs.

Chiron may also point to an area of your life in which you experience reversals—not necessarily painful but, rather, situations in which you realize you are not going where you intended. For example, you go to an artists' colony to write a novel and produce a film instead. Training you to trust options is a common way in which Chiron helps you develop a new bridge to the sacred. Chiron trains us to become initiators into higher levels of consciousness without faking a single step.

Find Chiron ⚷ at work in your life by completing this sentence:

I most want to be a healer in this area of my life: _____.

To further define your Chiron, answer the following questions:

Where am I discovering that I am truly connected, capable of breaking the glass ceiling, and raising the vibration?

Where in my life have I felt like a crippled giant, walking around on my knees, who suddenly discovered the cosmic joke: There is nothing wrong with my legs?

In recalling a new learning experience, I remember my frustration and the moment when the connection amazingly offered itself to me. Where has this new skill taken me, allowing me to serve as a "missing link" in a situation capable of serving a higher order, a more inspired vision, than before?

When have I realized that I can stretch, become larger than a limited situation and solve problems from there?

Intuitive assignment:

Imagine that you are met by a centaur, a creature who is half human, half horse. He asks you if you'd like to go for a ride to an interesting place very nearby but outside of time. In this place, you can make miracles in the twinkling of an eye. What miracles would you make?

Your Chiron knows the answers to this question.

♅ URANUS:
The instinct to express truth

Uranus is your truth compass and your freedom to choose changes based on that compass. Uranus is electric individuality and universal truth at the root of your personal uniqueness. Uranus indicates your cutting edge, where you are bushwhacking your way into new behaviors with no scout or role model. Within your inner family, Uranus is the free thinker, the part of you owned by no one. In your village, Uranus is the pioneering entrepreneur or the genius. At times it is the misunderstood genius, precisely because the intelligence of Uranus is far ahead of the crowd.

Uranus is in charge of your authenticity. It rumbles like thunder in the psyche when it catches you giving rote answers about who you are and where you are going. Uranus is that inner voice saying: *What you just said is no longer true about yourself. You've grown. You can't deny it.*

Uranus is ultimately concerned with equal rights for everyone: the freedom of thought, freedom of speech, freedom of expression. Out of that freedom, Uranus encourages you to reinvent yourself on a regular basis to come to know your nature.

The gift of Uranus is the ability to see a larger truth rather than resting in a righteous opinion. Uranus asks: *Do you want to be right, or do you want to be free? Do you want to wake up to the next level of truth?*

Uranus has no interest in protecting the past but great interest in stepping into the shoes of the future self, to experience what is possible there. Uranus is the ongoing awakening behind an authentic life.

Find Uranus ♅ at work in your life by completing this sentence:

I feel most authentic, fresh, and free when I _____.

To further define your Uranus, answer the following questions:

Where am I incapable of being in denial, because my truth compass is so strong in this part of my life?

Where have others noticed that I have a spark of genius, that I can do something that no one else can duplicate exactly?

Where do I most enjoy playing by my own rules?

When I look at my family background, in what arena of my life do I see myself breaking through into new roles that may be foreign or unfamiliar to my family of origin?

What activities naturally lead me into a state of confidence that I am on my true path and am not an impostor?

Intuitive assignment:

Imagine yourself suddenly free of caring what anyone else thinks of you or the choices you make. Imagine that you can, at will, take the next step to do something you've never done before, whatever it might be: painting, singing, having a child on your own, running for public office. How does it feel to contemplate this choice and trust it?

Your Uranus knows the answers to this question.

Ψ NEPTUNE:
The instinct to express soul

Neptune is unconditional love for life. Neptune is where you know that your sensitivity, your capacity to feel, is a strength. The purest instinct of Neptune is to make sacred, to honor the spirit behind form. Neptune sees soul everywhere.

Within your inner family, Neptune is the psychic self and your imagination—imagination being the foot soldier of the soul. The soul is boundless, unlimited by time and mortality. Likewise, your imagination is boundless and can go anywhere. Your imagination forms bridges to possibilities through your beliefs. For example, if you believe you can move to a new location where you know no one and find a job and develop community, you probably can. If you do not believe it, you are unlikely to make even the first step because there is no bridge to this possibility in your imagination.

In your village, Neptune is the inspired artist whose paintings transport you outside of time; the inspired violinist whose music takes you there too. It is the priest, rabbi, or priestess who prays with you to bless the new baby or bury the dead. Neptune is also the bartender at the neighborhood pub, serving you a stiff drink to soften the hard edges of your day.

Neptune is the consciousness junkie, eager to transcend time and the material world through shifts in consciousness. Meditation, music, creative self-expression, all serve to train your dexterity as your spirit explores levels of consciousness and identity beyond the "I."

Addictions to getting high can be a part of the Neptunian education. The instinct to "get high" is the very basic instinct to unmask, to let go of, who you think you are so that you can remember who you are.

When you go to a bar to have a drink, for instance, and the one drink becomes two or three or four, you are enjoying the removal of the hard hat of identity, the Sun, the true center of your life story as a mortal on Earth. Much of the relief of getting high is this sense of reunion with the self behind the mask. However, this can become a detour, a hall of mirrors in which the self dissolves into the mist of the habit—the alcohol or marijuana or watching too much television—or whatever shortcut you choose. Addiction creates a Catch-22 of grief, as you yearn for the soul and separate from it, still further, through the addiction.

The richer instinct of Neptune is simply to dissolve the time barriers to inspiration so that you can experience and express it. Through the sharing of this inspiration, you contribute to the great flow of life, of love. Addictions fall away as you claim the rare and fine rose in your garden of talents, the talent you are meant to grow through a long-term high, choosing a functional path that regularly merges with the great flow of intuition. Neptune is your spiritual heart, who trusts that you know the way.

Neptune's deepest desire is for you to be guided by the soul itself; to get out of your own way and step into the flow, that great sea of intuition that connects us all. Neptune is the cosmic eraser. It dissolves habits, structures, and forms—including addictions, once they have lost their power.

Through Neptune, you can have compassion for your own suffering and others', but you are able to sidestep self-pity. Neptune shows you that the magnificence of the soul is larger than any suffering. Neptune knows that suffering will not last, that the nature of reality is eternal change. Neptune is the inner voice that tells you: *There are only two truths: everything changes, and the only thing that lasts is love.*

Find Neptune Ψ at work in your life by completing this sentence:

> I most easily get out of my own way and allow
> inspiration to flow through me when
> I: _____.

To further define your Neptune, answer the following questions:

When I listen to music that is timeless and it transports me, who do I become? Where do I go? What are the benefits of occupying this place?

Have I ever been blocked in solving a problem, gone to sleep, and dreamt the solution?

When I encounter great beauty as I move through my day—a child's face in a stroller, a tree in bloom in the park, a particular quality of light, purple mountains rising behind a river—who is it within me that slows me down and makes me pause to appreciate this loveliness?

Have I ever had a psychic experience and wondered how I was able to know the truth without any facts? Have I had spiritual contact with a deceased loved one and known with certainty that I was visited? How did this reassure me?

Have I ever had the experience of being in the right place at the right time and acted as an "angel in the street," with no forethought or planning at all? Which part of me instantly agreed to be there?

Have I ever deeply needed help, only to have it appear from out of nowhere—in the form of a person, a phone call, or a silent reassurance from deep within? From where did that reassurance come?

Intuitive assignment:

Imagine that the most loving part of you has always been and always will be. This love is aware of itself but needs no mask. Imagine that every contact you have ever had with love—through your family, animals, or strangers—has merged with the love you already were. Imagine this love as unstoppable and creative, yet one that rides light in the saddle despite its power. Imagine that love appearing to you as a face—a version of your face. This face smiles at you with an ancient tenderness and love deeper than the ocean. What do you feel as you smile back?

Your Neptune knows the answers to this question.

♀ PLUTO:
The instinct to express power

Pluto's role begins with your conception: the sexual fusion of sperm and egg. Pluto knows every secret of the seed of your beginning. For the rest of your life, Pluto signifies the mystery of why you are here. Pluto knows your secret mission, slowly revealing it to you as you die and are reborn again and again. Pluto also reveals your fears about being powerless as well as about being powerful. Ultimately, Pluto educates you about empowerment and purpose.

Wherever Pluto is in your chart, it unveils your potential. It teaches you to claim your power and choose to change, even if you can't control every facet of the outcome. Your Pluto potential has been composting, building for centuries through your genes and ancestry. Now that compost is ripe and ready to fertilize your life, as an old self dies and a new one is born through Pluto. Catharsis is part of the transformation too, as impulsive yet purposeful instincts emerge.

Within your inner family, Pluto is the mission maker, the passionate part of you that wants to make a difference in the world. In your village, Pluto might be the Great Mother, the Powerful Communicator, the Powerful Recycler of Garbage—figurehead identities for people of purpose.

Pluto knows the secret of the seed of you as well as the mystery of your death—and every death/rebirth in between. Sexuality is deeply intertwined with Pluto, because it is through Pluto that you are most fertile not just for your own life but for all life. The sexuality of Pluto can be unfocused and raw, its emphasis on desire and the seductive moves. Pluto's sexuality can also be transcendent, however, such as when the attraction between two people defies explanation and becomes a choiceless choice to explore what has pulled you together, with sexuality the first language of intimacy.

Piggybacking on your own secret mission, through Pluto, is the larger master plan known only by God. When we ask: *Is life meaningful or meaningless?* we are knocking on Pluto's door, asking for information. Pluto is the deeply ingrained collective unconscious and collective mystery within each of us.

Pluto is about learning to manage your power, about which you may be unaware. Your Pluto talent can seem "too much," or "too intense"—overpowering—for a small audience. In a larger forum, your Pluto talent can stretch into its archetypal expression, and when it does, it not only makes your life more meaningful but all the lives that touch yours as well.

Find Pluto ♀ at work in your life by completing this sentence:

> I want to understand and work with
> my own power around _____.

To further define your Pluto, answer the following questions:

When I feel most powerful, what am I doing?

When I feel most powerless, what am I doing?

When control issues come up in my life, what is the context? When I feel the need to control others' perceptions of something, what is the context?

When I feel a drive deeper than desire, a compulsion, what am I being asked to do?

Have I ever taken a trip that was inconvenient but important because of someone I met or something I learned that was unexpected and extremely meaningful? How did this meeting or event link me to a larger purpose or life question that I feel I am spending my life answering?

When have I felt so powerfully sexual with another person that I could think of nothing but him or her? When have I felt deeply connected beyond explanation? How did my life shift as a consequence of that connection?

When have I been at the birth of a child, at the doorway to another world that alerts me to the power behind physical form? When have I witnessed the moment of death, been at the doorway to another world, alerting me to the power behind physical form?

Intuitive assignment:

Imagine that you are a snake, and as that snake you are wise, from living so close to the ground. Yet your power scares people. Others may want to kill you—or your power. How quickly would you strike, if someone tried to kill you?

Your (primal) Pluto knows the answer to this question.

☋ THE SOUTH NODE OF THE MOON:
What have I inherited from the past?

Each of us enters this life with a presence. Ask any new parents about their infant and they will tell you: *This is an old soul.* The south node of the Moon reflects what you have inherited from your ancestors, your ancientness, or both. Within your inner family, the south node of the Moon is your preconditioned actor or actress who already knows the lines to a play and has a full steamer trunk of character traits inherited from the past: your grandmother's talent for dancing, your grandfather's attitude, or your mother's penchant for saving the world. In your village, the south node of the Moon is the town historian who can guide you to the gravestones of your ancestors in the cemetery on the hill, as well as the older villagers who recognize you and say, "You are the spitting image of your great-grandmother."

What have you inherited from the past? Some people believe the only inheritance takes place genetically and through the physical experience of being alive, as parents pass their knowledge on to their children in a hands-on way.

Others believe in the evolution of the soul—individual spiritual growth and change that are beyond the personality but also include it. This belief hinges on the premise that spirit always precedes and survives form—soul is bigger than the body. The body is a husk the soul outgrows. The soul, embodied as a personality, is constantly growing and becoming more aware, and the soul free of the body continues to grow after death.

Some people view the evolution of the soul through the lens of reincarnation, speaking of past lives. Others consider reincarnation to be too simplistic and linear an explanation, yet remain convinced that they are somehow ancient and bring into this life talents and tendencies from another time and place, a more complex inheritance than through genes or the family environment.

Through any of these lenses, within your inner family the south node is your past-life storyteller with a full list of longings, accomplishments, vulnerabilities, and expertise. All of these inheritances can be both a resource and a potential prison. If you already have a great deal of experience and mastery in something, you may be tempted to replay it over and over simply because you can do it well. Though this inherited skill is a resource, it can also trap you in its familiarity and limit your further growth. To free yourself, explore the unfamiliar through the north node.

☊ THE NORTH NODE OF THE MOON: Where am I going?

The north node of the Moon is the perfect balance to the south. We all experience the north node of the Moon every time we gaze at the future and ask: *Where am I going?* Within your inner family, the north node of the Moon is the future self, ready to be born, who says: *Come on! Let's go!* It symbolizes new talent, unfamiliar and yet somehow a part of you—an unclaimed part of you, beckoning to you now. Within your village, the north node is the foreign visitor with a fresh outlook on life. She will not ask you to stay in character or be who everyone you know expects you to be. The north node is your liberation from the past. It gives you permission to bushwhack your way into a new role in which you can flower, without the weight of habit and past orientations.

You are creating a new pathway that cannot be created overnight but deserves grounding, over time. Your task is to stick your big toe into this new territory, begin to cultivate habits there, and let them take root. Enjoy the view from this new frontier and enjoy creating the next step, and the next, and the next.

Find the south node ☋ at work in your life by completing this sentence:

When I open my steamer trunk from the past, I find:

_____.

To further define your south node, answer the following questions:

Where do I feel most controlled by the past or by others' expectations of me?

What work or behavior comes most naturally to me, as if I'd done it a thousand times? books

What belongings have I consistently guarded as precious? What stories that are related to my past live around these belongings?

What gifts do I value from my past?

What do others seem to value in me that I do well but that prevent me from developing new skills?

Intuitive assignment:

Imagine that your bones can talk—that they are a sacred library that know in their cells every story you have ever lived, in this life or any other. Ask your bones to tell you a story about where they sing with happiness at life well lived in the past. Ask your bones to tell you a story about where they are burdened with unresolved pain. Ask your bones to tell you a story about where they are extremely bored with certain activities you do automatically because it's familiar territory. What do they say?

Your south node knows the answers to this question.

Find the north node ☊ at work in your life by completing this sentence:

When I gaze at my future and trust that I can become who I always intended to be, I am becoming

_____.

To further define your north node, answer the following questions:

What do I yearn to do that I have never done before?

What activities have I naturally gravitated toward that are new and seem to call to me?

Who are the people I admire and consider role models for myself in my new path?

Where do gates just seem to open at times, even though I may not have earned the opportunity or have the skills?

If I had no past to protect and could create my life freely, what would I do? Where would I go?

Intuitive assignment:

Imagine that your future self—a very happy one—comes to see you, and says with enthusiastic urgency: *Come on! You have friends, peers, loved ones, waiting for you. We have trainers and classes waiting for you to help you begin your next phase of development. We are so excited you are coming!*

Who are these future friends? What are these future classes? What will you be doing?

Your north node knows the answers to these questions.

Now you have met your inner community of storytellers with whom you will travel for the rest of the book. But before they begin to weave their tale, let's learn to locate them as they appear in signs and houses in your birthchart.

CHAPTER 3

How to Read
Your Birthchart

This book is designed to give you an intuitive grasp of the symbols in a birthchart through the lives of real people as well as your own life, but to begin that process you need to be able to read your birthchart.

The birthchart is a picture of the sky at the moment of birth, reflecting three major components: planets, zodiac signs, and house positions. The planets are the key focus, with the signs and houses providing context for the planetary instincts.

In looking at a chart, what should you examine first? Professional astrologers study the Sun first, to see what sign and house it is in. Then they look at the Moon, followed by the other planets.

Most beginners stumble over the zodiac signs at first because the glyphs are new to them; understanding the houses, which are simply numbered first through twelfth, goes much more quickly. In this chapter we will become familiar with both, as well as give you an opportunity to fill out a simple worksheet listing your planets in signs and houses for use throughout the rest of this book.

If you don't have a copy of your birthchart, don't worry that you will have to take up astronomy and calculate one by hand. There are many technical texts that can teach you to do that, but it is unnecessary. Again, you can get a copy of your chart quickly and inexpensively by mail, phone, or from the Internet (see resources guide).

You've already been introduced to the planets and are familiar with their glyphs. Next let's learn to recognize the houses of the birthchart, followed by the signs.

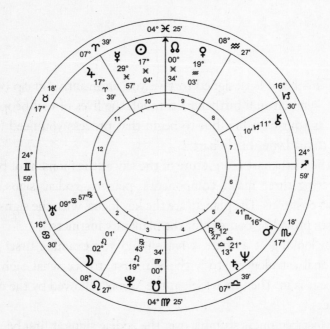

This sample chart is a picture of the sky (both above the horizon and below the horizon) on March 7, 1952, at 11:35 A.M. in Rocky Mount, North Carolina. The perspective is as if you were standing on top of the world facing south; therefore, east is on the left and west on the right.

The Houses

Finding the houses in your chart is very easy. In the sample chart, locate the horizontal line across the middle of the chart, and look at the far left line. You will see 24° ♊ 59'. (We'll explore a clear way to read both sets of numbers in a moment.) That is the beginning, or cusp, of the first house. The house below it is the second house, and so on. Most charts will have the houses numbered anyway.

The house symbolizes the stage, or *life arena*, upon which the action of the planets plays out. Technically, houses simply describe your position on Earth relative to the heavens. The twelve houses form a vertical circle of sky divided into twelve pie slices. The house system is a picture of the sky at the moment of birth, *as seen from the location on Earth at which you were born.*

Each house represents a particular location in the sky that is associated with specific settings for life experience. Symbolically, a house is like a theater stage, a large backdrop for the action of the planets in the signs. We will explore the symbolism of the houses fully in chapter 5.

The horizontal and vertical angles of the twelve houses are superhighways of energy. These are the main coordinates by which the houses are set up. To visualize them, go outside and look straight up, where the Sun would be at noon. That is the midheaven (appearing at the top of the sample chart at 4° ♓ 25'). The **midheaven**, often abbreviated to m.c. for medium coeli (Latin for "middle of the sky"), represents the most public point of your identity (again, chapter 5 covers the symbolism more fully).

Likewise, if you look straight down between your legs and imagine a point beneath the earth that is the opposite of the midheaven, this is the i.c. (imum coeli, Latin for "bottom of the sky"). I call that point the **taproot**, as it symbolizes the deepest point of nurturance. The taproot is the cusp of (or doorway to) the fourth house and is located at 4° ♍ 25' on the sample chart.

Similarly, you can locate east and west, the cusp of the first house running to the cusp of the seventh. Go outside and gaze due east along the horizon where the Sun rose earlier today. You are gazing at the ascendant point of the birthchart for this particular moment. (On the sample chart, it is located at 24° ♊ 59'.)

Just as the day dawns when the sun rises, the qualities of the ascendant in your birthchart reflect how your presence will "dawn" on others. The ascendant symbolizes the immediate vibration you put out into the world. It's the mask you wear when you step out the front door. It is also called the **rising sign**.

The western horizon line is the **descendant** (at 24° ♐ 59' on the sample chart) and symbolizes the way you seek life partners (you will learn much more about this in chapter 5, as the cusp to the seventh house). Everything above the horizon line was in the visible sky when you were born and everything below the horizon line represents the half of the sky beneath the earth.

The Tropical Zodiac

You'll see the words *tropical zodiac* emblazoned on most birthcharts. This refers to a twelvefold equal division of Earth's orbit around the Sun, which takes one year. The 360 degrees of that orbit are divided by 12 to create the signs:

Aries ♈
Taurus ♉
Gemini ♊

Cancer ♋
Leo ♌
Virgo ♍
Libra ♎
Scorpio ♏
Sagittarius ♐
Capricorn ♑
Aquarius ♒
Pisces ♓

This tropical zodiac sums up the fact that specific periods of the year have a particular energy that is describable and repeats yearly. These twelve seasons of the earth energize us and create a twelve-step cycle of maturation. (There is nothing "tropical" about this zodiac; it is simply the technical term used to describe a zodiac that shows a planet *in relation to the equinoxes* rather than in relation to the constellations, with which they have nothing in common but their name. See *constellations* and *tropical zodiac* in the glossary for a complete explanation.)

The zodiac signs are literally the belts each planet's energy moved through in order to reach you on the day of your birth. Whereas the planets are focused personifications of particular instincts, the signs are filters that energize the planets with particular purpose. In other words, think of the planets as actors and the signs as verbs seeking expression. We'll take a closer look at the agenda of each sign in the next chapter.

Locating the Zodiac Signs in Your Chart

Beginners often distinguish between signs and houses by remembering that the houses are linked to the local horizon, *whereas signs are linked to space itself.* The wheel of signs is slowly spinning around the steady local position of the houses.

Most commonly, the span of a sign will spill over two houses, not just one, in the same way that some people have property that is partially in one county and partially in another by virtue of where the county line falls. Likewise, the cusp of a new sign is not necessarily going to fall on the cusp of a house. That's why, on the sample chart, you can see that the sign of Pisces spans sections of the ninth house and the tenth. Likewise, the signs of Aries and Taurus both occur in the eleventh house, and so on. This is quite common.

Notice that there are two sets of numbers around each appearance of a zodiac glyph on your chart. The first set of numbers describes the degree; the second set is called minutes. For example, on the midheaven of the sample chart, you see 4° ♓ 25'. There are 4 degrees and 25 minutes of Pisces on the midheaven.

Consider that there are 360 degrees in a circle. Each sign therefore has 30 degrees in it (360 ÷ 12); a degree is further divided into 60 minutes. Minutes describe a more precise location of the planet in a sign.

The thirtieth degree of one sign becomes zero degrees of the next. For example, Aries is degree 0 through 29. The degree 30 of Aries becomes degree 0 of Taurus, and so on. The beginning of each sign is called the *cusp*.

Always read the numbers starting with the degree. Due to the circular nature of a chart, this may be right to left or left to right, depending on which side of the chart you are viewing. For example, on the sample chart, the Moon is at 2 degrees of Leo and 1 minute. Jupiter is at 17 degrees of Aries and 39 minutes. Pluto is at 19 degrees of Leo and 43 minutes. Chiron is at 11 degrees of Capricorn and 10 minutes. To abbreviate, astrologers often round the minutes to degrees. In other words, Jupiter rounded off would be 18 degrees of Aries because 39 minutes is well over half of 60 minutes.

The signs move counterclockwise, covering all 360 degrees of the zodiac over 24 hours, as the earth turns on its axis and faces a different part of the zodiac. So at 11:35 A.M. in the sample chart 4° Pisces 25' is on the midheaven, but in another ten minutes, the midheaven will be at 7° Pisces 5' and the ascendant at 27° Gemini 20'. An accurate birth time is preferable precisely because the zodiac signs shift quickly along the wheel of the houses.

Using your own chart, take a moment to notice which planet is in which sign. Don't worry if you have no planets in a sign or house. You're not "deficient" in that sign or house. After reading chapters 4 and 5, you'll understand why, as you learn about planetary rulerships of houses and signs.

What if you have more than one planet in a sign? It means you have a concentrated focus around that sign's purpose. If the two planets are within 7 degrees of each other, this is called a conjunction. Conjunctions are fusions of purposes. In chapter 7, you will learn more about conjunctions and other aspects, which are the angles planets form to one another.

You may wonder about planets in your chart at the very extreme degree of a sign, such as 29° Taurus or 0° Gemini. These planets are said to be on the cusp. For example, if you were born around June 21 your chart would show the Sun at 0° Cancer, the very end of the sign of Gemini. You would therefore carry the qualities of both Gemini and Cancer. Think of a person who is half Irish and half Scottish. They are both.

Sometimes an entire sign will fall within a house. This is called an interception. It is thought that intercepted signs are slightly slower to manifest in a person than a sign that is on the cusp. (Imagine a store with no sign out front or even at the back door announcing "the store is here." Planets in intercepted signs behave similarly. Other people may not pick up on these parts of you as readily.)

The technicalities of astrology are endless, and the resources guide lists books for those who want to explore them more fully.

For our purposes, you simply need to fill out the worksheet below.

Reading Your Birthchart

Using your birthchart, take the time now to fill out your worksheet. Try writing the glyphs for the signs as well as their names. If you want to include degrees and minutes for the signs, you can, but it's not vital as we begin our adventure around the symbolic meaning of planets in signs and houses.

⊙ My **SUN** is in the sign of _____ in the ____ house.

☽ My **MOON** is in the sign of _____ in the _____ house.

☿ My **MERCURY** is in the sign of _____ in the _____ house.

♀ My **VENUS** is in the sign of _____ in the _____ house.

♂ My **MARS** is in the sign of _____ in the _____ house.

♃ My **JUPITER** is in the sign of _____ in the _____ house.

♄ My **SATURN** is in the sign of _____ in the _____ house.

⚷ My **CHIRON** is in the sign of _____ in the _____ house.

♅ My **URANUS** is in the sign of _____ in the _____ house.

♆ My **NEPTUNE** is in the sign of _____ in the _____ house.

♇ My **PLUTO** is in the sign of _____ in the _____ house.

☋ My **SOUTH NODE** is in the sign of _____ in the _____ house.

☊ My **NORTH NODE** is in the sign of _____ in the _____ house.

My rising sign (the ascendant, or cusp of the first house) is _____.

My midheaven (the m.c., or cusp of the tenth house) is _____.

My descendant (the desc., or cusp of the seventh house) is _____.

My taproot (or i.c., the cusp of the fourth house) is _____.

The information available from these seventeen sentences is enough to lay a strong foundation for a lifetime of study. If you still have questions, don't worry. Everyone does at the early stage of absorbing the technology of a birthchart. But let's move on to the real adventure—the planets as instincts as they operate in the signs and the houses. How does this work in the lives of real people? How might it work in your life? In the next few chapters, you'll find out.

CHAPTER 4

The Signs:
Instinctual Energizers

You've just learned about the planets and how to read your birthchart. Now you are ready to add an additional dimension: the signs. *The sign acts as a filter for the planet, energizing that planet with an additional purpose.* Each planet is purposeful on its own but becomes animated in a particular way as it filters through a sign and takes on its agenda—an *active* agenda.

You may remember from chapter 3 that the signs of the zodiac are based on a twelvefold division of the year in time, beginning with the spring equinox around March 21. Aries, the first sign of the zodiac, marks this first day of spring. Pisces completes the cycle of the astrological year, running from, approximately, February 18 to March 20. We will move through this chapter in the exact order of the astrological year, beginning with Aries and ending with Pisces.

Our tour of each sign will begin with identifying its dominant purpose and exploring the creativity inherent in that purpose as expressed in the lives of real people. Then you'll have the opportunity to consider the planets you have in this particular sign.

But before we begin the tour of the signs, let's create a shorthand for each of them, just as we did for the planets. Take a moment now to note the theme of each sign in the table below.

As you read about the signs' respective purposes, you may notice similarities between them and the planets' purposes you read about in chapter 2. Planets are said to *rule the sign that maximizes the natural function of the planet.* The ruling planet of a sign is a focused distillation of the larger energy of the sign it rules. You will appreciate this principle more in later chapters as we build the living language of astrology, chapter by chapter.

THE SIGNS OF THE ZODIAC

SIGN	SYMBOL	PURPOSE	RULING PLANET
Aries	♈	To act	♂ (Mars)
Taurus	♉	To produce	♀ (Venus)
Gemini	♊	To listen	☿ (Mercury)
Cancer	♋	To nourish	☽ (Moon)
Leo	♌	To celebrate	☉ (Sun)
Virgo	♍	To serve	⚷ (Chiron)
Libra	♎	To balance	♀ (Venus)
Scorpio	♏	To transform	♇ (Pluto)
Sagittarius	♐	To unify	♃ (Jupiter)
Capricorn	♑	To teach	♄ (Saturn)
Aquarius	♒	To liberate	♅ (Uranus)
Pisces	♓	To let go	♆ (Neptune)

It will become clear why each planet rules the sign that it does, but keep in mind that the planets are fertile and creative in *every* sign.

♈ Aries: To Act

March 21 to April 20*

Aries encourages *clear intention*, and the claiming of your courage to act on those intentions, *to grow*. Aries is a fuel designed for people with a goal in mind, who can clearly voice *yes* and *no*. Aries explores obstacles and becomes the spiritual warrior who knows there are no enemies except the self. With that knowledge, Aries is unstoppable, the will focused into a laser capable of expressing harmlessness and power simultaneously.

♈ Aries Explores Will

March 21 through April 20 is when seeds of new growth sprout deep under the ground. The seedling pushes up against the force of gravity to find the light; the seedling knows what it wants to become. Aries grows quickly, like fire, and is therefore known as a *fire sign*. As the first sign, Aries has the strength of a crisp, peak period called *cardinal* by astrologers. Aries is ruled by the planet Mars, because Mars, like Aries, loves action. Mars is at home in Aries as he filters through it, and that gives Mars permission to act out, full throttle.

Without a direction into which to channel its strength, Aries cannot be healthy. Choosing the right challenge is key. If Aries plays small, he becomes a bully, trying to control everyone around him. But if Aries chooses a larger context in which there is plenty of room to grow in self-leadership and the leadership of others,

---

*Start and end dates of the zodiac vary slightly year to year. That is why start dates for a sign often overlap with the end date for the previous sign. Due to this variability, different texts state different start and end dates.

the resistance Aries encounters engenders courage and philosophical growth. Aries must constantly ask themselves: *Is my goal and its achievement life-giving for myself and others?*

Aries' first goal is physical survival, to embody sheer life force. For example, John Stokes, with Sun ☉ in Aries ♈, radiates physical vitality. With the exception of occasional visits and consultations with medicine men, he hasn't seen a doctor in thirty years. A teacher of animal tracking and outdoor survival skills in New Mexico, John has trained thousands of children and teenagers to respect the life force (Aries) and to listen to the earth.

John values process as much as reaching the goal. In demonstrating fire making, he explains that it is the quality of the stroke that is the essence of fire making. "We can use fire making to see where we are," John says. "Are we wobbly on the stick? Do we lose patience easily? You have to be very centered to make a fire." You have to have *clear intention.*

Sun ☉ in Aries ♈ can create business entrepreneurs capable of surviving and thriving. Restaurateur Mildred Council of Chapel Hill, North Carolina, is a good example. "I was born a colored baby girl in 1929, grew up a Negro in my youth, lived my adult life as black, and am now a seventy-year-old American," she writes in her book, *Mama Dip's Kitchen.* She opened her restaurant with $64 in 1976. Twenty years later her restaurant was reviewed in *The New York Times* and praised on ABC's *Good Morning America* for its authenticity. "Farm fresh is the highlight of country cooking," she says. Freshness is the Aries recipe for life on every level.

Aries creates activists. Aries must ask: *What is the good fight? What is the optimal way to win? What role does ethics play in conflict?* For example, Bill Monning, with Sun ☉ in Aries ♈, shines as a human rights activist and professor in conflict resolution at a California university. "As a grown man," he explains, "I am less concerned with winning and more concerned with taking good aim and moving toward a goal, aware of the waves I make as I move toward it." An attorney by training, he has negotiated with human rights violators around the globe. "The best negotiators have the ability to invent options to circumnavigate the challenges people face, rather than just blowing a fuse emotionally," Bill says.

Those whose Sun sign is Aries shine as they integrate their life story through the path of developing will and trail-blazing into new territories. But of course you can be another sign and still embody Aries energy by having planets other than the Sun in Aries.

For example, Peter Kater, a composer, has Venus ♀ in Aries ♈. Venus represents his love affair with creativity; Aries is head-strong and wants to follow its own lead. Peter says, "At age seven, I began piano lessons. I was terrible because I never wanted to play things the way they were written on the page. I wanted to play them the way I *felt* like playing them." He received a college scholarship in the arts but quit after two months, preferring to trail-blaze his own creative life. By age forty-two, Peter had sold more than a million albums worldwide. His capacity to flower as an artist is directly related to being a self-starter, needing no permission from anyone else to proceed.

♈ Find Aries at Work in Your Life

Locate individual planets you have in Aries below, and consider how they focus your life:

SUN IN ♈: Where is my *yes* to life? What circumstances activate my clear *no, absolutely not?*

MOON IN ♈: When I act out my caring for others, how does that energize me?

MERCURY IN ♈: How do my words stimulate actions?

MARS IN ♈: In what area of my life do I love to win and why?

VENUS IN ♈: Whom does my love move toward like a laser light?

JUPITER IN ♈: How can I be a role model for fighting fair and finding win-win solutions?

SATURN IN ♈: What steady path have I embarked on that gives me a clear *yes* and simultaneously requires I maintain firm boundaries?

CHIRON IN ♈: What healing experiences have I had as I allowed myself to choose a direction whether it pleased others or not?

URANUS IN ♈: Where in my life have I made pioneering decisions that opened options?

Neptune and Pluto were not in Aries in the twentieth century—nor will they be until the second quarter of the twenty-first.

SOUTH NODE IN ♈: How can I transform urgency or the need to control others into an awareness of options?

NORTH NODE IN ♈: How can I stick to a path once I've chosen it?

To Encourage Intuitive Flow for Aries

Play with Aries as part of your purpose if you have the Sun or other planets in that sign.

Imagine yourself as a fire—the flame of life. What aspects of yourself need more fire, more flame, more courage, a deeper and more fiery yes to life? Imagine you can pass on courage to others through the flame of you. Whom would you "fire up"? *Pass on courage, through the flow....*

♉ Taurus: To Produce

April 20 to May 21

Taurus seeks to stabilize growth, to encourage seedlings to take root so that they can ultimately produce abundant resources. Just as plants need predictable weather cycles to fully flower, every person born under the sign of Taurus develops patient, predictable work cycles aimed at a ripe end worth the work. The result? Resources that reflect the values of the creative person who built them. Taurus takes on a task and cultivates the habits necessary for the harvest, whatever form it takes: a row of corn, a rock garden, a well-made story.

♉ Taurus Stabilizes Growth

Once the new growth has been launched every spring during Aries, it begins to stabilize, to take root. Taurus is more methodical than Aries as it slows down into a routine, a rhythm, and builds a momentum designed to produce abundant resources. A great deal of work is involved.

In April and May the earth needs consistent conditions to fully flower, and every ecosystem predictably works toward that fullness. That determination has a *fixed* quality to it—the season is consistent as it stabilizes the growth.

Taurus is also said to be an *earth sign*, because of its productivity and groundedness. People who were born between April 20 and May 21 are wonderful workers, able to recognize the importance of reliable tools and the practical conditions under which the product of their efforts may grow. The planet Venus rules Taurus because the fertile and sensuous side of Venus is totally at home there. Just as the earth grows resources, Taureans become resources within their communities.

Christian McEwen, a writer with Sun ☉ in Taurus ♉, perfectly voices the rhythm of Taurus when she writes, "I've had to learn again and again the power of good basic habits in terms of managing a day, a week, a month, which then, with any luck, translates into managing my writing. When I am at home, my day is fairly structured. I get up, I have a modest breakfast, I meditate, and then I write. Only after that does the business of the day begin. . . . I give the cream of the day to the writing."

The coauthor of a book on nature writing, McEwen often writes about the role of the earth for each of us, as an early and important context for understanding the value of roots and place. About her own childhood in Scotland she writes, "I remember precisely how happy I was, lying in the field with the tall corn rustling overhead, or hunched in the long grass examining a grasshopper. I never lacked for new things to investigate, from the bright-eyed forget-me-nots under the barn to the plump crimson cushions of the spindleberry, each one shaped like a tiny four-cornered hat. There was a perfect match between my own curiosity and strength, and the woods and fields and hedges that were mine to explore."

Taurus can also embody the business world—resources taken to the economic level. Many corporations have branches around the world, influencing several cultures at once. What qualities should they have? What qualities should their leaders have? Executive coach for corporate leaders Ellen Wingard has Sun ☉ in Taurus ♉ and has spent her professional life exploring values in the workplace. She says, "Leaders who awaken to their own values and aspirations create committed cultures and extraordinary results. As leaders look at the legacy they are leaving, they are asking bigger questions outside of their personal success:

Beyond our corporate interests, how are we contributing to our communities?" Ellen is a builder; she coaches leaders who set the tone for their corporations.

Someone whose Moon ☽ is in Taurus ♉ tends to focus on building resources for the home. For example, urban visionary Marie Runyon recognized the value of turning abandoned buildings in Harlem into housing. As a result she spent decades organizing and fund-raising to house hundreds of homeless people. None of this would have happened without Marie's good work habits and fund-raising skills. The tangible results make her emotional center—her Moon—happy.

The planet Mars is much like an engine, and in Taurus it loves tangible results and at times earthy results. My father had Mars ♂ in Taurus ♉, and nothing energized him more than gathering and hauling materials he could compost—peanut hulls, corn husks, and manure, which he turned into rich soil for the organic vegetable garden that fed his family.

Taurus and native peoples of the earth are deeply connected; Saturn by its nature honors what has endured over time historically. Saturn in Taurus can reflect earth history, indigenous people, and their history. With her Saturn ♄ in Taurus ♉, native-education activist Gail Bruce has played a significant role in supervising the building of cultural learning centers at twenty-nine tribal colleges on Indian reservations in twelve states.

People with south node ☋ in Taurus ♉ typically have an inherent appreciation for the earth's resources and dislike waste. My mother is a good example. In her sixties, she joined a plant rescue group that dug up wildflowers and ferns from fields and forests about to be bulldozed for industrial sites. She transplanted them to the grounds of her home, which became a wildflower paradise.

People with north node ☊ in Taurus ♉ are learning to choose work that grounds them, helps them stabilize as resources themselves and take root in some regard. For example, health advocate and educator Patrick Reynolds maintains a busy public speaking schedule encouraging young people to value themselves enough to invest in a healthy lifestyle. As founder of the Foundation for a Smokefree America, he educates youth about the advertising strategies the tobacco industry uses to hook them.

The practicality of Taurus fully registered with me one day when my truck broke down. I called a Taurean friend to help me, a carpenter who was working nearby. After we opened the hood, he turned to me and said, "Where are your tools?" "Tools?" I answered blankly. "Don't you have any tools to work on the truck?" he said incredulously. I looked sheepish and said, "No, I'm sorry, I have no tools." I have no planets in Taurus at all.

♉ Find Taurus at Work in Your Life

Locate individual planets you have in Taurus below, and consider how they focus your life:

SUN IN ♉: What do my possessions tell me about my values? How am I a promoter or producer for a particular value system? What is my relationship to nature, to the earth?

MOON IN ♉: What are the rhythms of my day that make me happy?

MERCURY IN ♉: How has my mind carefully cultivated practical information?

MARS IN ♉: How does the harvest of my work amplify my sense of direction?

VENUS IN ♉: To whom or what do I bring my steady love?

JUPITER IN ♉: Which of my resources do I enjoy sharing with others, offering a Big Picture commentary with the gift?

SATURN IN ♉: What is most important for me to pass on to future generations that reflects the teachings of my work, my values?

CHIRON IN ♉: How can I learn to see the exchange of money as a sacred and meaningful transaction?

URANUS IN ♉: Where in my life am I an innovative builder? Who am I as a prototype producer?

Neptune and Pluto were not in Taurus in the twentieth century—nor will they be until the second half of the twenty-first.

SOUTH NODE IN ♉: How can I transform the desire to remain stable into making changes that encourage passionate purpose?

NORTH NODE IN ♉: How can I trust the magic of stabilizing around a specific role and growing a garden there?

To Encourage Intuitive Flow for Taurus

Play with Taurus as part of your purpose if you have the Sun or other planets in that sign.

Imagine you are the earth itself on a warm spring day, green with abundance. What aspects of yourself need more earth, more abundance, gained through work that mirrors your values? Imagine you can pass on that abundance to others. Whom would you endow? *Pass on abundance, through the flow....*

♊ Gemini: To Listen

May 21 to June 21

Gemini encourages deep listening as well as sight and touch that can tell the tale, translate the inner perception to the outer. Gemini has a thousand eyes, a thousand ears, and intelligence that seeks to communicate: to deliver the message, the painting, the letter, the music, the sound. To create signs and symbols that make contact—that is the business of Gemini.

♊ Gemini Listens, Perceives, Communicates

Gemini gathers information as intelligence in motion. With its ear to the ground, its eyes open and witnessing, its throat clear and ready to speak, Gemini articulates the abundance begun by Aries and stabilized by Taurus. Gemini is the communicator who can walk through the forest and say, "This is an oak, this is an elm, this is a poplar tree." The planet Mercury rules Gemini because Mercury personifies the same qualities that Gemini offers energetically.

In May and June, the seasons are in motion again; spring is about to mutate into summer. For that reason, Gemini is considered to be a *mutable sign*. People who have planets in Gemini can shift easily. An *air sign*, Gemini looks up, around, everywhere; Geminis are information gatherers, excellent reporters or scribes, and good listeners and storytellers. Focusing is their challenge; they have to choose a medium—music, words, images, or choreography. Without a focus, the grass is always greener on the other side of the fence for Gemini.

Once focused, Gemini can be profoundly creative. Composer Peter Kater, with Sun ☉ in Gemini ♊, says, "The creative process is all about listening. It's not about doing, it's about listening and responding." He is articulate about the role of silence as well. "Even if I'm driving in the car for long distances, I rarely put on music. I'd rather just sit there, listening. I'm aware that silence doesn't really exist, ever. Even when I sit and meditate, my head is full of sounds, constantly."

Kater found a medium—music—through which to translate those sounds into stories that transport the listener. His soundtrack to *How the West Was Lost*, a Discovery Channel series, became a bestselling album.

Other Geminis favor a more verbal medium, like novelist

Allan Gurganus, author of *Oldest Living Confederate Widow Tells All*. With Sun ☉ in Gemini ♊, Allan had no problem inventing consummate storyteller Lucy Marsden, who takes the reader from her marriage at age fifteen to her days in a nursing home. Gurganus writes "six days a week, and when I start I don't stop for anything. I won't even take calls until late afternoon when I finish for the day."

Gemini produces both writers who create stories and storytellers who voice them. Gioia Timpanelli, with Sun ☉ in Gemini ♊, has played both roles. Considered the dean of America's professional storytellers, she has also written a book of fiction called *Sometimes the Soul—Two Novellas of Sicily*. In it a character writes in her diary, "Writing and telling—they don't compare easily. Birds and stones."

Describing her life as storyteller and writer, Gioia says, "For both telling and writing you've got to put yourself in the position to allow whatever wants to come in, to come in. To unite the worlds is what the story desires . . . the story is *alive*."

Gemini communicators are as good at producing reports and data as music, stories, or novels. Social scientist Cindy Waszak conducts research on family health, and with Mercury ☿ in Gemini ♊, her intelligence and focus take on extra clarity. She reports vital information back to her employer, Family Health International. She also has Venus ♀ in Gemini ♊, which invites her to involve her aesthetics—to discover beauty as she gathers information. She does this with a camera, shooting photos of people on her travels in Egypt, Zambia, and Nepal. Cindy's photographs have a healing impact on those who see them; the images tell stories from the heart, not the head.

Gemini can be an authoritative voice. With Saturn ♄ in Gemini ♊, urban activist Marie Runyon is highly vocal, with firm opinions. She is a woman who will not be silenced about the issues she feels need to be aired. As a tenant of powerful Columbia University in New York City, she did battle with them often over numerous issues; one trustee there called her "an impossible woman . . . a real rabble organizer." Her Saturn insisted that she be heard.

And what about those who have inherited Gemini inclinations from the past? Writer Christian McEwen was born with south node ☋ in Gemini ♊, and she describes an early childhood need for a place of her own to write. She chose a woodshed behind her home and "hauled my two white bookcases out there and put all my little paperback books in a row on the shelves, and I sat there, somehow expecting to know what to write—I didn't know what. I had this sense of extreme familiarity, as if I'd made a studio for myself many times in many lifetimes, and here I was, as a child, making my studio again, and I knew that one day I would work out what to do in it."

Gemini can be profoundly perceptive. For years two of my closest friends were Geminis born May 29—one in 1914, the other in 1960. Both were painters. One evening the three of us were looking at slides of the younger Gemini's paintings, and as one particularly busy painting came on the screen, the older Gemini joked, "A thousand ways to avoid a problem." We all laughed. She said the painting portrayed the retreat of his intelligence from a focus rather than the advance of his intelligence to a focus. The agile mind of a Gemini can have remarkably accurate perceptions—particularly about another Gemini.

♊ Find Gemini at Work in Your Life

Locate individual planets you have in Gemini below, and consider how they focus your life:

SUN IN ♊: As an interpreter of my life story, what experiences do I routinely go to, to clarify that story?

MOON IN ♊: Who nourishes me when I talk to them? Who do I enjoy nourishing through images or words?

MERCURY IN ♊: Where and when do I feel the quicksilver skill of my mind?

VENUS IN ♊: How do I fall in love with life through storytelling or offering images that create a language of love?

MARS IN ♊: Where do I go for stimulating conversation that will give me a chance to fine-tune my thoughts?

JUPITER IN ♊: How do I play educator/philosopher with others around particular focuses?

SATURN IN ♊: What commitments have I made in my life to be sure that I am heard?

CHIRON IN ♊: When do I feel the sacred moving through me as I speak, or touch someone?

URANUS IN ♊: As a communicator, what truths am I passing on that have developed from my own "ahas"?

NEPTUNE IN ♊: What poetic perspective do I most enjoy sharing with others?

PLUTO IN ♊: What powerful story do I tell and retell because it is meaningful to others, not just to me?

SOUTH NODE IN ♊: How can I let go of a need for excessive detail in order to make an intuitive leap to the Big Picture?

NORTH NODE IN ♊: How can I discover the fine grain of the photograph or story in order to understand the details of the Big Picture?

To Encourage Intuitive Flow for Gemini

Play with Gemini as part of your purpose if you have Sun or other planets in that sign.

Imagine yourself as the original sound, the first word, capable of expressing a clear and lucid intelligence. What parts of your life could use that clarity? To what parts of the world would you send that clarity? *Pass on clarity, through the flow....*

♋ Cancer: To Nourish

June 21 to July 22

Cancer expresses the capacity to care, to nourish. Cancer, like the womb of a woman, knows how to create a safe place in which new life may grow. Cancer builds the web of emotional connection that results in family, no matter the form—a mother, father, and child; a department within an organization; a film crew. Cancer understands inner essence as a fertile world worth exploring.

♋ Cancer Nourishes, Cares, Incubates

After the seeding stage of Aries, the stabilizing stage of Taurus, and the communicative stage of Gemini, Cancer's job is to build the nest. The sensitivity of Cancer expresses itself through umbilical cords of connection, the emotional depth of true caring, which in turn produces families and atmospheres that are incubators for a healthy humanity. The Moon is the ruling planet of Cancer. Strongly affiliated with qualities of the mother, Cancer has an inner creative power that invokes new life rather than commanding it to come. The soft fullness of early summer reflects the lushness of Cancer, as a growing season that is peaking and therefore considered *cardinal*. Just as Aries is the peak of early spring, Cancer is the peak of early summer.

Cancer, a *water sign*, seeks to connect through flowing. That flow of connection creates family and friendships with an emotional bond. To care, to nourish, is the business of Cancer.

Parent-child relationships and reproductive health are all Cancer concerns. Public health educator and mother Cindy Waszak embodies all of those concerns with her Sun ☉ in Cancer ♋. Based in North Carolina, she has traveled the globe helping women understand family planning as an important life option. Women who become mothers by choice feel more connected to their children. Cindy offers information to women who otherwise would not understand their options around family planning. She particularly likes focusing on the lives of girls as they grow into women in cultures that are changing from traditional to modern. How will they build self-esteem? Cindy says, "I believe I can help young girls with these issues, as a compassionate adult who can hold up a mirror of a young woman's potential. Girls are often left out and in certain countries virtually ignored, as if they were invisible. I want girls all over the world to recognize their gifts."

Cindy not only serves as a mother-at-large but also as mother of a son and daughter. She says, "Motherhood is more pleasant in theory than in practice, but [it] has taught me amazing lessons about myself and love and responsibility."

Cancer men can be as nurturing as their female counterparts, carefully cultivating the essence of a situation, the life of an organization or project. For example, James Kullander, with Sun ☉ in Cancer ♋, is managing editor of publications at a seminar center in Upstate New York that focuses on nurturance through the healing and creative arts. The center, Omega Institute for Holistic Studies, offers courses in health, healing, the arts, and spirituality. James's work not only involves the cultivation of high-quality publications but also requires sensitivity toward the people he serves who come to Omega seeking nourishment on many levels. He brings the same sensitivity to the restoration of his home, where he also gardens and enjoys cooking meals for friends.

The sensitivity of Cancer often calls for a private exploration of the capacity to care. For example, Moon in Cancer treasures sisterhood—the bond of woman to woman or mother to daughter. Author of *The Rhythm of Compassion—Caring for Self, Connecting with Society*, Gail Straub has Moon ☽ in Cancer ♋. In addition to nurturing students in her workshops, Gail walks her talk about the importance of self-care. For more than a decade, she has belonged to a women's group that has met regularly, an informal sisterhood whose members are dedicated to supporting one another.

Pluto ♀ often creates figurehead identities, and in the sign of Cancer ♋, powerful caregivers. Marie Runyon has been called "Harlem's Unlikely Hero" for her community work there. "I am not going to let my whiteness interfere with what I think I can do," she says.

People with south node ☋ in Cancer ♋ frequently have deep ties to the mother or the female line of the family, like storyteller Gioia Timpanelli. She speaks with love of her mother and her grandmother, who gave her a deep appreciation for the ineffable. Gioia says, "The ineffable might be the most valuable thing we have. For example, look at a woman who is a most incredible person, who is taking care of a house, loving and teaching children both the practical and ephemeral works of a family. She's given no pay for it, she's given no value, unless she's married to a very smart man.

"No radio reports: *Now here's Margaret Smith's stock market worth. Today she has actually earned for this family some points that are so incredibly high that no one has ever seen them on the stock market.* This society is so materialistic that it undervalues the ineffable and so endangers the value of women."

My father, a Cancer, had that ineffable quality and could build trust faster than anyone I have ever known, because he enjoyed being emotionally present for people. By trade he was a furniture dealer, but he also bought run-down houses, cared for them, brought them back to prime, and rented them. He did all the maintenance work on the rental houses himself, and it was not uncommon to see him driving around town in his truck with six children in the back—none of them his own. They were neighborhood children he "mothered" just by including them in his life, as worthy of his time.

♋ Find Cancer At Work in Your Life

Locate individual planets you have in Cancer below, and consider how they focus your life:

Sun in ♋: How do I use my sensitive side to offer quality care? How do I value the essence of things, even if that essence is invisible?

MOON IN ♋: How have I made my house, my home, and my food vitally important components of my happiness?

MERCURY IN ♋: How can I listen deeply through emotional tones rather than clinical data? How can I honor a knowing that does not translate into words?

VENUS IN ♋: Who taught me to express tender love, and how does that love still flow through me to specific people?

MARS IN ♋: How can I own my feelings and not bury them, particularly when I'm angry?

JUPITER IN ♋: How can I use my philosophical gifts to explore the essence of a matter, including the emotional context?

SATURN IN ♋: How can I maintain a discipline that informs me what I need (on any level) to be well-nourished?

CHIRON IN ♋: How can I discover the knack for being present for those in need without taking on their wounds?

URANUS IN ♋: How can I learn to be emotionally connected to others and simultaneously authentic and truthful about who I really am?

NEPTUNE IN ♋: How can I learn to tune in to my own psychic ability about my family or home?

PLUTO IN ♋: How have I played the role of the archetypal caregiver and what have I learned about my power issues as a consequence?

SOUTH NODE IN ♋: How can I develop boundaries that prevent me from giving too much?

NORTH NODE IN ♋: How can I learn to trust my feelings more, as valuable informants requiring no justification?

To Encourage Intuitive Flow for Cancer

Play with Cancer as part of your purpose if you have Sun or other planets in that sign.

Imagine yourself as the giver of life, one who understands the importance of creating a safe place in which new life can grow. Which parts of you need this safe place, in order to incubate the best of you? Imagine you can send the spirit of the mother anywhere in the world, to put her arms around a person or situation, offering emotional safety to heal or to grow. Where would you send her? Pass on nourishment through the flow.

♌ Leo: To Celebrate

July 22 to August 23

Leo loves life with an open heart and contagious laughter and all the courage of one born a colorful character. Leo understands the pleasure of creating and, as an extrovert, of giving the creation away in generous gestures. Leo comprehends the nobility of heart behind every living creature. Leo grasps the importance of the child within each of us, who loves freely, with abandon.

♌ Leo Creates and Celebrates

Leo says: *Celebrate life—and while you're at it, be somebody.* After the nest-building agenda of the sign of Cancer, the eggs in the nest hatch. The powerful child is born who knows she has a right to exist, she has a right to shine; life is good, life is grand. Leo, a fixed sign, is affiliated with the lion for the regal power of the heart, strong and steady, carrying through the purpose of the season—celebration! This celebration wants to be seen and shared, and those born under the sign of Leo flourish when there is applause and appreciation for the creative gesture, the gift.

A *fire sign*, Leo is active, extroverted, bigger than life. The fire of Leo is the fire of the Sun, the constancy of life smiling upon itself and its own nature—and, not suprisingly, the Sun is the ruling planet of Leo. To celebrate life and creativity is the business of Leo.

Spontaneity and surprise are the simple pleasures Leo employs to create the celebration. The spirit of play is huge with Leo. But every playful person needs a form—something or someone to play with.

Stuart Quimby, with Sun ☉ in Leo ♌, is a good example. A toy maker based in Upstate New York, Stuart is the founder of Design Science Toys, which are based on the shapes and forces of nature. The first toy design was inspired when Stuart and his wife tried to duplicate with soda straws and thread a structure designed by visionary architect Buckminster Fuller.

"It had a magical quality," Stuart says. "The straws were floating, suspended in a tensile web of thread, none of them touching, and yet the whole featherlight structure possessed tremendous strength. Our fascination with the model led to making another, and another." More than a decade later, Stuart's company has gained international stature as one of the few toy companies in the world focused on bridging the gap between art and science.

Leo's spirit of play naturally includes the animal kingdom. The lion has been most traditionally associated with Leo. His nobility as a creature is clear. Many people would agree animals often have more dignity than humans, and Mary Bloom is one of them. An animal photographer with Sun ☉ in Leo ♌, Mary's love affair with animals led to her having a small menagerie in her New York City apartment, to the delight of neighborhood children.

One of those children was the daughter of children's author Aliki. Inspired by her daughter's magical experience with Mary, Aliki wrote *At Mary Bloom's* and *Overnight at Mary Bloom's*.

Mary says, "Aliki and I would sometimes go to children's classes, and she would talk, as a children's book writer, and would bring me as the living illustration of the book. I would bring my hedgehog or skunk or armadillo and teach the children that these animals had a unique way of protecting themselves in a nonviolent way. Doing that, I began to realize that my life's work—that which pleased me and made me feel fulfilled—was to help animals."

The creativity of Leo sometimes calls for unexpected and dramatic expression, particularly with Uranus in Leo. Uranus encourages taking the next step. In Leo, Uranus is unlikely to rest on past laurels. Composer Peter Kater has Uranus ♅ in Leo ♌ and avoids standardized roles. He says, "I redefine myself and my music periodically, and that refuels me more than anything else." He has birthed more than two dozen musical releases as a result.

Neptune ♆ in Leo ♌ takes on a softer expression, often with love of God and laughter merging. For example, restaurateur Mama Dip has Neptune in Leo and in her book *Mama Dip's*

Kitchen, she describes the feasts at her church in the 1930s and 1940s.

"The second Sunday in August was the time for one of my favorite occasions—the homecoming feast at church. The women dressed so gracefully with their handmade broomstick shirtwaist dresses covered by starched and ironed feed sack aprons to keep their dresses clean. Their hair would be shining with grease and rolled up with hair pins, with a straw hat pressing on their forehead. They served dinner on a long wooden table nailed between two cedar trees near the church well and laughed and chattered as they spread fried chicken and vegetables of every kind on the table, cutting up pies and cakes to feed an army of hungry men, women, and children."

People with south node ☋ in Leo ♌ frequently have ancestors who are bigger than life, sometimes of the privileged or aristocratic class, and—depending on their values—either self-important with power or benevolent.

Housing visionary Marie Runyon has south node in Leo. Marie's great-great-great-grandfather gave some of his land holdings to help anchor the Cherokee Nation in western North Carolina in 1861, protecting a segment of the Cherokees from deportation. His nobility of heart was passed on to Marie, who one hundred years later was determined to share what she had and to do what she could to create homes in Harlem for people who don't have them.

♌ Find Leo at Work in Your Life

Locate individual planets you have in Leo below and consider how they focus your life:

SUN IN ♌: How do I enjoy opening my heart to the fullness of life? What is it about my life path that makes me smile and feel generous?

MOON IN ♌: Can I see my need for affirmation and applause as healthy when it alerts me to where I am appreciated?

MERCURY IN ♌: How does my voice communicate my pleasure in life?

VENUS IN ♌: How do my love relationships reflect my love for play, creativity, and color?

MARS IN ♌: How do I express a hearty confidence-at-the-core? How can I encourage myself and others to accept joy as the great motivator?

JUPITER IN ♌: How am I eager to play ambassador to the good life? How can I bring enthusiastic heart to situations that have grown too sober or stale?

SATURN IN ♌: How can I trust that my spontaneity will find its own discipline without imposing too much order on it from the first effort?

CHIRON IN ♌: How can I trust my creativity as a link to the sacred, even if it doesn't always fit into a mainstream context of "creativity"?

URANUS IN ♌: How can I embody the creative spirit in a fresh and original way that has never been expressed before?

NEPTUNE IN ♌: How does my soul shine through every time I laugh or love?

PLUTO IN ♌: Who am I as the king or queen? Do I pull rank, or am I a role model of dignity as I act on my self-confidence?

SOUTH NODE IN ♌: How can I use my ability to entertain people but not let it prevent me from becoming more authentic?

NORTH NODE IN ♌: How can I cultivate a sense of humor and heart rather than depend so heavily on my intellect?

To Encourage Intuitive Flow for Leo

Play with Leo as part of your purpose if you have the Sun or other planets in that sign.

Imagine yourself as the Santa Claus of creativity, capable of bringing more spontaneous joy into an area of your life. Where would you like to receive that joy? If you could send the generous heart of creativity to anyone in the world, give them a sense of humor and pleasure in life, who would it be? *Pass on your celebration of life, through the flow....*

♍ Virgo: To Serve

August 22 to September 22

Virgo loves ecosystems and recognizes that the whole is more than the sum of the parts. Virgo serves community as it discovers this gestalt. Virgo loves the human body, a miraculous design of efficiency and sensuous order. Virgo enjoys function, what works well: a dependable person, a computer, a corporation, a prosthetic limb that allows someone to walk who otherwise wouldn't. Virgo wishes to be of use, always.

♍ Virgo Explores the Finest of Functions

After the glorious profusion of celebration in the sign of Leo in late summer, Virgo signals a return to order, with the agenda of making full use of resources in order to better the community. Virgo signals a transition between summer and fall, a shift, and is for that reason considered a *mutable sign*.

Food is harvested before the first frost of fall ruins the last crops. Gardens are cleaned up; school and work schedules resume. Rather than the party being over, the true joy begins, in a more quiet way of developing the best base possible for the working order of your life. The productivity of Virgo makes it an *earth sign*, with the agenda of dependability, a building block of life support. Both Mercury and Chiron are considered to rule Virgo. Virgo's love of order enhances Mercury's capacity to gather information, and so it thrives in the sign of Virgo. Virgo enhances Chiron's healing gifts, particularly with health, and so it too blossoms in Virgo.

More than any other sign, Virgo looks to the body as teacher and friend. The first ecosystem one encounters upon birth is that of the body. The human body is a magnificent creation. For that reason many Virgos naturally gravitate to medicine, health care, or yoga as a profession.

For example, author Judith Berger has Sun ☉ in Virgo ♍ and has been a resource in New York City for more than a decade as a yoga teacher, massage therapist, and herbalist. The art and science of yoga is dedicated to the health of the body and spirit, working with the breath as the unifying factor in the health of both. Virgo loves quality, and the quality of the breath can create health or disease. Virgo also loves the power of ritual, because it creates a container for meaning, for function endowed with a shift toward a better state. Berger combined her love of ritual and herbs in her book *Herbal Rituals*, a journey through the calendar year, exploring the physical and spiritual power of herbs.

The human body may be the immediate ecosystem we find ourselves in upon birth, but that rapidly expands to become the body of the planet. Virgo naturally gravitates to that body as equally interesting. Abraham Oort is a good example of Sun ☉ in Virgo ♍. As a climate scientist for thirty years, Abraham studied the global system of the earth and its environment—including the ways in which the atmosphere, oceans, cryosphere, biosphere, and lithosphere interact to create climate.

Later in life, Abraham's Virgo interests shifted to the body and its optimal health. He became a shiatsu practitioner as one way to explore the body. Shiatsu originated in Japan as a form of massage using thumb, finger, and palm to apply pressure to the body in order to balance vital energy.

Virgo loves to organize, and this tendency can take on a very serious focus when Saturn ♄ is in Virgo ♍. For example, human rights activist Bill Monning has Saturn in Virgo and says, "I learned the practical tools of organizing when I worked for a year with the United Farm Workers of America, AFL-CIO. The union had perfected the art and science of mobilizing people to organize in their own self-interest through the power of united action." Bill learned to build political ecosystems that improved the quality of life for that group.

The ecosystem of the body begins with the ultimate organizer: DNA. When Neptune ♆ is in Virgo ♍, an interpretation of that event can be inspired. For example, native-education activist Gail Bruce has Neptune in Virgo and she says, "Indian culture talks about the Creator in all living things. With the discovery of DNA, scientists found the spiral and they discovered that every living thing breaks down to the same molecular structure. So what Native Americans have been saying forever is indeed true: *The Creator is in all of us.* We are all exactly the same. My DNA structure breaks down to the same structure as a plant, tree, or bird. I went, *Wow, they knew it all along. God is in everything.*"

♍ Find Virgo at Work in Your Life

Locate individual planets you have in Virgo below, and consider how they focus your life:

SUN IN ♍: How can I shine as I discover a whole system and endow it with a shift toward a better state? How does my discovery of a whole system allow me to be of service to others?

MOON IN ♍: How can I choose a line of work that encourages emotional attunement to details?

MERCURY IN ♍: What books and magazines on my shelves reflect the how-to details of my focus?

VENUS IN ♍: What creative collaborations can I participate in that have healing or aesthetic consequences?

MARS IN ♍: How can I lead a team without lapsing into irritation around the imperfect aspects of their work or mine?

JUPITER IN ♍: How do I enjoy playing educator about the finer functions of my work focus?

SATURN IN ♍: How can I bring discipline to my love of order and build the base for a skill I can share with the community around me?

CHIRON IN ♍: Does my perfectionism prevent me from aligning with a path that could unleash a sacred gift in me and connect me with people I normally wouldn't contact, as community?

URANUS IN ♍: How can I reinvent my craft and make it contemporary and useful for present and future purposes?

NEPTUNE IN ♍: How can I bring a right-brained gift to a left-brained process?

PLUTO IN ♍: What do I passionately love breaking down and rebuilding to unleash its potential? A manuscript? An old house? A corporation? A motorcycle? A musical composition?

SOUTH NODE IN ♍: How well do I weather the situation when someone steals my to-do list? Can I let go of any compulsive need to control and order life?

NORTH NODE IN ♍: How can I craft a role for myself as a grounded practitioner or public servant who has mastered a body of knowledge?

To Encourage Intuitive Flow for Virgo

Play with Virgo as part of your purpose if you have the Sun or other planets in that sign.

Contemplate the miraculous working order of your body, even if you suffer from disease, scars, or aging. Imagine that your body is part of a larger body that has no disease at all—the original imprint for the radiant health of the human form. Imagine that you can rebalance what is out of balance in your body by calibrating to this original imprint. How does it feel? What shifts in diet or work environment or lifestyle does the recalibration whisper to you to try?

If this original imprint for radiant health could be sent on a mission to encourage well-being in someone else, to whom would you send it? *Pass on radiant health, through the flow....*

♎ Libra: To Balance

September 22 to October 23

Libra loves beauty that blends the inner and outer. Libra creates art and relationships that rebalance all involved. Libra recognizes the beauty of justice and fair play. Above all, Libra understands the value of intimacy between equals—true partnership and the larger life one can live when well partnered.

♎ Libra Loves Beauty, Balance, and Fair Play

After the hard work of Virgo, with its agenda of service, fine function, and the building of the body, community, ecosystems, and environment, the time is ripe to rebalance, relate, socialize, and introduce aesthetics into the situation. Libra is the artist as well as the diplomat, both of whom are interested in synthesizing opposites in some regard. Libra the lover embraces that same dance with opposites.

Libra is 180 degrees from Aries, its opposite, and just as Aries is a *cardinal sign*, a peak season, Libra too is cardinal, the peak season of the fall. Aries the activist and Libra the lover are two halves of a whole. When Aries suffers from partial insight, it is concerned only with its own aim and has no appreciation for diplomacy. When Libra suffers from partial insight it has too much diplomacy, able to see two sides of a situation and feel agreeable to both, endlessly circling, unable to take aim and act.

Libra's primary ruling planet is Venus, as the planet of the arts and love, activities Libra naturally encourages. Saturn also thrives in Libra. The Libran capacity for balance allows Saturn to express graceful commitment, which softens that planet's hard edges.

Like Gemini, Libra is an *air sign*, intelligence in motion, seeking expression. The intelligence of Libra is attuned to true balance—the scales of justice and fair play in the world or at home, the true balance of intimacy between equals—in marriage or in partnerships of any kind. The artistry of Libra emanates from the individual's ability to be in balance from the inside out and to project that balance as beauty.

As a consequence, many Librans are physically attractive, such as Gail Bruce. Currently a native-education activist, grandmother, and painter in New York City, in her youth Gail was a fashion model who appeared on the cover of *Vogue* and other magazines. Later she balanced the emphasis on her outer beauty by becoming a painter, working to create from her inner beauty.

Librans excel as diplomats; Gail has been a bridge between the Native American community and mainstream culture. She has also explored the Libran role of lover fully. Gail says, "One of the most instinctive moves I have ever made was to walk out of my entire life in less than a week to be with Murray, the man who would become my husband. We were married a year later. We've been together thirty years. I would marry him again in a second."

The Libran love for relating and intimacy can express itself as much through friendship or family as the lover relationship. John and Jim Thornton, identical twins with Sun ☉ in Libra ♎, are a case in point. As colicky infants, their crying ceased immediately when they were allowed to sleep side by side. They were inseparable throughout childhood and called each other *Udder Man* ("Other Man"). Like many twins, they invented their own secret speech as children (for example, *hantaast* meant "good luck to you"). As adults, they have each married but stay in close contact. Both have chosen the arts as a profession, Jim as a writer and John as an artist. They still sometimes bid each other farewell with, "Hantaast, Udder Man!"

The Libran preference for relating well can also express itself as a love for justice. For example, former Judge Jerry Leonard with Sun ☉ in Libra ♎ learned that he would rather hand out a community service verdict than jail time. "The easiest thing in the world is to throw the book at people," he says. "It doesn't take any creative thinking."

Currently he runs a mediation practice, using many of the listening skills he developed as a judge. "I see angry people all the time, but if you can get them comfortable talking about their problems, you may discover a complicated solution is unnecessary. Sometimes an apology goes a long way."

Marriage partners inevitably learn mediation skills but ideally they also explore the unique beauty of their partnership as well. Particularly when the Moon ☽ is in Libra ♎ is the instinct to explore that beauty strong. Social scientist and documentary photographer Cindy Waszak has Moon in Libra and is frank about the importance of her partner as key in her happiness. She says, "My romance with my partner is directly connected to the ways we complement each other as a man and woman. His masculine self is so big that my feminine side naturally expands to meet him. That nurtures me more than I can say." In her travels she frequently photographs couples, with an eye for the romantic moment and the tenderness inherent in a simple gesture.

When Jupiter ♃ is in Libra ♎, the collaborative instinct often expands beyond the personal partnership into professional ones. Composer Peter Kater has Jupiter in Libra and says, "I think some of the best music I've written has been composed for other people's projects. Sometimes I get out of the way more personally when I'm working on someone else's thing because it usually involves a visual, like film or television. When I compose for another art form, it has more space and rhythm in it so that the other art form has room to express itself equally well."

Libra requires a light touch, whether it is expressing its energy through the arts or through healing; Libra is not demanding or controlling. Healer and herbalist Susun Weed has Chiron ⚷ in Libra ♎. Chiron heals through allowance. Weed insists that imbalance can be as healing as balance and that, in fact, perfect balance doesn't exist. Chiron allows what *isn't* balanced to become the step to healing. She says, "The difference between a rescuer and a healer is that the rescuer has a set state of perfection they want that person to be in, and the healer—if the healer wants anything at all—wants the person to incorporate more of their wholeness. So if a person is protecting themselves in an inelegant way (like alcohol or drug abuse, or overeating), the healer might help the person find a more elegant way to protect themselves but without taking away the protection."

The light touch of Libra invites one to unify opposites by

dancing with paradox, sidestepping the polarized position of demand.

♎ Find Libra at Work in Your Life

Locate individual planets you have in Libra below, and consider how they focus your life:

SUN IN ♎: How can I organize my life around beauty and balance, yet trusting the moments when I am off-balance as part of the dance too?

MOON IN ♎: How do I nurture myself through intimacy with equals? Who do I contact when I need a mirror of my own beauty and grace?

MERCURY IN ♎: How do I listen to life with an ear for what is fair and just?

VENUS IN ♎: How do I love bringing people together to promote good feeling, no matter the context—a party, a meeting, or in bed with a lover?

MARS IN ♎: How am I able to hold my position when challenged by others, rather than reversing my opinion to keep the peace at all costs?

JUPITER IN ♎: How am I a benevolent matchmaker for people and purposes that will refine the world rather than making it more coarse?

SATURN IN ♎: How have I contracted to be a lifelong student of the artist I am? The lover? The healer?

CHIRON IN ♎: How can I embody the gifted healer able to take relationships to an inspired level by trusting the crises that may come up as the relationship grows?

URANUS IN ♎: My inner male and female both have big truths to tell me. What do they say, and how do they want to balance each other?

NEPTUNE IN ♎: How are my most soulful relationships an art form, light as a feather yet embodying timeless love?

PLUTO IN ♎: How can I explore the hidden purpose of partnership? What have I discovered about dancing with two opposites within myself and synthesizing them into one?

SOUTH NODE IN ♎: How can I release any dependence on a partner to create a life path while retaining my strength as a skilled partner?

NORTH NODE IN ♎: Can I recognize my readiness to set aside heavy-handed opinions so that subtle harmonies can unfold between myself and others?

To Encourage Intuitive Flow for Libra

Play with Libra as part of your purpose if you have Sun or other planets in that sign.

Imagine that you always have an invisible partner hovering near you who sees your beauty and grace and encourages you to share that beauty and grace in specific ways. What does your partner suggest? *Pass on grace and beauty, through the flow....*

♏ Scorpio: To Transform

October 23 to November 22.

The passion of Scorpio is to understand the source of life—the secret of the seed. To appreciate the power of the seed, Scorpio must comprehend its opposite: the power of death and the energy that flows from source to seed, to life, to death, and to rebirth. Scorpio studies energy, which is power, and learns to transform power. Scorpio knows power's true purpose—to be life-giving, to bring more trust into the world, not more fear.

♏ Scorpio Knows Through Feeling

Scorpio feels, and therefore knows, like a sorcerer or psychic, and is considered a *water sign* due to its emotional depth. A *fixed sign*, the season of Scorpio is autumn enduring, building upon the process of Libra as it brought autumn to its peak.

Scorpio is about not just what it knows but also what it suspects, as it psychically touches potentialities, both positive and negative. Scorpio explores the palette of power in the human psyche and has us touch the full range from light to dark and back to light again. As a consequence, the phoenix rising out of the ashes is a common symbol for Scorpio.

Mars and Pluto rule Scorpio. Mars, with its strong will, takes on rich depth in Scorpio and unleashes hidden reserves of energy to meet a goal. Likewise, Scorpio is the perfect fuel to burn in Pluto, given that Pluto is the personification of power.

Scorpio teaches that those who seek power for its own sake will always meet a greater power, which inevitably leads to fear (of losing power). The wise Scorpio understands how to have power without needing to display or use it. The power struggle with others is replaced by the idea of empowering others.

How is this done? Psychologists ask that question when working with clients who have suffered abuse or are abusers themselves, and political analysts ask that question in multinational power struggles as well. For that reason, many Scorpios become psychologists and political analysts.

Marty Rosenbluth is a good example. With Sun ☉ in Scorpio ♏, the political analyst and documentary filmmaker has explored the Israeli/Palestinian conflict, among others. Born Jewish in Brooklyn, New York, Marty spent his youth hating Palestinians—until he spent a few years living on the West Bank after graduating from college. Seeing the complexity of the situation, he made an insightful film about the conflict (*Jerusalem: An Occupation Set in Stone?*). He says, "[We] have to make sure that *nobody's* human rights are ever violated, regardless of their politics. I am passionate about magnifying that message. Passion is what gives life meaning."

Marty also has Neptune Ψ (which rules filmmaking) in Scorpio ♏. His film illuminates patterns of abuse so they can be recognized and released. He holds a mirror up to abused people who retaliate with abuse and simply asks, "Aren't you doing the same thing?"

Scorpio is also the part of pure spirit that is rascal. Scorpio can seem crazy as it asks you to claim all of who you are—the jealous one, the passionate one, the wild one—but the untamable look of Scorpio is really a portrait of human wholeness. Scorpio explores emotion, and when that emotion is wedded to music, the music pulls the listener in, like a hypnotic induction.

With Sun ☉ in Scorpio ♏, cellist and composer Giovanni Sollima embodies this. Born in Palermo, Italy, in 1962 into a family of musicians, Giovanni had years of classical training and slowly transformed his relationship to music to match his nature. Giovanni's desire was to be a conduit for other dimensions in a way he could not be if he remained totally true to his classical training. To reach these other dimensions, he needed to include his wild side. He says, "As a consequence, every piece I compose is a new experience for me, and some are quite metaphysical. For example, when composing the pieces for my CD, *Aquilarco*, I wanted to describe stories about flying and traveling through the air. I thought of the Victorian mathematician Charles H. Hinton, who developed, through tales and drawings, an extravagant theory of a fourth dimension."

The music in *Aquilarco* includes repetitive spirals, sounds of circling, and a subtly altered rhythm with each reentry into the refrain. The technique creates for the listener a playful and hypnotic doorway to that fourth dimension.

Paintings can embody Scorpio dimensionality as well as music. Painter Gail Bruce has Venus♀ in Scorpio ♏, and she says, "Through art and painting, I have experienced not only beauty but the balance necessary to be whole. Sometimes that balance includes darkness, jagged edges, and a kind of walk-the-plank uncertainty where there are no guarantees." As a consequence, her paintings have more power.

One of Scorpio's powers is fertility—the secret of the seed. *Where do we come from? What role does sexuality play in identity?* When Saturn ♄ is in Scorpio ♏, such questions are crystallized in the mind. With Saturn's love of developing authority, it is not uncommon for those with Saturn in Scorpio to become credentialed investigators, professional researchers. Scientist Cindy Waszak has Saturn in Scorpio and got her Ph.D. in social psychology—demonstrating her commitment to becoming expert at human behavior. Her thesis tested a theoretical model of how adolescents process information about pregnancy prevention from TV. (Scorpio reflects fertility issues.) Over the course of her career, she has evolved into a dedicated family-planning educator.

Whereas Saturn loves to structure the secret knowledge of Scorpio, Neptune ♆ in Scorpio ♏ enjoys the flow of consciousness as it moves in every direction uniting the sacred and the profane. Composer Peter Kater has Neptune in Scorpio and says, "A perspective I often have is: *It's either all God or it's not, whether it's buying gasoline at the gas station or going out on stage to perform.* And so at one point I started to rebel against doing anything special around my creative process. I would just treat it as the next thing that I was doing. As a result I started going into projects and recording sessions comically unprepared, as a way of exercising this desire to really see what information is available intuitively without thinking that I needed to manipulate time and space in some way."

Scorpio often expresses its transformative power through the healing arts. In 1991 I had an allergic reaction to a medication and developed a heart arrhythmia that lasted days. The doctors wanted to give it time to correct itself before taking additional measures, but my sense was that time wouldn't help. I went to a masseuse who'd trained extensively in the healing arts and asked for help. Linda used a combination of polarity (a gentle rocking motion), massage, reiki (a form of energy healing), and other modalities, including tuning forks strategically placed over the chakras—the energy centers of the body. Two hours later my heartbeat was normal.

Scorpio knows what is possible when you work with the energy behind form and the extraordinary becomes available ordinarily.

♏ Find Scorpio at Work in Your Life

Locate individual planets you have in Scorpio below, and consider how they focus your life:

SUN IN ♏: How can I trust my emotional intensity, whether I reveal that intensity or not? How do my depths inform me of my nature and empower me to choose change rather than waiting for it to come to me?

MOON IN ♏: How can I trust that I have little capacity to repress emotions and, subsequently, my emotional life is a rich roller-coaster ride? How does this help me build powerful emotional bonds?

MERCURY IN ♏: What policies have I developed around discretion, or the power of the spoken word, as a consequence of my skill at picking up subtext?

VENUS IN ♏: How can my charisma become a meaningful gift for those swayed by the power of my beauty or grace?

MARS IN ♏: How do I experience my passion as an unstoppable force that can do both great good and great harm?

JUPITER IN ♏: How can I cultivate deep faith in certain powers and share knowledge with others about these powers?

SATURN IN ♏: How can I become an expert at exploring a labyrinth of powerful information, some of it hidden within me? How can I remember that if I try to control every outcome I will miss a lot of magic?

CHIRON IN ♏: How can I sidestep power struggles by not taking things personally? How is this healing for me? For the other person?

URANUS IN ♏: How can I create honest relationships that are also passionate and have depth?

NEPTUNE IN ♏: How have I discovered that in the search for power, love is the greatest power of all?

PLUTO IN ♏: How often do I inexplicably know that I am on track, plugged into an activity that draws from my depths?

SOUTH NODE IN ♏: How can I transcend old fears of loss and stabilize my life through embodying a skill no one can take from me as I craft it from within and share it in the larger world?

NORTH NODE IN ♏: How can I release a fixed notion of who I am or where I belong and begin to trust major changes in my life on a more regular basis?

To Encourage Intuitive Flow for Scorpio

Play with Scorpio as part of your purpose if you have the Sun or other planets in that sign.

Imagine yourself a shaman whose job is to occupy the dark of night and the bright of day and in both places to remember power's true purpose: to be life-giving, to bring more trust into the world—not more fear. Yet fear is part of life. How can your shaman empower the most fearful part of yourself? What must you let go of? What comes in its place? If you, as shaman, could remove power struggle anywhere in the world, where would it be?

Pass on power that is life-giving, through the flow....

♐ Sagittarius: To Unify

November 22 to December 21

Sagittarius seeks the Big Picture that enlightens and gives hope based on the interconnection of all life. Within the unity of life lies the ultimate safety: the freedom to connect with the wisdom of that unity. Sagittarius is the optimistic messenger about the Big Picture it discovers; a philosopher with an unforgettable overview.

♐ Sagittarius Unifies by Making a Map

Sagittarius explores the unity of life and then makes a map about it—whether as educator or musician or writer or outdoor adventurer or street philosopher. After the dive to the depths of the human psyche in Scorpio, we're ready to move toward the sky, the open marketplace, the world, and explore the intersection of all paths, instincts fully in place. Sagittarius is the ultimate optimist, who knows: *There are no aliens, anywhere.* We are all part of a great unity and, within that unity, anything that is hurt can heal; any fragmented situation can rediscover a context in which it can be understood as a piece of a whole. The pieces of the puzzle come together.

Sagittarius is 180 degrees from Gemini, its opposite, and just as Gemini is a *mutable sign*, so is Sagittarius: a transitional phase toward the peak of winter with plenty of room built in for flexible interpretations. Thematically, the two signs are deeply connected as well—Sagittarius as universal voice, Gemini as personal voice. Both are intelligence in motion, seeking expression— to tell a story, be the messenger. Sagittarius is a *fire sign*, energetic and fast-moving; nothing is hidden. Horses are frequently associated with Sagittarius for precisely that reason: their moving energy and freedom of motion to explore, to journey, to cross from one dimension to another. Remember the planet Jupiter's capacity to embody Blue Sky Mind? Jupiter rules Sagittarius because it feels totally at home with its open-mindedness.

The universal voice of Sagittarius often chooses to reach many people at once, through public speaking or the media, pivoting from a basic theme anyone can identify with. Health advocate Patrick Reynolds, with Sun ☉ in Sagittarius ♐ is a good example. An inspirational speaker and educator, he coaches young people on thinking positively about their future and choosing a healthy lifestyle so that they can enjoy that future, specifically by saying no to cigarettes. The mastermind behind Foundation for a Smokefree America, Patrick is the grandson of the founder of R.J. Reynolds Tobacco Company. His own father's death from emphysema (caused by smoking) affected Patrick enormously. Despite a difficult family life growing up, by his late teens Patrick already had discovered an inner map, a self-image as a stabilizing, positive force for good in the community. It was inevitable that the lineage of the tobacco industry and his own self-image would collide, but what was not inevitable was the way he negotiated that collision. Patrick chose to testify before Congress, offering information on how the tobacco industry tried to suppress information linking smoking with chronic illness and death. He shed an irreversible light on the situation. The Sagittarian map is much like a light—its openness carries no agenda of manipulation and, therefore, it cannot be battled very well by special interest groups.

Sometimes Sagittarians choose to make maps literally, such as John Mickelson, whose Sun ⊙ is in Sagittarius ♐. A landscape cartographer, John spends his time assessing and compiling detailed conservation maps. With a degree in landscape ecology and remote sensing, he has been trained to study the ecological patterns and processes of regional landscapes—but from an outer-space perspective. For example, in 2000, he worked exclusively for a 7,000-acre forest in Connecticut. "What I love about my work is that I get to spend half of my time wandering around in woods and swamps doing detailed field surveys and the other half in the computer lab, performing high-tech image processing of satellite imagery and algorithmic analysis of the field data. This work allows us to better understand the locations, functions, and relationships within the natural systems that support us and is slowly allowing us to become better stewards of the earth," Mickelson says. His work is an expression of his faith in the interconnectedness of all life.

When Venus ♀ is in Sagittarius ♐, Sagittarian faith takes on personal charm and the words are rich with the heart and possibility of the ultimate optimist. Political analyst Marty Rosenbluth has Venus in Sagittarius and says, "As an activist, I always go into a situation believing I'm going to win. Always. I never go into a situation believing failure is possible."

Saturn ♄ in Sagittarius ♐ can be more cautious, unless an attitude of slow, steady progress is adopted to serve Saturn's need to be thorough. Composer Peter Kater describes how he combines Saturn's discipline and realism with the expansive desire of Sagittarius to expand and make a map—or in his case, a musical composition. Peter says, "I never go into a project knowing what I am going to do. I have thoughts and ideas of where I want to arrive eventually, but I really never know how I am going to get there. All I need to know is what's next. I don't need to know what's next after next. I just need to know the next step. The closer I stay to that, the happier I am in the process." That Saturnian approach enables Peter to build a cohesive musical composition whether he can see the whole from the beginning or not.

Those born with north node ☊ in Sagittarius ♐ are frequently pulled toward a path or philosophy that unifies their focus. Stuart Quimby, the toy maker, is a good example. With north node in Sagittarius, the healthiest path to his future includes recognizing the unifying field. Stuart says, "Discovering Buckminster Fuller's Synergetics was a turning point in my life." Synergetics is Fuller's name for the geometry he advanced based on the patterns of energy that he saw in nature. Stuart's business, Design Science Toys, was founded on these principles, and with the production and sale of every toy, he is introducing a child to "the unifying field"—an education in interconnection. Hopefully, these children as adults will create a more conscious culture.

♐ Find Sagittarius at Work in Your Life

Locate individual planets you have in Sagittarius below, and consider how they focus your life:

SUN IN ♐: How can I live life as an optimist and be a symbol of possibility to others? Where has that optimism led me? What maps do I pass on to others?

MOON IN ♐: As a traveler, how have I discovered that home is everywhere? How have I created expansive spaces, through light or spatial arrangement of furniture in my home?

MERCURY IN ♐: How do I express my eloquence as a speaker and my sense of philosophical adventure simultaneously?

VENUS IN ♐: How do I create social adventures with diverse groups of open-minded people? Artistic adventures?

MARS IN ♐: How am I like a galloping horse crossing an open field, unafraid of speed or space? How am I energized when I help others find a reason to expand philosophically?

JUPITER IN ♐: How am I a generous educator? How do I play the role of good guide to those seeking new maps, good ideas, or better resources?

SATURN IN ♐: How can my cautious optimism help me trust travel rather than tethering me to too small a territory? As the practical idealist, what philosophy have I steadily explored, testing its limits, with an ordered approach to building faith in that path?

CHIRON IN ♐: How well do I remember that one person's faith or map of possibility is not necessarily mine; mine is unique? How can I trust that a journey involving detours may offer more than the main road?

URANUS IN ♐: How does my life resemble an experimental journey? How am I brilliant at expanding the map of what is possible (culturally, philosophically, literally)?

NEPTUNE IN ♐: How do I act on my faith in the unity of all cultures, in one world? How does the universe whisper to me about my sacred place in it?

PLUTO IN ♐: What compelling stories do I want to pass on to future generations which describe the great changes of the time in which I lived?

SOUTH NODE IN ♐: How can I resist being in perpetual motion and focus on rich detail?

NORTH NODE IN ♐: Am I ready to trust that there is a unifying principle, and this whole is more interesting than my capacity to deconstruct the whole into intellectual exercises?

To Encourage Intuitive Flow for Sagittarius

Play with Sagittarius as part of your purpose if you have the Sun or other planets in that sign.

Imagine yourself as the cosmic travel agent able to write yourself free tickets for any trip. You are also able to do this for everyone you love and even people you don't (but who might improve if they took a trip and got a fresh perspective). As you write your own ticket, fear falls away about the unknowns involved. Where would you go? Who would you gift with a trip? What *ahas* would you like to have on your trip? What *ahas* would you like the others to have?

Pass on faith in the adventure of life and every aha! *through the flow....*

♑ Capricorn: To Teach

December 21 to January 20

Capricorn excels at discipline and therefore, completion. As a consequence, Capricorn completions can be tested by time, credibility earned, standards of mastery made real. Capricorn builds traditions that support those standards. Capricorn creates teachers who choose a tradition to embody, as impeccably as possible.

♑ Capricorn Supports Standards of Mastery

Key questions to every Capricorn are: *What tradition do you serve? What boundaries do you need in place to serve that tradition? What are the firm stepping-stones upon your path?*

Capricorn carefully contemplates and then embodies a certainty, which is part of why Capricorn is a *cardinal sign*—a peak period of winter. The days are short; the night is long; the hermit has work to do, building what can be built only with careful contemplation. Capricorn is considered to be an *earth sign* because it has the ability to build structures—schools, college departments, corporations, small businesses, research companies, symphonies. Capricorn's difficulty may be as a creator who needs too much control over the creation, or the crippling critic who has such high standards that no one can qualify.

Capricorn is 180 degrees from the sign of Cancer; the two are halves of a whole. Cancer's agenda to nourish from the inside out is much like the agenda of a mother emotionally attuned to her offspring. Capricorn is more concerned with the final form something will take—and giving it support through clearly defined standards. Like a father figure, Capricorn is a role model of self-responsibility and accountability. Saturn, with its penchant for discipline, thrives in Capricorn and therefore rules it. Capricorn must continually redefine inner and outer authority, sidestepping know-it-all attitudes and embodying instead the teacher who can be taught.

The most interesting Capricorns are risk-takers in lifelong learning. Author and teacher Gail Straub is a good example of a Capricorn skilled at identifying limits and yet continuing to grow. With Sun ⊙ in Capricorn ♑, she has spent two decades helping people identify and transform limiting beliefs in order to manifest a vision. She and her husband coach people all over the world through their Empowerment Training Programs.

Yet Gail's own health and happiness have hinged on finding the grace to love her deepest vulnerabilities—the person behind the mask of the teacher. Finding that grace for herself has similarly enabled her to help her students. "So very many people try to mask their needs and vulnerabilities. We all think we need to be perfect in order to be loved," says Gail. "But once we recognize that the suffering in our story links us to the suffering of all living things, our own drama is less consuming."

It is commitment to character that Capricorn seeks to breed, an appreciation for what is good and strong, with faults falling away on their own, in their own time. Capricorn becomes the old growth tree, certain of its goodness and every gnarled branch.

That same commitment to character breeds in Capricorn a love of consistency and certainty, and the scientific community loves Capricorns for precisely that reason. Biochemist and author Kary Mullis, with Sun ☉ in Capricorn ♑, is a good example. Kary established a new tradition in science when he discovered PCR (polymerase chain reaction), which enabled DNA testing to become a reality in 1983 and forever changed the worlds of medicine, biotechnology, genetics, and forensics. He won the Nobel Prize for that discovery in 1993 and wrote a book about it, *Dancing Naked in the Mind Field.*

Kary explains why the scientific method requires such certainty and commitment:

"Scientists submit articles in order to report their work. Preparing articles describing their work and having them published is crucial to a scientist's career. In primary journals, every single experimental detail has to be there either directly or by reference, so that somebody else could repeat exactly what was done and find out whether it comes out the same way in their hands. If it doesn't, somebody will report that, and the conflict usually has to be resolved so that when we go on from here, we know where *here* is."

Capricorn loves the knowledge of where "here" is, no matter

the tradition. The question with Capricorn is: *Which authority can we trust? On whose shoulders can we safely stand?*

Capricorn, with its desire to teach, inevitably explores self-mastery. The first step in self-mastery is essentially a Capricorn wisdom: to keep an open mind, to be the teacher who can be taught, so as not to be permanently stunted by one's own opinions.

It is that same destiny of self-mastery that inspirational speaker Patrick Reynolds encourages in teenagers across America, as he fathers and mothers them, with his Moon ☽ in Capricorn ♑. Reynolds reminds these teenagers that they are guardians of their own health. They must learn to parent themselves.

When Venus ♀ is in Capricorn ♑, the grace of Venus wants to teach principles of grace and beauty. Teacher Gail Straub, whose Venus is in Capricorn, has created a spiritual training literally called Grace. Her book *The Rhythm of Compassion* is based on her experiences teaching that training.

When Mars ♂ is in Capricorn ♑, leadership qualities (Mars) merge with an appreciation for executing solid plans right on time. My mother has Mars in Capricorn and she made sure our family was not only on time but a little early for school, church, weddings, funerals, parties, or travel. We not only arrived with spare time, but we had a spare tire in the trunk and spare clothes in the event plans shifted. That is how she internalized her Mars.

♑ Find Capricorn at Work in Your Life

Locate individual planets you have in Capricorn below, and consider how they focus your life:

SUN IN ♑: How can I commit to building character, appreciating what is good and strong, and letting faults fall away on their own, in their own time?

MOON IN ♑: How can I produce a pearl—beautiful and solid—from my solitude that others will recognize as my emotional autonomy, my completeness within myself?

MERCURY IN ♑: How do my communications skills build solid projects that are clearly complete?

VENUS IN ♑: Do I wear the golden ring of commitment, proclaiming my long-term marriage to the healing or creative arts? Who will win my love by wearing the same ring, wedded to similar purposes?

MARS IN ♑: How can I aim my ambition at projects that will give me credibility and, therefore, authority in the culture?

JUPITER IN ♑: What work gives me faith in my mastery as a builder of clear form?

SATURN IN ♑: How can I find the sculpture hiding in the marble of me, wanting to be revealed through work I commit to, as I parent or teach or mentor or build?

CHIRON IN ♑: How can I be a healer as I infiltrate ranks of authority figures who have forgotten that a series of imperfect stepping-stones can lead directly to the top of the mountain as they spiral up the hill?

URANUS IN ♑: How can I be a catalyst in the traditional world, retranslating old methods and approaches so that they are suitable for the needs of a contemporary culture?

NEPTUNE IN ♑: What do I most want to build and what support do I need from the Muse to build it?

PLUTO IN ♑: How can I help birth training schools for teachers destined to teach teachers?

SOUTH NODE IN ♑: How can I relax into trusting the essence-oriented side of myself who creates in the dark, aware the form will take care of itself if the essence is seeded with care?

NORTH NODE IN ♑: How can I learn to find form and stand steady in the role of teacher?

To Encourage Intuitive Flow for Capricorn

Play with Capricorn as part of your purpose if you have the Sun or other planets in that sign.

Imagine that before you entered this life you went through training with a teacher who was the best of the best at a particular focus, and who loved you like a son or daughter. This teacher taught you everything about this focus, reminding you, "You won't remember a thing consciously, but it will all be there in your subconscious, waiting to be reawakened, once you get to Earth and your nature is stimulated to grow." What did this teacher train you to cultivate and grow? Do you remember the part of the training that reiterated: *Try and fail a hundred times, rather than playing too small, repeating what you have already perfectly mastered?*

Pass on trust in life-long learning, through the flow....

≈ Aquarius: To Liberate

January 20 to February 18

Aquarius is the undeniable truth. Aquarius has no interest in protecting reputation or any tradition, unless the tradition liberates one into a larger truth. Aquarius is the scout on a constant reconnaissance mission to wake up. Aquarius gives everyone permission to reinvent him- or herself.

≈ Aquarius Liberates by Revealing the Undeniable Truth

After all the Capricorn completions, a new beginning is essential, a fresh step: Aquarius is that step. Capricorn can be so in love with certainty that it is deaf to the possibility of change. Aquarius liberates us into amazement again, giving us permission to do what we have never done before.

Aquarius is a *fixed sign*, carrying through the purpose of the season—liberation—after a spell of extreme order (Capricorn). Aquarius is high intelligence, crystal clear and, therefore, an *air sign*, which carries intelligence. Air signs (Gemini, Libra, and Aquarius) mobilize the planets that occupy them and encourage them to move into heightened objectivity. Air signs encourage perceptual adjustment in response to what is seen.

One hundred and eighty degrees from Leo, Aquarius looks at its opposite, with its agenda of celebration and heart, and says: *You may wander far from the truth in order to please others or make up a better story. The truth cannot be improved upon; you do not need to exaggerate to tell the truth.* Leo says: *The truth is so big you must exaggerate to tell it.* Leo is also inclined to listen carefully for applause; Leo wants to be loved. Aquarius is free of that concern, so it can follow the liberating path without retreating in the face of public criticism (or no feedback at all). The permission of Aquarius to experiment is the perfect fuel for Uranus, and so Uranus is said to rule Aquarius.

Aquarians can be freethinkers, outlaws, or both. Ideally, Aquarians are freethinkers who use that intelligence to connect them to community rather than isolating them. That is precisely what Susun Weed, with Sun ☉ in Aquarius ♒, does. She writes, "Since 1986, I have lived in the Catskill Mountains of the Hudson River valley, where I grow most of my own food and herbs, heat with wood, and milk the goats twice a day. No radio, no recorded music, no TV, no newspapers intrude on my day or interrupt my thoughts. I listen to nature, to the plants, to the wisdom of the animals and my own body." She also offers that environment to the women who come to her teaching center, and the connection to community is complete.

Aquarians sometimes find themselves in the publishing business, spreading their truths around, giving people more options through information. Toward that end, Susun Weed built a publishing company featuring books on health and healing herbs as an important alternative to mainstream medicine. "I have been called a backward pioneer," she writes, "because I have reclaimed the oldest ways of healing—herbs and shamanic skills, women's ways of nourishing and relating—and made them accessible and workable for today."

Aquarius and the planet Uranus are literally electrical—the electricity of evolution, our ability to move freely toward our next stage of development. For that reason, Aquarius (and Uranus) are affiliated with acupuncture, which restores the authentic electrical system to the body, encouraging health.

Originating in China, acupuncture has been in use for more than twenty-three centuries. With Sun ☉ in Aquarius ♒, acupuncturist Miriam Cooper explains her fascination with the body's electrical system as based on much more than technical knowledge. She says, "Human beings are a web of energy and matter, a continuum of form and function. Chinese medicine particularly focuses on the energy end of the continuum. This energy is called Qi and is the life force that animates us and all living things. Qi, or life energy, is more subtle than the electrical energy it produces, but the two are deeply intertwined. I love my work because you really reach a person at an essential core."

Aquarius can be political as well, working with evolution (change from within) or revolution (change from without). Human rights activist Bill Monning, with Moon ☽ in Aquarius ♒, often finds himself caring deeply (Moon) about people who have lost their freedom, and acting out his caring by working for their release (Aquarius).

Aquarius can attract others to its ideas by voicing them persuasively, particularly with Venus ♀ in Aquarius ♒, which can beautifully describe truths bigger than the linear logical box (the box being more of a Capricorn mentality). It is not uncommon for those with Venus in Aquarius to be particularly open to astrology. Aquarius rules astrology because skillful use of astrology wakes people up.

To the shock of the scientific community, Nobel Prize winner Kary Mullis admits a respect for astrology in his book *Dancing Naked in the Mind Field*, devoting an entire chapter to "I Am A Capricorn." His Venus in Aquarius is showing as he writes:

"We consider ourselves to be sophisticated, intelligent, modern people. Our psychologists and sociologists consider astrology to be nonsense. Academic departments concerned with human behavior consider astrology to be a confusing distraction with no serious value to their pursuits. And it's not that they've never heard of it. They've noticed that every daily paper in the world has a column devoted to it and that lots of humans pay attention to it. The reason they don't pay attention to it is that it would embarrass them in front of their colleagues. There's no proven body of facts in the social sciences that says human behavior does not contain elements that relate to planetary positions at the time of birth. Instead there's a broad and arrogant understanding among social science professionals that folklore, like astrology, is for simpletons. Without doing any simple experiments to test some of the tenets of astrology, it has been completely ignored by psychologists in the last two centuries.... Most of them are under the false impression that it is nonscientific and not a fit subject for their serious study. They are dead wrong."

Aquarius can be intelligence on a high mental plane—clear and lucid, free of illusion—and when Uranus, ruler of Aquarius, is in its home sign, life-changing realizations can enter unexpectedly in the form of a book or a person or a guide, like lightning striking the old way of operating and introducing the new. My father had Uranus ♅ in Aquarius ♒ and when he read Norman Vincent Peale's *The Power of Positive Thinking*, he was electrified by the idea that we create our own reality by virtue of the thoughts we think.

I can remember politely listening at the age of eight while he read parts of Peale's book aloud to my sister and me, oblivious to the fact that he was voicing what would become a foundational assumption in my life as human being and astrologer: *Life doesn't just "happen" to you.* Your beliefs shape your experiences enormously. Thoughts are things, and when you think positively, you are taking responsibility for creating your best possible future.

♒ Find Aquarius at Work in Your Life

Locate individual planets you have in Aquarius below, and consider how they focus your life:

SUN IN ♒: How do I create a lifestyle that is totally my own? How do I gift my community with fresh ideas and entrepreneurial talent?

MOON IN ♒: How am I guided toward nourishing relationships with authentic people with whom I can be free as well?

MERCURY IN ♒: How does my intelligence seek innovative ways to express itself?

VENUS IN ♒: How does truth articulate itself through me with no sentimentality yet with unmistakable grace?

MARS IN ♒: How do I challenge myself regularly by updating my ideas when they become outdated? How do I serve others similarly?

JUPITER IN ♒: How do I express faith in my original ideas? How do I encourage others who are trying to do what they have never done before?

SATURN IN ♒: How do I build the foundational layer of my life on authenticity? How do I communicate to others that I am not for sale?

CHIRON IN ♒: How do I carry a truth that is a missing piece in a puzzle? When I offer that truth to others during puzzling times, how do I help them shift out of abstract thinking and into wisdom?

URANUS IN ♒: How do I embody the freethinker and act on the knowledge that thoughts are things?

NEPTUNE IN ♒: How can I express timeless truths as part of my soul's purpose?

PLUTO IN ♒: How can I be a "battery pack" for group creativity, generating the ultimate interactive form of empowered intelligence?

SOUTH NODE IN ♒: How can I honor the freethinker within me without getting trapped in intelligence that lacks heart?

NORTH NODE IN ♒: How can I cultivate the freethinker I am, the pioneer of my future?

To Encourage Intuitive Flow for Aquarius

Play with Aquarius as part of your purpose if you have the Sun or other planets in that sign.

Imagine yourself able to wave a magic wand over the entire planet, liberating countries from oppressive dictatorships, swinging wide prison doors for political prisoners, providing educational opportunities for all.

Imagine everyone listening as you say: *Each of us has an equal right to awaken to the path that is our unique gift. And at the root of that gift is deep connection to one another. May we move as one world toward freedom, toward an experiment in awakening.*

Pass on freedom to evolve, through the flow....

⌘ Pisces: To Let Go

February 20 to March 19

Pisces encourages letting go of who you think you are, so that you can remember who you are. As Pisces peels away the masks of identity, it reveals the face of compassion; it accesses the strength of benevolence. The heart of Pisces is supersensitive, and seeks to express the soul itself. The eyes of Pisces are visionary, the vision a reflection of the power of love.

⌘ Pisces encourages imagination

Imagination is the foot soldier of the soul. Pisces encourages soul in the cosmic scheme of things, and imagination in the day-to-day ordinary moment, allowing your consciousness to roam. The true goal of Piscean imagination is to encourage you to step into the flow that connects all life and allow the power of the universe to be channeled through you. Unlike Scorpio's exploration of power, which is primal, Pisces explores the power of the universe through an astonishing emotional range and heightened sensitivity, drawing first from spirit but also from sound, touch, smell, and sight. Inspired, Pisces can be the evangelical preacher, the masterful musician, or the advertising executive triggering the minds of the masses through skillful use of poetic words and images.

The Pisces face is a flexible one, capable of registering every human emotion. Pisces is ever-changing, a *mutable sign* reflecting the shift from one season to another in February and March. Those born under the sign of Pisces are often transparent, no matter how well masked they think they are, which can be endearing—or unnerving, depending on who is behind the mask.

Profoundly psychic, Pisces can empathize as no other sign can, as well as inspire. (Neptune is its planetary ruler given Neptune's personification of the Muse.) As a *water sign*, Pisces has the emotional depth of the ocean. With antennae finely tuned to know through feeling, the Pisces heart can break wide open to hold the entire world. Considered the zodiac sign at greatest risk, Pisces is sometimes called "the sign of self-undoing," due to its extreme sensitivity and imagination as well as those times when it unmasks unconsciously and loses face. Pisces can also get lost in playing messiah, in being a channel for infinite love and, subsequently, losing its basic instincts of self-preservation which results in martyrdom. Pisces functions best when its expression of infinite compassion is aimed at the self first, as it builds a fully functional life.

A Pisces grounded in self-care can be successful at anything—art, business, or human services—but frequently Pisces is the priest or priestess wearing no religious garb but bringing a new light to their communities. Urban visionary Marie Runyon, with Sun ☉ in ♓ Pisces, is such a light. She moved to Harlem in 1946, a southern white woman and single mother living in a black community. Making a living in a variety of fashions while she raised her daughter, Marie fell in love with Harlem and carried a vision of it as a community that could thrive. It bothered her in particular that there were so many homeless people on the streets, while abandoned buildings fell into deeper decay. In 1976 she began organizing to change that, and Marie's vision resulted in the Harlem Restoration Project: housing for hundreds of people who were otherwise homeless, built by ex-offenders who needed the work. Pisces does not see "dangerous criminal" when it looks at an ex-offender. Pisces sees with the eyes of the soul.

Nor does Marie waste time on people or situations that refuse to improve. She moves on to tackle a situation that does. "I don't want no leisure world," Marie says dryly. "I love my life. We deal with problems, of course, all the time. But I'm doing what I want to be doing. I'm hoping for a new renaissance in Harlem."

Ananda Apfelbaum, with Sun ☉ in ♓ Pisces, is another example of a Piscean priestess, acting out her compassion in ways that have changed the lives of hundreds of people. A photographer and masseuse by profession, Ananda was traveling in India in 1994 and visited Dharamsala where hundreds of Tibetan refugees were living; her heart opened to them all. She photographed extensively and then gave slide shows in the U.S. upon her return. Moved by the photos, people gave Ananda money to bring back to Dharamsala.

Ananda created a nonprofit organization, the Tibetan Relief Project. She and donors to her organization have helped hundreds of Tibetans survive. Pisces can become a gateway for compassion to flow wherever it needs to go.

Pisces favors visionary arts like photography, painting, film, or media that make eternal a moment. Pisces is the free flowing energy of the Muse, looking for expression.

The Piscean artist understands the full palette of color and, more important, the light behind the color. With Sun ☉ in

Pisces ♓, abstract expressionist painter Quita Brodhead worked with that light and color for over eighty years before her death in 2002 at the age of 101. Quita began painting in 1919 and described painting as the transfer of sensations, "and it is not easy to pin down a sensation."

She used color as one of her primary mediums to say what she saw as she attuned to the spirit behind the form. "It's just like writing," she said. "There are particular phrases that say exactly what you want, for that particular purpose, but each purpose is a little different. The colors I use change based on my location. I use different colors in the Canary Islands than in Pennsylvania. You are not conscious of it—you relate to the vibes of the atmosphere."

Quita did not believe one must have physical sight to be a visual artist, because of this ability to "relate to the vibes of the atmosphere" intuitively. Although not blind herself, she served on the board of directors of the National Exhibits by Blind Artists and was chairman of the exhibition committee.

Pisces, as the last sign, is about infinity as source and destination. Quita's series *The Endless Circle* reflected her philosophical questions about infinity and appeared in her show "Celebration of a Century" in New York City in 2001. *The New York Times*'s review of the show reflected the power of Pisces at its best: "[A] swirl of blue, like a comet in its tracks, dances on a hazy cosmic ground, an ethereal blend of lavenders, whites, and yellows. The gifts of long life and the talent to live it rewardingly do not go to many. Ms. Brodhead is simply a phenomenon." She was a Piscean phenomenon, having spent a lifetime learning to get out of her own way in order to paint such pictures.

Pisces can be political, particularly about the ocean, which it rules. With Jupiter ♃ in Pisces ♓, activist Bill Monning has a weekly radio show in California that is a forum for his community to discuss their feelings about local politics, the health of the ocean, and the local coast.

Pisces gives one access to deep universal waters yet can poignantly honor individuality as well, particularly with Uranus ♅ in Pisces ♓. My mother has Uranus in Pisces, and cries easily when moved, much more so than most people, and she has cultivated a natural way of excusing herself in public ("Don't mind me, I do this all the time"), dabbing at her eyes while simultaneously completing the cry. The tears may be about a performance she attended that was so inspiring it has stayed with her, or about someone else's great grief or joy—or her own. She has very little emotional backlog as a consequence of these cries. She trusts the truth of the flow.

♓ Find Pisces at Work in Your Life

Locate individual planets you have in Pisces below, and consider how they focus your life:

SUN IN ♓: How can I explore the spirit behind the mask of me? How have I discovered my sensitivity as strength and found a way to channel that sensitivity imaginatively?

MOON IN ♓: How does my happiness hinge directly upon my ability to follow my dreams? How does my emotional sensitivity inform me of where I really feel at home (or don't)?

MERCURY IN ♓: What means of communication have I chosen to focus my gift for articulating the spirit behind the form of things?

VENUS IN ♓: How do I treasure people who unmask and let the light of the soul shine through? How am I treasured when I unmask as well?

MARS IN ♓: How am I able to prioritize my intentions based on intuitive guidance rather than linear logic?

JUPITER IN ♓: How can I be a generous host to visionary possibilities?

SATURN IN ♓: How can I commit to boundaries that guard my sensitive spirit, understanding that there is a difference between a wall and a boundary? How can I build a container, a structure, a discipline for my remarkable Muse?

CHIRON IN ♓: How can I empathize with others without confusing their feelings with mine?

URANUS IN ♓: How am I continually surprised at the range of my emotions and the truth they communicate, no matter how many decades I have lived?

NEPTUNE IN ♓: How do I align with a source of inspiration so strongly communicative to me, I consider it my true home?

Pluto was not in Pisces in the twentieth century but will be by the middle of the twenty-first.

SOUTH NODE IN ♓: How am I more identified with spirit than being Someone In Particular? How can I trust my readiness to find form, to efficiently execute a plan rather than just going with the flow?

NORTH NODE IN ♓: How can I discover the secret sea of intuition afoot in the universe that I can step into at any time and gain guidance?

To Encourage Intuitive Flow for Pisces

Play with Pisces as part of your purpose if you have the Sun or other planets in that sign.

Imagine yourself discovering a giant circle in an open field. You step inside of it and suddenly begin to see every color of the rainbow as well as some you have never seen before. Every color corresponds to an emotion, a frequency of knowing through feeling that represents every stage of human development. As you move from color to color, each door to feeling you have ever shut down reopens. You cry, you laugh, you keep moving through the circle. At the center of the circle is a white light with a strong presence of unconditional love. This light animates every color in the circle. The light at the center telepathically says: "I can shrink to a small sparkling light and relocate instantaneously wherever you direct me to go, as a gift to someone else. Where would you like me to go? Which parts of your own life would benefit from regular visits from me?"

How do you answer this light?

Pass on wisdom of emotion, through the flow....

You've completed a tour of every sign, and identified your planets within each. Now let's move on to the third building block in astrological language: the houses, which set the stage for much of the action you've just articulated.

CHAPTER 5

The Houses:
Life Arenas for Each Instinct (Planet)

There are three dimensions to astrology: planets, signs, and houses. We've explored the planets as instincts, and the signs as energizers for those instincts. Now we'll explore the houses as *life arenas* in which each planet plays out its purpose. Each life arena is like a home territory for the planet to explore and represents a theme, such as career, home and family, spirituality, partnership, play, and others.

Many different analogies have been used to describe the houses. Some astrologers liken the twelve houses to twelve rooms in the house of your psyche. Others describe them as twelve stages, upon which the drama of your life is played out.

We'll begin our study of the twelve houses with a highlighting of the four major angles (at the beginning of the first, fourth, seventh, and tenth houses) which are superhighways of energy in the house system.

Then we will tour each house, its theme, and the creativity inherent there as reflected in the lives of the contemporary people you met in the last chapter. You will notice that houses thematically correspond to certain planets and signs. Planets *and* signs are said to "rule" the house that maximizes their natural function (a list of them appears on page 128, with the major themes of each house).

After touring each house, the section entitled "Find the First (Second, etc.) House at Work in Your Life" will help you identify the relevant life questions the houses bring to you. If you took notes in chapter 4 on how your planets operate in particular signs, you can now add the third dimension of how they operate in the houses, fleshing out your astrological mirror in a rich way.

If you have no planets in a house, looking at which sign (or planet) rules that house is another method for exploring that thematic material. Confusing? Just think of the *house*, the *life arena*, as a country, such as Russia. The *zodiacal sign* that rules the house would be *the energy* of that country at large, something inherently Russian (but not a Russian person), for example Russian clothes or food or anything carrying the cultural energy of Russia. The *planet* (remember a planet personifies) that rules that house would be the equivalent of a Russian person, *a personification of Russianness.*

In most cases your planets will not be in the sign they rule *or* in the house they rule, which creates the three-dimensionality of astrological symbolism. Just as you could be a Russian person dressed in Japanese clothing living in Canada, you could have Mars in Cancer (rather than Aries, the sign it rules) living in the third house (rather than the first, which it rules).

After you complete locating all of your planets in the houses and exploring the life questions they suggest, play with intuitive imagery for that house, just as you did in the last chapter on signs. You can apply this imagery to your Sun or any other planet in that house.

But before we begin the tour of the houses, let's create an easily remembered phrase for each of them and note the ruling planet and sign as well.

The twelve houses set the stage for these activities:

In the **first house** you **announce your identity**. This life arena symbolizes your choice to be someone in particular, out of free will, with a consistent mask as you face the exterior world. *(Mars and the sign of Aries rule the first house.)*

In the **second house** you learn to **pay your own way**. This life arena encourages you to stabilize self-resourcefulness and build self-esteem. *(Venus and Taurus rule the second house.)*

In the **third house** you learn to **trust your own eyes**, and **find your own voice**. This life arena encourages you to own your personal voice or vision. *(Mercury and Gemini rule the third house.)*

In the **fourth house** you create **home**. This life arena encourages self-care from the roots up. *(The Moon and Cancer rule the fourth house.)*

In the **fifth house** you **play**. This life arena encourages creativity, sport, spontaneity, joy, and a love affair with life in general. *(The Sun and Leo rule the fifth house.)*

In the **sixth house** you get back to **work, day-to-day**, and improve the quality of life for others. This life arena encourages a contribution to the community through your work. *(Chiron and Virgo rule the sixth house.)*

In the **seventh house** you **partner** with a significant other. This life arena encourages bonding with others as equals in relationships that endure over time. *(Venus and Libra rule the seventh house.)*

In the **eighth house** you **explore what is unseen**. This life arena encourages learning to respond—rather than react—to what you discover as you explore the unseen. *(Pluto and Scorpio rule the eighth house.)*

In the **ninth house** you discover **worldly wisdom**. This life arena encourages unifying all you have learned into a cosmology that guides you. (*Jupiter and Sagittarius rule the ninth house.*)

In the tenth house you create your public reputation and career path. This life arena is where you play out a public role based on the cosmology you developed in the ninth house. (*Saturn and Capricorn rule the tenth house.*)

In the eleventh house you recognize and respond to long-term goals. This life arena also encourages you to network with others who have the same goals. (*Uranus and Aquarius rule the eleventh house.*)

In the twelfth house you answer the spirit call. In this life arena, you step outside of time and merge with the Muse, infinite imagination, the source of the "I" birthed in the first house, and now the destination of that "I," free of every mask. (*Neptune and Pisces rule the twelfth house.*)

As you read about the houses in this chapter, note that meaning builds as you move from house to house. Particularly as we reach the eighth house, many different life experiences are synthesized (more information is given about that house than about the others, in deference to its complexity). Because the houses are vast theaters, their thematic range can be broader than the signs or the planets. Still, the houses as life arenas reflect a twelve-step path of unfoldment, just as the signs do. But to begin, let's look at the four primary angles that act as major gateways in these twelve steps.

The Four Angles

You may remember from chapter 3 that the horizontal and vertical angles of the twelve houses are superhighways of energy. Many astrologers look carefully at the zodiacal sign on the cusp of the first, fourth, seventh, and tenth houses that create this grand cross. They also look for any planet conjunct (within five degrees of) any of the major angles, because these planets become the equivalent of power brokers, playing a dominant role in a person's life story.

The ascendant deserves the most attention of the four angles, as it represents your self-presentation to others. **The qualities of the ascendant (the cusp of the first house)** in your birthchart reflect how your presence will "dawn" on others. The ascendant—the rising sign—symbolizes the immediate vibration you put out into the world. It's the mask you wear when you step out the front door and dawn on the world.

For example, educator Patrick Reynolds has *Scorpio rising*. His immediate presence communicates Scorpio's intensity. Anyone meeting him would understand that he has a passionate purpose—to transform the power politics around tobacco in America. Onstage, speaking to youth, he is direct and intense, sharing the story of his father's and brother's deaths caused by smoking.

Writer Christian McEwen has *Capricorn rising*. Her immediate presence is somewhat reserved, but the committed teacher of writing comes through quickly. The oldest of six children, she was the "elder" among them, their father figure in a sense, as is often the case with Capricorn (expressing parental responsibility for others).

A good example of a planet conjunct the ascendant is herbalist Susun Weed's Moon in Taurus, which casts her as Earth Mother in self-presentation. In effect, with her Moon conjunct her ascendant, Susun becomes a walking advertisement (first house presentation) for nourishment (Moon) from the earth (Taurus). She makes herself easily accessible to others as an herbalist.

Similarly, composer Peter Kater has *Leo rising* with Uranus on the ascendant. His immediate presence is creative yet experimental and individualistic with Uranus so strongly present. He says, "My *yes* to life comes from a willingness to periodically redefine what I think is important and how I present myself to the world. I tend to rebel against whatever bandwagon comes along. I *don't* jump on."

The qualities of the midheaven (the cusp of the tenth house) describe your public identity seen from a great distance, like a flag flying from the top of your identity announcing your reputation or larger life-purpose, particularly through career or profession.

For example, educator Patrick Reynolds has *Leo on the midheaven*, suggesting a dramatic public role in which nobility and color play a part. In fact, his public reputation is linked with his upbringing in the privileged upper class. With the planet Pluto less than a degree from his midheaven, he plays an archetypal role as a public person: He is more than a colorful actor; he is a symbolic king.

Writer Christian McEwen has *Saturn on the midheaven* in the sign of *Sagittarius.* As an adult, Christian has stabilized her sense of faith (Sagittarius) in her own authority (Saturn), become a respected teacher (tenth house) in her field of writing and teaching, and edited several anthologies.

As the ascendant symbolizes your own immediate vibration put out into the world, **the descendant (the cusp of the seventh house)** symbolizes the qualities you seek in long-term intimate or professional partnerships.

For example, artist Gail Bruce has *Aries on the descendant*, and she married an Aries. In addition, she has the planet Mars in Aries on the descendant, suggesting she partners best with strong-willed personalities (her husband is a director).

The i.c. or taproot (the cusp of the fourth house) symbol-izes qualities that you may find at the bottom of the well of your psyche, where all nurturance begins. The taproot correlates to the umbilical cord that once connected you to your mother, the least conscious point of nurturance—and the most primal. It also outlines the fast path to self-care whenever you are off-center. For example, composer Giovanni Sollima has *Leo on the fourth house cusp*. With Leo there, creativity, laughter, and heart make him feel at home and well nourished. "I come from a family of musicians, so music is in our DNA, in our blood. Every day, every moment, there is music in life."

Now let's take a deeper look at the individual houses, one through twelve, beginning with the first.

The First House: Announcement of Identity

The first-house life arena announces your identity, the way you dawn on others, the first impression you make. The ascendant is the sharpest image of that self-presentation, as you announce: *Hello, World! I'm here! This is who I am!*

Whatever planet you have in the first house encourages you to fully claim its qualities as your identity. Charlie Parker said, "If you don't live it, it won't come out of your horn," and this is true for planets in the first house as well. Out of free will, you become a representative of that planet in that sign, as if you were their walking billboard. The first-house identity is generally what a person offers in response to, "And who are you?" For ex-ample, I would answer, "I am an astrologer." I have Uranus in the first house in Cancer. Uranus, with its instinct to express truth, is affiliated with astrology. Cancer's purpose is to nourish.

I am a caring astrologer. My ad copy reads: "Intuitive Astrology—Compassionate coaching for optimal outcomes."

Mars rules the first house. Mars loves to lead, and the first house arena encourages free will, as you choose to announce who you are. Writer Christian McEwen has Mars in Aquarius in the first house. In the sign of Aquarius, Christian would consistently lead her life toward authenticity (Aquarius). Mars loves physical exercise; as a child, Christian would race round and round the house. Mars also indicates one's ability to be aggressive; when she was very young, Christian once bit a very proper lady on the ankle.

Public health educator Cindy Waszak has a first house Cancer Sun and is exploring her capacity to care. She is a walking billboard for family, and women in particular. In a first conversation with her, she might introduce herself with, "I do family-health work."

Filmmaker Marty Rosenbluth has Moon in Pisces in the first house. From the production studio in his home (Moon), his (Pisces) imagination cooks up films and videos. It makes him happy to be accessible to customers who want to drop by (first house) to discuss projects.

Marty also has Chiron in the first house, but in the sign of Aquarius. He heals himself and others (Chiron) as he voices his truth (Aquarius), in person (first house), in public, about his experiences as a Jew living in Palestine. He is learning to not take personally the demands of some audiences that he accept the ancient wounds of the Jews as "the only truth." With Chiron in the first house, he has to stand physically in front of the people who project their old wounds onto him, and remember: *There is nothing wrong with me.*

To some extent the first house rules the body and the health of the body. Quita Brodhead, the Piscean painter, had Saturn in the first in the sign of Capricorn (the elder). Her 101 years of life were marked by vigorous health. She committed (Saturn) to understanding her body and attributed her longevity (Saturn and Capricorn) to being her own authority figure about longevity, counting CoEnzyme Q10 and vitamin supplements as key. "Be sure and include choline and inositol—they go together—and avoid processed foods and meat with hormones or antibiotics in them, and walk two miles a day. Oxygenate!" she advised.

Find the First House at Work in Your Life

Locate individual planets you have in the first house below, and consider how they focus your life:

SUN IN THE FIRST HOUSE: How am I able to be a walking advertisement for my life path, my purpose, easily accessible to all?

MOON IN THE FIRST HOUSE: How is my caring reflected in my immediate self-presentation? How do people, friends and strangers, automatically look to me to take care of certain things?

MERCURY IN THE FIRST HOUSE: How am I a communicator up-front and in person? How do I represent a particular perspective or certain types of information?

VENUS IN THE FIRST HOUSE: How do I enjoy attracting people to me, who in turn may encourage me to grace certain situations with my skill or charm or artistry?

MARS IN THE FIRST HOUSE: How can I take a stand and be an open advocate for a particular issue?

JUPITER IN THE FIRST HOUSE: How can I be big in person, acting as the Jolly Green Giant for particular purposes? What are those purposes?

SATURN IN THE FIRST HOUSE: How can I represent, in person, the mastery of one who embodies a particular tradition?

CHIRON IN THE FIRST HOUSE: How do I volunteer to play a public role as a missing link in understanding so that a healing purpose can be fulfilled?

URANUS IN THE FIRST HOUSE: How can I embody authenticity, up-front and in person?

NEPTUNE IN THE FIRST HOUSE: How do I walk around in public with my soul hanging out?

PLUTO IN THE FIRST HOUSE: Who am I as a bigger than life personality?

SOUTH NODE IN THE FIRST HOUSE: How have I inherited a tendency to stay in charge, be comfortable as the leader? How can I begin to grow toward intimacy by relinquishing my leadership role?

NORTH NODE IN THE FIRST HOUSE: How am I ready to trust being complete unto myself, able to face the world without being dependent upon others for permission to make a move?

If you have no planets in the first house, look for your Mars, the ruler of the first house. Mars is the instinct of free will. Also look for any planets in the sign of Aries, which is the energy, or fuel, of free will. They will also inform you of what your will wants.

To Encourage Intuitive Flow for the First House

Play with the first house as part of your purpose if you have the Sun or other planets there.

Imagine a room in which you say over and over: *I am.* Consider that this room is a psychological state you can occupy at any time and that the affirmation becomes more potent every time you repeat it. A hundred times a day for decades you will use the words *I am* ... and become what you profess to be. You are able to be a walking advertisement for that particular quality. What is that quality, and what story does it tell you about why it is important for you to embody this quality, up-front and in person?

Pass on the affirmation I am, *the gift of identity. Pass on the gift of free will, through the flow....*

The Second House: Paying Your Way

Once you've established an identity (I am!) through the first house, you need confidence and grounding to continue your adventure on Earth. We all need a reserve of energy to stabilize us—a psychological or financial cushion that allows us to make moves that lead to fulfillment. To earn the confidence for such a cushion, the second house encourages you to explore what you value in yourself and then invest in it.

Because of the work involved in developing the natural resources you identify in yourself, the second house is often related to how you make your money and develop financial self-resourcefulness. The rewards of the second house are always the result of direct and steady work over time. Self-esteem grows as a consequence of having followed through with intention. There is no substitute for *doing*.

Planets in the second house outline aspects of identity that deserve development, in part through identifying with who we are and what we value. "These are my shoes, this is my rocking horse, this is my house," says the toddler. An emotional attachment and sense of values begin in childhood with possessions.

In adulthood, the second house encourages you to do more than acquire possessions with your "cushion cash." It encourages you to create your own reality. This requires recognizing your resources and working consciously with them, particularly your qualities as a human being. As a consequence of investing time and energy in them, they grow and become a resource, allowing you to be your own bank, your own fund of self-esteem and confidence—not to mention money. When you have an active second house, you are quite capable of paying your own way. Like the sign of Taurus (which rules the second house), you have the patience to move through seasons and cycles of regular, rhythmical productivity to create a harvest through doing.

Second house personal values are often colored by the part of the earth you live on; the landscape and the lifestyle. When you combine the second house and the sign of Taurus, the theme is magnified twofold. Writer Christian McEwen has a second house Taurus Sun, which encourages her to cultivate daily habits that allow her to know who she is, what she values about herself, and what she might build into a body of work. Her identity and values are shaped a great deal by the landscape of Scotland (where she grew up), the streams she waded in, the trees she climbed. As an adult, she has edited such books as *The Alphabet of the Trees: A Guide to Nature Writing*. She has taken what she values about herself—her love of nature—and devised a way to get paid for being herself.

Activist Bill Monning has Moon in Aquarius in the second house. He is most at home when he is able to build a base (second house) of self-confidence and resourcefulness that allows him freedom to remain true (Aquarius) to his values. When he ran for public office in California, he refused to accept PAC (political action committee) contributions and instead created a contract with the people, which made their contributions as voters the most powerful currency in the election process.

Artist Gail Bruce has Venus in Scorpio in the second house. She has worked as both a fashion model (Venusian beauty) and visual artist. She loves combining her creativity with her Scorpionic love of mystery—the energy behind the form of things. Her paintings and projects reflect this—and they sell, encouraging her to continue to be a productive artist. Venus is considered to be the planetary ruler of the second house, as fertile Venus makes productivity a rich possibility.

Patrick Reynolds has Mars in Capricorn in the second house and expresses his will readily as a leader interested in reforming government regulations concerning the tobacco industry. He asks authority figures in positions of power (Capricorn authority) *What does your will (Mars) want for your grandchildren, for future generations? Who are you as a parent (Capricorn)?* He is aggressively defining his own personal values and asking those in authority to do the same.

Social scientist Cindy Waszak has Jupiter in Leo in the second house. She feels most expansive, able to see the Big Picture, when she's grounded in work that matches her values, pays her well (Jupiter), and gives her an opportunity to be generous (Jupiter) and creative (Leo). Despite the need for statistics and hard data in her work in international family health, she brings a strong sense of creativity and enthusiasm for each project to the process.

Cindy consistently invests in her creative side (Leo) and every time she does, it earns results (Jupiter in the second house). Soon after she began shooting pictures, she entered a photo in a competition and it won first prize.

Chemist Kary Mullis has Uranus in Gemini in the second house. The second house teaches self-esteem, asking you to trust the value of your work even if no one affirms it right away. Kary had great difficulty getting his research published (Gemini) on his discovery (Uranus) of PCR. "This experience taught me a thing or two," he writes, "and I grew up some more.... We have to make it on the basis of our own wit ... the media are at the mercy of the scientists who have the ability to summon them and the scientists who have such ability are not often minding the store."

Educator Gail Straub has south node in Scorpio in the second house, suggesting a deep inheritance from the past that causes her to trust the ground from which she grew, having a well-developed value system. In her book *The Rhythm of Compassion*, she writes, "I was blessed to find a sense of belonging early in my life.... The natural world was my soul food, my true church, and my first and oldest love. In nature, I felt completely at home, and yet surrounded by immense mystery [Scorpio]. My love of the earth [second house is ruled by Taurus] was fierce and passionate [Scorpio]."

Scorpio includes the cycle of death and rebirth; not surprisingly, with south node in the second house (her turf, the land she owns) she composts and creates a new resource for herself from her waste.

Find the Second House at Work in Your Life

Locate individual planets you have in the second house below, and consider how they focus your life:

SUN IN THE SECOND HOUSE: How am I productive, regularly working the fields, preparing the soil, and tending the garden of a product, service, or skill that matches my inner values? What is my crop?

MOON IN THE SECOND HOUSE: How can I invest in my capacity to care? How do I nurture the harvest of my work and how does it nurture me?

MERCURY IN THE SECOND HOUSE: What products or services do I cultivate that promote information or clarity?

VENUS IN THE SECOND HOUSE: How do I invest time and energy in cultivating the healer, lover, or artist that I am (or all three)?

MARS IN THE SECOND HOUSE: How do I take advantage of a strong life force to work with great focus at something that makes me say *yes*?

JUPITER IN THE SECOND HOUSE: How can I invest in the self that is part mentor, part philosopher, part producer, capable of building anything at all?

SATURN IN THE SECOND HOUSE: How can I invest in the realist I am who loves completions, solid accomplishments that hold up over time?

CHIRON IN THE SECOND HOUSE: How can I cultivate sacred wisdom as the character quality I grow, and bring that wisdom into the practical world as a healing force through my work?

URANUS IN THE SECOND HOUSE: How can I invest in my own brilliance, which no one else can see, and become an entrepreneur?

NEPTUNE IN THE SECOND HOUSE: How does my imagination inspire me to be productive? How can the Muse merge with my daily work in the real world?

PLUTO IN THE SECOND HOUSE: How can I invest in the part of me that is a powerful battery pack, capable of recharging or rebuilding situations?

SOUTH NODE IN THE SECOND HOUSE: How can I use my work skills and resulting harvest and possessions as a resource but not be overly attached to them?

NORTH NODE IN THE SECOND HOUSE: How can I be my

own resource, stabilize on my own terms, and survive and thrive? What character qualities would I like to invest in that would become my grounding, my anchor of identity that no one can take from me?

If you have no planets in the second house, look for your Venus, which is the ruler or planetary focalizer of the second house. Venus is the flower of the earth—fertile and productive. Also look for any planets in the sign of Taurus, which is the energy of productivity. Both of them will inform you about how you are resourceful and productive.

To Encourage Intuitive Flow for the Second House

Play with the second house as part of your purpose if you have the Sun or other planets there.

Imagine swinging wide the doors to a bank. This bank contains great wealth. Its assets are the character qualities within you that represent what you are meant to grow, to gift the world and yourself with, through repetitive seasons and cycles of work. Patience is called for to bring the harvest to fruition.

Now imagine yourself walking into a huge vault that has many rough-cut diamonds inside. Imagine each one has a quality, such as creativity, steady focus, stamina, organizational skills, communication skills, managerial skills, or brilliance teaching children. Pick up a few diamonds, aware that you now have the responsibility to polish them. Cultivate these qualities day in and day out, as steady and predictable as the earth orbiting the Sun. What did you pick?

Pass on confidence in the jewel you are, your earned worth, through the flow....

The Third House: Trust Your Own Eyes, Find Your Own Voice

The third-house life arena encourages you to trust your own eyes so that they can embody clarity. With that clarity, when you say what you see, you will do so with the integrity of the personal voice. The third house involves a two-way exchange—the "in" breath of listening, of being observant, and the "out" breath, which delivers accurate detailed communications. Mercury is the personification of the third house; Gemini is its energy in motion—therefore, both are rulers of the third house.

After having declared "I'm here!" in the first house and then done inventory on character qualities in which to invest, in this third of twelve steps the call to communicate sets in. The third house is the life arena in which you develop trust in your own eyes and ears, as well as the ability to translate what you see. Many writers, teachers, and reporters have active third houses in their birthcharts. Singers, musicians, dancers, and choreographers may also have active third houses, as they discover the perfect pitch of their personal voice or rhythm.

Information gathered through the third house is often immediately relevant, particularly in your local neighborhood and among your circle of friends.

Activist Bill Monning has Sun in Aries in the third house. He is unrelenting (Aries) as a communicator (third house) in his effort to stimulate a dialogue that creates clarity. As a professional negotiator, Bill says, "The worst day at the negotiating table is preferable to the alternative, which may often be war, protracted conflict, or continued exploitation and abuse. Get people to talk and get people to *listen*" (the double action of the third house—talking and listening).

Composer Peter Kater has Moon in Libra in the third house. He is most at home (Moon) when he can listen (third house) as an artist to the life around him and explore balance and beauty and creative collaboration (Libra).

Chemist Kary Mullis has Saturn in Cancer in the third house. The third house is our database, our memory bank; with Saturn in Cancer there, many of the memories are of family, women, and umbilical cords—what kept them in place, what severed them. Kary says, "There is a general place in your brain, I think, reserved for melancholy of relationships past. It grows and prospers as life progresses, forcing you finally, against your better judgment, to listen to country music."

Tracker John Stokes has Chiron in the third house in Capricorn. Chiron seeks the sacred, the third house calls for clearly articulated sounds, and Capricorn wants information that can be mastered and taught. "I love language," John says. "Listening to different languages was the whole gateway to the native people for me, because I think the ear that you cultivate in language is the same ear for music and for imitating the sounds of the animals to call them in the woods."

With Chiron in Capricorn, the ideal context in which he would learn to hear would be with an elder teacher who did not *command* him to learn but *allowed* him to learn. He lived in Australia for seven years and became part of the Aboriginal community—working at an Aboriginal college for urban people and for tribal Pitjantjatjara from the central desert. "They thought I was a riot, and the old men began to teach me just as if I were a two-year-old. With most native people ... the kids just need to sit next to you and watch you in order to learn. Just by being with the didgeridoo player, you would resonate with him," which is what John did and what young men now do with him.

Find the Third House at Work in Your Life

Locate planets you have in the third house below, and consider how they focus your life.

SUN IN THE THIRD HOUSE: How is my life path that of translator of what I see, hear, or feel? Do I trust my own eyes? Ears? Voice?

MOON IN THE THIRD HOUSE: What stories do I tell that nourish the essence of my home (Moon), my neighborhood?

MERCURY IN THE THIRD HOUSE: How can I be a state-of-the-art communicator voicing clarity and share it with those immediately around me?

VENUS IN THE THIRD HOUSE: How can I express beauty or healing purposes through my voice, my eyes, my dancing feet, or a personal painting?

MARS IN THE THIRD HOUSE: How can I take a lead in directing perceptions—mine or other people's? How do I sharpen my attention into a laser focus designed to deliver a message?

JUPITER IN THE THIRD HOUSE: How can I swing wide the gate to a particular perspective and initiate others into it through my personal philosophy?

SATURN IN THE THIRD HOUSE: How can I be a lifelong student—or teacher—of a particular focus? What are my strengths here? My weaknesses?

CHIRON IN THE THIRD HOUSE: How can I be a healing messenger who has a piece of the story that has previously been unheard?

URANUS IN THE THIRD HOUSE: How can I see the truth of a situation with laserlike accuracy and voice it in some way?

NEPTUNE IN THE THIRD HOUSE: How can I honor intuition as a primary source of information around me?

PLUTO IN THE THIRD HOUSE: How can I access the buried secret in personal perspective and use my voice or pictures as a regenerative power for those who hear that voice, see those pictures?

SOUTH NODE IN THE THIRD HOUSE: How can I make an intuitive leap to seeing the Big Picture without becoming addicted to replaying new takes on details?

NORTH NODE IN THE THIRD HOUSE: How can I trust that if I take care of details in a focused manner, the Big Picture will take care of itself?

If you have no planets in the third house, look for your Mercury, ruler of the third house. Mercury personifies the communicator and will tell a story about your instinct to communicate. Look for planets you may have in the sign of Gemini, which will inform you of communication agendas being carried by particular planets.

To Encourage Intuitive Flow for the Third House

Play with the third house as part of your purpose if you have the Sun or other planets there.

Imagine yourself longing to relate, to communicate. You cry out "Hello!" to the rest of the world. As you do, you realize the uniqueness of your voice. You put your hand on your throat and cry out again to feel the vibration there. You place your fingertips over your eyes and feel their sensitivity. You blink and recover the power of perception and remember the gift of sight. Your ears enjoy the gift of sound. You are capable of witnessing every moment, recording it with personal perspective and memory. The experience is so rich you want to pass it on through your eyes, your voice, your feet, or your touch. Which do you choose?

What is the rich experience your witness, your reporter, wants to pass on?

Pass on the integrity of the personal voice, through the flow....

The Fourth House: Home

The fourth-house life arena encourages self-care from the root level up and describes your answers to the questions: *Where is my home? Who is my family?* Like the sign of Cancer and the Moon, which rule the fourth house, this life arena encourages profound sensitivity. We each grew from the safe space that is the womb. The fourth house suggests what you in turn will grow. It also reflects the inner family that every psychotherapist is trying to access when you have a session: *Who are the private cast of characters in your psyche who tell you who you are? From what well, symbolically, do you drink?*

The i.c. or taproot is on the cusp of the fourth house. The taproot has primal power because it includes the memory of your birth and your mother. Though the umbilical cord was severed, ancestral memory still flows through the superhighway of the taproot, shaping your approach to home and family.

However, you have been updating that approach since you drew your first breath. The fourth house is a birthing room for deeper identity: Every time your consciousness reenters after sleep, you renew the private conversation with self about identity. The unconscious mind becomes conscious, every day.

Your outer family also fits into the fourth house—your family of origin and the ways in which they shaped your psyche as you grew out of that nest, as well as your current family. The goal of the fourth-house arena is to create a well-made nest for any of these purposes: raising a family; self-care; nurturance from the root level up.

When Venus is in the fourth house, this nest takes on an extra glow and fertility, with a particular propensity toward sharing the gift of home. Marie Runyon has Venus in the fourth house in Aquarius and she loves entertaining freethinkers—artists, politicians, blue-collar workers, human rights activists—around her dinner table. She has become well known in Harlem for her yearly Thanksgiving dinner, a potluck extravaganza for her egalitarian (Aquarian) community, opening the proceedings with a cowbell and the call, "Shaddup!"

Uranus in the fourth house can involve ongoing revelations about one's own psyche or family. Composer Giovanni Sollima has Uranus in Virgo in the fourth house. In Virgo, his community of Palermo, Italy, is his extended family. Giovanni says, "Sometimes I am surprised as I discover the ancient past of my town. This is amazing because I was born here. I'm thirty-seven years old, and even today, it's possible to discover a church or place or painting I've never seen before."

Neptune in the fourth house can open a floodgate of intuitive skills. Composer Peter Kater has Neptune in Scorpio there, which suggests his intuitive ability (Neptune) to explore the deep (Scorpio) inner spaces of the psyche (fourth house). He says, "There's nothing external, period, and so the more that we think that there's anything to be done outside of ourselves, the more we're just digging deeper into the illusion."

Pluto in the fourth house can link one's personal home with a larger destiny. Susun Weed has Pluto in Leo in the fourth house. "My home is my teaching center, where I teach women how to be bitches, witches, dykes, and sluts (and herbalists and goddesses)," she says. "White mainstream culture takes these words, which describe women's power, and makes them into vile things you would be embarrassed to be. I want to reclaim those words and those powers for myself and other women." Her Pluto empowers women (fourth house) dramatically (Leo).

The south node in the fourth house suggests a deep inheritance from the family of origin or identification with the role of mothering. Mary Bloom has south node in Aries in the fourth house and says, "I always identified with my mother, and mothers everywhere—including the mother Mary, my protector." With south node in Aries, Mary has inherited (south node) great strength of will and the capacity to survive and thrive, through the mother role (fourth house).

Find the Fourth House at Work in Your Life

Locate planets you have in the fourth house below, and consider how they focus your life.

SUN IN THE FOURTH HOUSE: Who are the characters in my subconscious that become my inner family (the worker, the housecleaner, the priestess or priest who keeps the fire in the hearth going, the mother, the psychologist who mothers his or her clients?) How does the inner family relate to my outer family?

MOON IN THE FOURTH HOUSE: How can I touch base with my own feelings, digest them fully as the basis for my self-care?

MERCURY IN THE FOURTH HOUSE: How can I pay close attention to the language of my own psyche and to domestic details? What is my dream language? What's on the grocery list?

VENUS IN THE FOURTH HOUSE: How can I fall in love with

the private person I am who loves entertaining at
the one who makes home artful?

MARS IN THE FOURTH HOUSE: How can I keep a priority
list around self-care, with exercise close to number one?
How do I nurture myself by firing up the engines of
the will?

JUPITER IN THE FOURTH HOUSE: How can I create a generous and expansive nest for myself and my family? How do I
give others faith in this kind of self-care?

SATURN IN THE FOURTH HOUSE: How can I have clear
boundaries with family members so that I can remember
what I am emotionally responsible for and what I am not?
How can I ritualize self-care?

CHIRON IN THE FOURTH HOUSE: How am I able to break
through to a definition of self-care beyond what my family
of origin taught me was possible?

URANUS IN THE FOURTH HOUSE: How do I exercise the
muscle of self-honesty routinely, in the privacy of my own
home? How does my honesty encourage other people's personal growth as well?

NEPTUNE IN THE FOURTH HOUSE: How is the Muse my
mother?

PLUTO IN THE FOURTH HOUSE: How do I privately trust
my own complexity?

SOUTH NODE IN THE FOURTH HOUSE: How can I begin
to trust that I have something to offer beyond my own
home turf, while honoring my rich roots in home and
family?

NORTH NODE IN THE FOURTH HOUSE: How have I discovered my own inner life and family as a rich arena to explore, relinquishing my public image as the power point of
my identity?

If you have no planets in the fourth house, look for your Moon. The Moon will provide information about your homing instinct. Look for any planets in the sign of Cancer. They express the energy of caring and nourishment.

To Encourage Intuitive Flow for the Fourth House

Play with the fourth house as part of your purpose if you have the Sun or other planets there.

Imagine a deep well of clear clean cold water outside your house. Imagine yourself thirsty, lowering the bucket deep into the well, and drawing water. As you drink this water, your eyes grow heavy with sleep and you curl up on the grass next to the well. Immediately you begin to dream of the ancestral memory of the mother line as it passes through you, of your current family life, and especially of your deepest needs right now. These needs speak to you through images of houses and rooms in houses, particularly the basement, where a psychiatrist's couch lies before a crackling fire in the hearth. There is no psychiatrist there, only a soft pillow upon which to lay your head. Someone has left a diary there to read by the firelight. The first line reads: *Home is where you are understood.* What does the next line say?

Pass on the wealth of the subconscious, through the flow....

The Fifth House: Play

The fifth house, the house of play, describes the ignition point of joy behind art, sport, and spontaneity. The fifth house is also about the simplicity of presence, of just being. Of creativity, the fifth house says: *Be it and, therefore, birth it.* The creative child is conceived in joy out of spontaneity, and so the fifth house rules children too.

The common denominator for all fifth-house activities is the ability to be in the present. Animals and children are master teachers of that ability and so are affiliated with the fifth house. People who play sports often talk about "the zone"—a mental space in which they are perfectly poised in the now, at one with the game. That is a fifth-house moment. Likewise, fine artists cannot manufacture "art" on demand—it is a spontaneous occurrence. The same is true for healing artists. The healing is spontaneous.

The creativity of the fifth house very much involves "thinking outside the box," entering "beginner's mind," and seeing with new eyes—experiencing life as fresh and amazing. The expression on the face of a one-year-old as he sees everything for the first time is very fifth house.

The fifth house is also associated with romantic love. You are very much in the moment when you unexpectedly make eye contact with an attractive stranger in the grocery store check-out line and fall in love.

The fifth house sponsors the space to love life, moment by moment, and those with the Sun in the fifth house tend to be warm personalities who shine particularly brightly, as the Sun rules the fifth house (along with the sign of Leo). They are naturals for the creative or healing arts, sports, or the entertainment world.

Teacher Gail Straub has both Sun and Jupiter in the fifth house in the sign of Capricorn. She is the ultimate optimist (Jupiter) when she teaches people the joy of self-responsibility (Capricorn) and helps them understand the play (fifth house) within the work of that. She gains faith in herself and her life as she does this, learning as much from her students as they learn from her. She says. "I'm a very serious teacher, but I'm an outrageous player. I played hard in childhood—climbed trees, had puppet shows, canoed, sailed, made circuses—and I still play hard, including with my students. Also, I love theater, music, and culture."

Gail also has Mars in Aquarius in the fifth house. Aquarius tends to pioneer the ground it occupies, and Mars loves to lead. Gail was the first female East Coast trainer of New Games, which began in California in the 1970s as part of the movement toward play for all ages through creative and noncompetitive games. "For five or six years I taught thousands of people to play—blind people, handicapped people, regular people, young people, old people," she explains.

Social scientist Cindy Waszak also has three planets in the fifth house—Moon and Neptune in Libra and Saturn in Scorpio. Her Moon in Libra suggests she is deeply nourished by creative activities; Neptune rules photography, and so she naturally chooses that as a creative focus. Sometimes the fifth house is associated with youth; Cindy takes a special interest in teaching them responsibility (Saturn) around procreation (Scorpio).

Giovanni Sollima has Mercury in Libra in the fifth house. "I was attracted to the cello because it is like a body fifty percent male and fifty percent female." Libra reflects the balance of masculine and feminine energy; Mercury is sound, and the fifth house is the creative space in which Giovanni can develop this balance, through his cello. When he performs, he exchanges communications with his audience. His cello tells them a story, communicates to them, and the audience replies. The cello can have a spontaneous (fifth house) conversation with a thousand people at a time, without one word ever being spoken.

Peter Kater has Saturn in the fifth house in Sagittarius. His Saturn encourages him to work hard at playing and to combine discipline and spontaneity, leading to an end result he can share with others. He correlates *doing nothing* strongly with creativity:

"My version of doing nothing is going for a long bike ride or just hanging out. It's the most significant part of the creative process. That's when it all comes into play. It's not that I *will get a creative idea because I am doing nothing*. It's that you have to create the space to allow creativity to surface.

"On the other hand, some creative people never finish anything because they're always on to the next thing. It's very important to finish something. The completion creates an alchemical shift in you and everything around you in some inexplicable way."

Saturn loves completions; many artists with Saturn in the fifth house are professional artists for that reason.

Storyteller Gioia Timpanelli has Uranus in Taurus in the fifth house. About her storytelling performances she says, "People think I've memorized the stories. I have never memorized a story in my life. I'll retell it in a different way, each time, always. Never the same. That's my work [Taurus]—improvisational storytelling." The fifth house spawns improvisation and her Uranus casts her as a pioneer in improvisation.

Find the Fifth House at Work in Your Life

Locate planets you have in the fifth house below, and consider how they focus your life.

> **SUN IN THE FIFTH HOUSE:** How does my life shine through my creativity? Through the healing arts? Creative arts? Birthing children? Playing golf? Raising dogs?
>
> **MOON IN THE FIFTH HOUSE:** Who are my playmates with whom I share an emotional bond? What creative activities nourish me?
>
> **MERCURY IN THE FIFTH HOUSE:** What joy do I articulate most often?

VENUS IN THE FIFTH HOUSE: How does a garden of delight invite me in every day to smell the flowers and to give some away?

MARS IN THE FIFTH HOUSE: How can I find the fast path to the heart of pleasure, creativity, and healing? Do I do this through sport? Art? Playing hard with my children?

JUPITER IN THE FIFTH HOUSE: How do I instigate special moments, memories that take on more meaning because everyone is unified by my generosity as hostess to the party?

SATURN IN THE FIFTH HOUSE: How can I discover that spontaneity naturally discovers its own discipline?

CHIRON IN THE FIFTH HOUSE: How can I express my creativity in a context that no one else can control, so that sacred wisdom comes through me as artist or healer?

URANUS IN THE FIFTH HOUSE: How can I trust the radically innovative artist or healer I can be?

NEPTUNE IN THE FIFTH HOUSE: How can I discover my private sanctuary of worship through the creative arts?

PLUTO IN THE FIFTH HOUSE: How can I act as a battery pack for myself and others, charging the atmosphere with permission to play, to enjoy life?

SOUTH NODE IN THE FIFTH HOUSE: How can I value my love of spontaneity yet not be controlled by it either? How can I begin to see beyond the power of the moment?

NORTH NODE IN THE FIFTH HOUSE: How can I give myself the space and time to develop spontaneity, personal joy, and creativity?

If you have no planets in the fifth house: Look for planets in Leo, the sign of creativity. If you have no planets in Leo, look to your Sun as creative by nature, no matter what sign it is in. Also look to Venus, which loves life magnificently.

To Encourage Intuitive Flow for the Fifth House

Play with the fifth house as part of your purpose if you have the Sun or other planets there.

Imagine you are in a favorite place in loose clothing and comfortable shoes and a perfect temperature and nothing to do. Then you think of something you've been wanting to do.

The pleasure of the day takes over as you move like a dancer from moment to moment doing this thing. You laugh out loud, a long ho-ho-ho from deep in the belly. It is the sound of inner happiness and confirmation that life is good—no, grand. That belief seems to stand tall on your head like a black top hat, a clownish presence of *Yes, it is real, the continuity of my being is rooted in joy, and pleasure is no sin.* There is no sorrow, no loneliness, no aching or hunger. You are full and your cup is very definitely running over.

What are you doing that has brought such a deep laugh, such pleasure? With whom are you playing, if there is someone else there?

Pass on foolish fun, ecstasy, and creative abundance, through the flow....

The Sixth House: Work

The sixth house sponsors the space in which to work. It is your day-to-day workplace and your service to community. In the first house you created an identity (I'm here!) In the second house, you discovered inner resources to develop so that you could pay your own way. In the third house you claimed your voice. In the fourth house, you built a nest, made a home. In the fifth house, you claimed creativity. In the sixth house, you take the sum of yourself to community and join a group that is your support as you are theirs. Any planets in the sixth house illuminate what talents you may bring to that interdependence with community, as well as what tools you need to make your contribution.

For example, tracker John Stokes has Mercury in the sixth house in Aries, which encourages him to communicate in a way that is active and grassroots (Aries). He founded a community mentor program in New Mexico called Nurturing the Roots, which is based on the idea that the roots of any community are its elders, culture, language, history, and the ability to transmit this information to its youth. Mohawks, Navajos, Hawaiians, Chinese, Swedes, Aborigines are just some of the people who come from across the globe to New Mexico to exchange ideas on developing the program in their local community.

Writer Gioia Timpanelli speaks through her Venus in Taurus in the sixth house when she describes the importance of loving your work. She says, "Everybody has something they absolutely love that they want to follow, and that's what they must do. Follow it down. It will tell you where to go next; it's full of more information, more learning. And if you don't honor the work you are doing, what are you doing? Almost every work has honor in it. If you have something that has some value, some understanding for people, then look for that good part of it that is transcendent, that might bring you to something which is more meaningful. Study, figure it out, and then express it. The most important thing in true work I have found is that it comes from your being willing to start with exactly where you are right now."

The sixth house encourages teamwork and, like its ruling sign, Virgo, the sixth house explores the delicacy of fine functions, ecosystems, your own body. *How does my body work, and how can I help it work better?* These are sixth-house questions. Due to the importance of good health, Chiron, the healer, rules the sixth house. Herbalist Susun Weed, with Chiron in the sixth house in Libra speaks eloquently for Chiron when she says, "I think that the healing energy that exists in the universe is the best placebo there ever was. A placebo is something that works but isn't measurable. We cannot measure the healing energy of the universe, the Veriditas, as Hildegard von Bingen called it—the greening power. We can't measure what it is that makes things grow. But I know if I cut myself and do nothing, it will heal. Even if I look at it and say, 'Don't heal, don't heal, don't heal,' it will heal.... Healing energy is so much bigger than our thought. To believe we can control it is a very interesting kind of hubris. We can *engage* the energy but we can't control it."

Susun suggests that healing is more likely to occur as we stop pushing away what we don't want, stop clinging to what we think we want, and occupy a place of I *don't know*, "which also happens to be open to the universe." Chiron heals through engaging the energy and then allowing for a healing, through the openness of "I don't know."

Not surprisingly, many health practitioners have planets in the sixth house, as do computer specialists, mechanics, and organizational consultants, since bodies take all shapes and forms.

Chemist Kary Mullis, with Jupiter in Virgo in the sixth house writes about his body in *Dancing Naked in the Mind Field:* "Nothing is more fun or interesting to me than human bodies [Virgo and sixth house] . . . I want my eyes to keep focusing, my heart to keep beating, and that thrilling sexual function my body engages in to keep working night after night....

"The most important principle [Jupiter] is that living systems are modular [Virgo]. They are collections of cells, and the cells are collections of parts, and we have a rapidly growing familiarity with the nature of the parts and the ability to make them...."

Cellist Giovanni Sollima, with Sun in Scorpio in the sixth house, works with the body of a cello as an extension of himself. They are in passionate (Scorpio) relationship to each other. Giovanni says,

"It is a very physical relationship. My whole body is involved." His sixth-house musical community is reflected when he describes why he likes to write music for friends to play in Palermo, Italy: "I know the eyes of these people. I know their hands. I know the thinking of these people. I know the way they eat. So I feel great when I write music for them. I feel very comfortable with this kind of a community, my little ensemble band."

Because the sixth house supports community, it can birth ideals for that community, with perfectionistic standards. The beauty of the sixth-house ideal is that it can set a standard for what is possible and inspire teamwork and mutual respect.

For example, Marie Runyon, with Pisces Sun in the sixth house, shines as a light of inspiration (Pisces) to people who need it. The success of the Harlem Restoration Project was its ability to help people help themselves and, in turn, help the project. Marie says, "The most important allies were those countless community members who became the recipients of our efforts. With a roof over their heads, they improved themselves and therefore bettered the community."

That is the key purpose of the sixth house: to link personal well-being with the health of the community.

Find the Sixth House at Work in Your Life

Locate individual planets you have in the sixth house below, and consider how they focus your life:

SUN IN THE SIXTH HOUSE: How does my work teach me to appreciate synergy—a concept that suggests we are more than the sum of our parts?

MOON IN THE SIXTH HOUSE: How do I combine my capacity to care with the service I offer community? Through a corporation? A restaurant? Health care?

MERCURY IN THE SIXTH HOUSE: How can I be the quality-control person around communications? What are too many words? Too few words?

VENUS IN THE SIXTH HOUSE: How can I express beauty or healing intentions through my work? How is my work my art?

MARS IN THE SIXTH HOUSE: How do I set priorities around my work that keep me personally refueled so I can stay on track as leader?

JUPITER IN THE SIXTH HOUSE: How am I an educator about my work, inspiring those around me?

SATURN IN THE SIXTH HOUSE: How do I create stability and a lasting lineage in my life through my work? How do I share this focus with my community?

CHIRON IN THE SIXTH HOUSE: How am I able to raise awareness in my workplace about what is possible there?

URANUS IN THE SIXTH HOUSE: How do I introduce others to the freshest function of my work?

NEPTUNE IN THE SIXTH HOUSE: How can I choose work that honors my sensitivity to surroundings as a strength rather than a weakness?

PLUTO IN THE SIXTH HOUSE: How do I serve as a battery pack, charging my community with new life?

SOUTH NODE IN THE SIXTH HOUSE: How can I let go of an overdeveloped sense of responsibility while retaining my wisdom about work well-done?

NORTH NODE IN THE SIXTH HOUSE: How can I cultivate a hands-on approach to my work in a specific community, offering dependable and grounded service?

If you have no planets in the sixth house, look for planets in the sign of Virgo, which will provide information about your relationship to community and work. Explore the function of Chiron (the healer) as informant about your unique gift to community.

To Encourage Intuitive Flow for the Sixth House

Play with the sixth house as part of your purpose if you have the Sun or other planets there.

Imagine yourself about to train 200 new people who are joining a seasonal support staff for a large seminar center. You must write a welcome booklet that outlines dos and don'ts for living in community there, suggestions on what teamwork really is, and information on self-care both on and off the job while they work for this facility. You must remind your workers that there are many benefits to living in community; however, there are also responsibilities. You say, "Everything we do creates a ripple effect that impacts many others," and then you tell a story about your first real work experience in which you understood how much you needed cooperation from your coworkers, and they needed yours. What was this story?

Pass on good works, through the flow....

The Seventh House: Partnership

The seventh-house life arena encourages partnership with an equal, whether that be marriage partner, business partner, or close friend. Commitment is key for the partnership to survive and thrive. The cusp of the seventh house, the descendant, symbolizes the qualities you seek in long-term partnerships, whether you have any planets in the seventh house or not. The seventh house is ruled by Libra; though Libran planets do not necessarily require long-term growth for a relationship, the seventh house does.

On a more basic level, the seventh house is a mirror for one's relationship to the "other"—including one's adversaries. We are as married to our enemies as we are to our spouses; there is an emotional bond there that is highly charged and has much to teach us about who we are. But most typically the seventh house invites significant others to come into our lives for lasting intimacy.

Venus, planet of love, rules the seventh house and so, not surprisingly, it often appears in the seventh house of those married for decades. Scientist Abraham Oort has Venus and Mars in the seventh house in the sign of Leo, and has been married more than thirty years. Venus fertilizes and Mars forges, and with both planets in the seventh house, Abraham's partnerships would always be in an active growth process. About his thirty-year marriage he says, "My wife, [Bineke], and I have explored partnership deeply through Thich Nhat Hanh's book *Teachings on Love*. He mentions that there are four elements to true love: love or loving kindness, compassion, joy, and equanimity.

"Equanimity means accepting the person you love with both his or her good and not-so-good qualities (the same holds for loving yourself). You may start to understand the not-so-good qualities of your loved one and perhaps the roots of them. Without understanding, love is not real love. Similarly, without joy, love is not real love.

"I am learning to grasp all these aspects of true love and it has helped tremendously in my relationship with Bineke. It's more fun to be together."

Writer Christian McEwen has Jupiter in Leo in the seventh house and finds faith (Jupiter) flowing freely in herself and her life when she reflects creative power (Leo) to people who may not know they have it, and they in turn do the same for her. Generosity (Jupiter) plays a major role in the contracts she creates with loved ones and long-term professional partners. (*Can we be generous with one another?*) She has a significant number of artist friends who are her intimates, many of whom she has collaborated with in teaching and theater work.

When Pluto is in the seventh house, a person may be led to a mission that brings that person in touch with many collaborators who are connected to that purpose; if he or she marries as well, ideally the partner also has a mission. If the marriage itself becomes the Pluto mission, power issues may escalate into an exercise in domination/submission.

Marty Rosenbluth has Pluto in Virgo in the seventh house and perceives his wife as a major source of his power (Pluto), giving depth and meaning to his life story. He is quick to admit that the success of their marriage has been helped by the fact that they both have work that gives their lives meaning. Marty explains, "Our political work is a major part of who we both are, so there isn't this reaction of 'Oh, you're going to this meeting? You don't care about me.' That happens in a lot of relationships where there's a competition between the couple and the outside world. To both of us the outside world is very much a part of who we are. What makes our partnership work is that it is more than just equal—our larger life-purposes are symbiotic. Liz is the most important ally in my life. I don't think it would be possible for me to do the work I do if it wasn't for the level of support I have from her."

Seventh-house partnerships bring into the world possibilities that could never be birthed by one person alone, including the experience the Sanskrit word *namaste* describes: *I honor the place within you where if you are in that place in you and I am in that place in me, there is only one of us.*

Find the Seventh House at Work in Your Life

Locate individual planets you have in the seventh house below, and consider how they focus your life:

SUN IN THE SEVENTH HOUSE: How can I build a lifetime of alliances with intimate and professional partners with whom I can cultivate what cannot be cultivated alone?

MOON IN THE SEVENTH HOUSE: How can I share a home with significant others and honor domestic life as a ritual of partnership?

MERCURY IN THE SEVENTH HOUSE: How can I cultivate the language of love, and develop a special skill for articulating contracts, deals, or clear understanding between people, whether professionally or personally?

VENUS IN THE SEVENTH HOUSE: How do my relationships act as a fertile advertisement to others to form loving alliances?

MARS IN THE SEVENTH HOUSE: How can I choose equals to partner with who will challenge me, as I challenge them, so that the relationship will grow toward a passionate *yes!* that reenergizes both parties even if we don't agree on every point?

JUPITER IN THE SEVENTH HOUSE: How can I honor partnership and my relationship skills as the most generous teacher in my life?

SATURN IN THE SEVENTH HOUSE: How can I partner first with my own self-responsibility and then partner with a worthy equal? Is that person someone with whom I would like to grow old?

CHIRON IN THE SEVENTH HOUSE: May I find a partner or long-term friend with whom I make this vow: *We will make each other better people as a consequence of our partnership; we share a sacred path but that path does not require we take on each other's wounds.*

URANUS IN THE SEVENTH HOUSE: Can I choose partners who give me a lot of personal freedom and ask me to give them the same? What contracts do I create with people who are awakeners, either personally or professionally?

NEPTUNE IN THE SEVENTH HOUSE: How can my partner and I share a creative path with a powerful Muse, or a spiritual path that serves as the guiding light for the partnership? How can I sidestep anchoring the higher potential of my partner while my partner daydreams about it and lives off my love?

PLUTO IN THE SEVENTH HOUSE: How can I marry a mission that can help many people, and find a partner who has also married a mission? How can I take care not to turn the partnership itself into a mission?

SOUTH NODE IN THE SEVENTH HOUSE: How can I enjoy relationships without being dependent upon them for my identity?

NORTH NODE IN THE SEVENTH HOUSE: How am I ready to begin to explore intimacy with an equal, without controlling the terms of when and where that happens?

If you have no planets in the seventh house, look for planets in the sign of Libra, which reflects relationship patterns, as well as your Venus, which is the personification of the lover you are. Your Mars can tell a story or two also about to whom you are attracted with a clear *yes!* who will energize you as partner or lover, or who can make you mad, as intimate enemy (possibly the same person).

To Encourage Intuitive Flow for the Seventh House

Play with the seventh house as part of your purpose if you have the Sun or other planets there.

Imagine yourself near the end of your life looking back, specifically at the people you loved longest and who loved you in return. Consider your lineage of love, tested by time, which taught you how precious twenty or thirty years of friendship or partnership can be. Consider that there is no way to create that kind of intimacy instantly; it must be earned. You understand that the ultimate schoolroom is the heart, as it creates a working love for another person, love in action. Can you see the ways in which your heart has ripened, your character grown, through these relationships? Can you see the ways in which these relationships have made you lovely, as you have made them lovely? Who are these people?

Pass on the art of lasting intimacy, through the flow….

The Eighth House: The Unseen World

After the intimacy of the seventh house, the mirror of the Other needs to disappear, for a full education into the energy behind the form of things (including the Other), but on a broader scale than one person. The unseen world the eighth house describes includes anything that resembles a source of power (sex, money, the power to give life, the power to end life, the power to protect you against the unknown). For example, the eighth house rules the insurance industry, which is a corporation designed to guard against the unknown. The planet of power, Pluto, and the sexual sign of Scorpio rule the eighth house. In the same way that they are multidimensional and mysterious, so is the eighth house, as the summation in many ways of every life arena that has preceded it. Study of its complexity yields rich rewards that serve as the integration of those arenas, before moving to study of the ninth, tenth, eleventh, and twelfth houses.

The eighth house is Eros at large, that greater sea of sexuality that is afoot everywhere. Storyteller Gioia Timpanelli is articulate about the nourishing capacity of this power through her eighth house Pluto in Cancer. She says, "Eros is when the spirit of life itself comes into something—a passion, a love of beauty. It can just be an absolutely strong feeling of a creative force. It is in everything that creates, because it desires to make connection. It desires to have two things that are not the same meet to create a third thing. A lot of it is unawares, a lot of it is not business as usual, a lot of it is why you believe there is something more than an equation.

"The trouble occurs when people think that Eros is passion that they can own, that it's theirs—actually, that's not the point. Always, with the true spirit of Eros, things given are generous— the gift given for the other. It can't be something for yourself. It has to be something that you give because something has been given to you. It is from great abundance, from a true feeling of loving generosity, that you have received this gift. That's why it's a holy thing.

"Eros is the understanding that there is something present that is giving you this gift. That's why ancestors or even our parents believed that lovemaking has to be made holy by marriage, by serious commitment. It has to be sanctified. You have to feel that this is a holy thing you are doing, because indeed it is, and not take it lightly.

"There is Eros in all aspects of our lives. I've seen people make improvisational dinners for everybody out of nothing—that's

Eros, that's great love at work. That sort of generosity of spirit cannot be measured."

That sort of generosity can take on archetypal purposes in the eighth house, doing extraordinary good, at times even reversing evil.

In the eighth house, we discover that archetypal purpose is a living power. Like a force of nature, it can shift the group dream almost instantaneously as awareness reaches critical mass on some unseen level.

People with planets in the eighth house often set that shift in motion, whether knowingly or unknowingly. A good example is photographer Mary Bloom, with Sun in Leo in the eighth house. She has taken photos that shift people's perceptions, even mass belief about our values as a culture, and the price we pay to have what we want. Traveling with a team of animal rights investigators in the late 1970s, she shot photos in northern Canada of the killing of baby harp seals; the Associated Press distributed Mary's picture of a mother seal trying to rouse her dead baby, stripped of its skin, and it was published globally. Her photo made visible what was unseen in the collective unconscious. She contributed to a wave of protest worldwide.

The eighth house can also describe what is hidden and unseen in quite mundane areas—the fact that we do not know what others will do, how things will work out, and how circumstances will respond to us. The old English saying "You places yer bets and gets yer outcomes" refers precisely to this. Just as the weatherman makes his best guess at what the weather will be next week, the truth is, he doesn't know.

Scientist Abraham Oort, with Sun in Virgo in the eighth house, understands this fully. He dedicated thirty years to studying the weather. As a climatologist, much of what Abraham studied were the unexpected variables that create climate. He studied the interrelationships of the parts to the whole and the ways in which a life is more than the sum of its parts (Virgo). He studied the unseen energy behind the form of things.

The eighth house is often called the house of death and rebirth or the house of crisis because it can involve sudden accelerated shifts as energy changes form. Energy enters the seed of conception. At the moment of death, it leaves the body. If you have eighth-house planets, this does not mean you need to live in fear of an unexpected death, but the life/death paradox will be explored either metaphorically or literally. For example, when Mary shot the pictures of the baby seal carcasses, she was surrounded by death but felt "more alive than I had ever been before. I was energized as I realized my images could show the world the atrocity taking place for the sake of a winter coat. I could be a voice for a creature that had none."

The eighth house encourages empowerment and purpose, but in order for it to do that, you must acknowledge that you are part of a great and powerful energetic river that includes death and dark waters. Did you personally create the entirety of its reality? Not at all. But you are a part of it.

In its raw state, the eighth house is chaotic energy, a tumult of white water cascading down the archetypal river. How can chaos be converted to connection? Through learning new rules of power. Usually this is preceded by crisis, and the new connection to power is discovered through the invention of integrity on the spot.

A simple example of such invention of integrity is recognizing the difference between privacy and secrets. Your energy is your own, and you may be private about it. But if you have a commitment with someone and something going on with you changes your commitment, if you fail to tell that person, you are keeping a secret.

Secrets always involve energy loss for the person who is shielded from knowing the secret. When the power of full knowing is being withheld, manipulation is the result. Manipulation creates domination/submission contexts and control issues, which destroy trust and guarantee a rise in inner fear (the secret is always there to defend). This contributes to collective fear. **The eighth house is the territory in which you learn how to convert the chaos of your motives into connection and to enrich the group dream in the process.**

Human rights activist Bill Monning is a good example, as he explores trust and power issues through his eighth house Pluto in Leo. With brave heart (Leo), he has entered situations with human rights and negotiation teams in which he could literally die. He says, "In some of the prisoner releases going into El Salvador we had to wear bulletproof vests. The fiction was we were being protected from the guerrillas, when everyone knew it was the right-wing death squads that posed the risk. A weird dynamic occurs internally for me in situations that are scary like that. My adrenaline is elevated but I just translate it to the focus of the mission [Pluto] and a strange calm takes over. I function well when the risks are higher, when there are stresses I can't control, because I *know* I can't control them." But Bill is meant to be there, and that's part of the source of his calm. He is playing out his eighth-house destiny through Pluto.

Fear can loom large in the eighth house, precisely because it reflects the collective unconscious of the culture of which you are a part. When you go to the movies and sit in an audience, the audience becomes one body, experiencing a group dream. The eighth house is similar—it is a group dream about power and life source and every topic in between, with *connection* to life source— or its disconnection (evil, scary, BOO!)—being the thematic material.

With Neptune in Libra in the eighth house, Christian McEwen explores the dream (Neptune) of relationship (Libra). A lesbian from an early age, Christian's writing explores sexuality with the boundary between male and female dissolved, and she has edited anthologies about the topic in both Great Britain and the United States (*Naming the Waves: Contemporary Lesbian Poetry* and *Out the Other Side: Contemporary Lesbian Writing.*) She feeds the dream world of the global culture about human sexuality.

The eighth house is also a training ground for being able to track spirit as it changes form. When loved ones die, the eighth house is an access point for contact with them on an energy level. Christian says, "I think, more than most people my age, I'm aware that the dead are as interesting as the living. I pray fairly consistently to my beloved dead. I have three uncles and three immediate family members dead."

The eighth house is the arena of multidimensionality, and you must give up some control to enter. The eighth house asks: *Which barriers between which dimensions do you want to break? Who are you as risk-taker?* Libran twins John and Jim Thornton answer through their Mars in adventurous Sagittarius in the eighth house. As teens, they drove their Grand Prix through Pittsburgh at 125 miles per hour. Later, they took up skydiving as a safer alternative for the adrenaline rush. As grown men, they each play archetypal roles in the culture as philosophers (Sagittarius) in their field, with a penchant for pushing (Mars) the envelope: John's paintings often reveal the deeper psychodynamics of sexuality; Jim's magazine articles are often first-person accounts of dangerous adventures such as paragliding.

The eighth house is also the arena of the stock market. Who are you as you take risks and gamble there? Whereas the second house might reflect your retail store (you have control over the inventory and hours, and it is *your store*), the eighth house would reflect the wholesale dealer. The wholesale dealer works with collective resources at higher risk and greater gain. Fund-raisers for larger purposes are much like wholesalers, and Harlem's Marie Runyon is a good example. With Moon in Taurus in the eighth house, Marie has raised millions of dollars (Taurus) for housing for the homeless (Moon). In the eighth house you can shape-shift the culture, much like a wholesale dealer, by defining group values through your art, your product, or the way you call energy to you—the way you convert chaos to connection.

The eighth house rules shamanism and sorcery, as a means of converting that chaos to connection. The magician understands the balance between powerful intention (which engages the archetypal energies to fertilize it) and the power of non-attachment as the best environment in which to spawn results. The magician understands the field of resonance between self-trust and trusting the unknown Out There.

The eighth-house theater eloquently reveals that absolute power has no fertility. Absolute power is fear-based. Fear is rooted in ignorance of archetypal creativity, which seeks to regenerate, from the dark fertile soil of current chaos, new combinations of meaning—chaos converted to creativity.

A skilled shaman recognizes the interconnection of everything that exists, including what is unconscious, unseen, or scary. Those with south node in the eighth house may understand this particularly well. With south node in Sagittarius there, Susun Weed was born with an innate ability to negotiate archetypal energies. She has a very articulate life philosophy (Sagittarius) about how to respond to challenging surprises, from negotiating illness to being audited by the IRS. (The eighth house rules the IRS because when we pay taxes, it is as if we are anteing up for the collective resources.)

Susun was audited by the IRS because she had claimed 87 percent of her house as office space. (She teaches classes in her home, almost year-round.) They investigated and approved her claim. But, like most people, prior to their visit to her home, Susun was anxious and tempted to be defensive. To prepare, she fell back on "a very simple formula taught to me a long time ago." She said to herself, "I exist in the universe. The IRS exists in the universe. There is a connection between us that benefits all." She describes this acknowledgment as "engaging the energy" rather than trying to control the situation.

Susun's formula of acknowledging interconnection converts chaos to connection and reduces the possibility of power games, which in the eighth house casts your vote for a cultural dream that is creative and not fear-based.

The basic lesson of the eighth house is to learn to respond, rather than react, to the unknown element, as you explore what is unseen. By virtue of incarnating, you agreed to play in the outfield of the collective unconscious, willing to catch the fly ball of the unknown whether you asked for it or not. As you catch the ball, you convert chaos to connection—as the ball connects with you, you respond in a meaningful (rather than meaningless) way on behalf of everyone. And, if you cannot, shrug your shoulders, and say, "I gave my best effort. Only a fool stays in a fire that is too hot." In order to thrive in the eighth house, you must recognize that you belong to a purposeful story larger than your own. Yet you have to realize that not every story that comes your way is yours to enter. *Is this my story?* you must ask yourself over and over with planets in the eighth house. *Should I be plugged in to this story, this current of unseen energy, or break the trance?*

We all deserve a deep mystery to solve. With the eighth house, you will live that mystery.

Find the Eighth House at Work in Your Life

Locate individual planets you have in the eighth house below, and consider how they focus your life:

SUN IN THE EIGHTH HOUSE: How do I create a life that explores Eros, risk, purpose, and power? How does it bring me in touch with the dream of the culture, as the world around me declares what is valuable, purposeful, powerful?

MOON IN THE EIGHTH HOUSE: How do I find nurturance by owning my own light and dark? How do I nurture the culture as I honor human complexity as a source of power?

MERCURY IN THE EIGHTH HOUSE: How can I be a communicator who can listen for the deepest intention in a situation and speak to it? How do I express clarity in the midst of many voices, many perceptions?

VENUS IN THE EIGHTH HOUSE: How can I combine my charisma and passion to create fertile possibilities behind the scenes for many people?

MARS IN THE EIGHTH HOUSE: How can I be a powerful advocate behind the scenes, skillfully aligning my will with possible outcomes in my culture?

JUPITER IN THE EIGHTH HOUSE: How can I be the benevolent behind-the-scenes philosopher who teaches empowerment principles through my actions?

SATURN IN THE EIGHTH HOUSE: How can I trust the cautious student of power that I am, while also trusting that I am simultaneously in training to be a teacher of power who takes risks?

CHIRON IN THE EIGHTH HOUSE: How can I express a new variety of healing power that is missing from the group dream I share with others?

URANUS IN THE EIGHTH HOUSE: How can I trust my brilliance at recognizing the truth in highly complex situations?

NEPTUNE IN THE EIGHTH HOUSE: What inspires me enough to be open to guidance not only on a personal level but an archetypal one?

PLUTO IN THE EIGHTH HOUSE: How can I be a behind-the-scenes power broker in the culture on whatever scale suits my nature?

SOUTH NODE IN THE EIGHTH HOUSE: How can I trust my skill at surviving unexpected change but release expectations of routine upheaval? How can I find the firm ground within me upon which to stand?

NORTH NODE IN THE EIGHTH HOUSE: How can I take risks that allow me to experience a wider spectrum of my talent? How can I enter the dream of the culture as cocreator there, aware I cannot command outcomes and must dance with the unknown?

If you have no planets in the eighth house, look for any planet in the sign of Scorpio. If you have no planets in Scorpio, invite your Pluto to describe your relationship with power. It will tell the tale.

To Encourage Intuitive Flow for the Eighth House

Play with the eighth house as part of your purpose if you have the Sun or other planets there.

Imagine yourself with a shaman friend taking a walk through the forest on a spring day. The dogwoods are in full bloom. The friend shares a bottle of water with you and suddenly you realize it wasn't water but a magic potion that has lifted the veil on reality; everything starts to move around you. Together you sit down on a large rock to steady yourselves. Nothing is still. Forest, sky, and earth vibrate with life before you. The concept of "vibration" becomes a living, visible entity that swallows up your sense of time and space and solid matter, penetrating everything with light. You also experience your essence as a distinct, unique vibration.

You sit for a long time, intensely aware of the effect that every vibration—your thoughts, tree thoughts, earth thoughts—has on the others. Suddenly you realize you are not your thoughts. Your feelings and perceptions, like little wild animals, move through you and hang for a moment in the air and then vanish. Who is it that is watching? You don't know, but you realize that you are powerful beyond measure, and with that power you wish to do no harm. With a rush of desire, you want to communicate with everything around you—to connect with the source of life itself. Instantaneously, you feel a response. What happens next?

Pass on trust in the mystery, through the flow....

The Ninth House: Worldly Wisdom

The ninth house encourages unifying all you have learned. Often called the house of holistic thinking, the ninth house synthesizes your life experience into beliefs that become the guiding principles you look to—your cosmology.

The ninth house is the natural step beyond the intensity of the eighth house, just as Sagittarius is the next step beyond Scorpio. In the eighth house and Scorpio, we often encounter unknowns we cannot control but need to learn to relate to. From that experience, deep recognitions accrue, and as you step into the ninth house, these recognitions gel into a philosophical framework that allows you to make sense of them. As a result, you expand and recognize yourself as part of a vast pattern.

The ninth-house life arena provides experiences that encourage universal perspective—the counterpart to third-house experiences, which engender personal perspective. The ninth house is often affiliated with communications that can travel anywhere, circling the globe—newspapers, magazines, films, television. It represents any professional activity—such as the law, politics, theology, or the evening news—that claims to speak for what is ultimately true.

Of course thousands of philosophies and paths lead to what is ultimately true. Teilhard de Chardin coined the phrase Omega Point to describe the intersection of all paths of consciousness. He believed that all paths are part of the same unifying field. The ninth house is very much about that unity.

Rather than being about an intellectual truth, the ninth house describes living wisdom that is always active on every level, not just by climbing the mountain for the overview. The ninth house ultimately asks you to explore the truth that is so big it is written on our inner parts. It asks you to integrate those truths, to act upon your knowledge until it deepens and becomes wisdom. Yet wisdom has no shelf life. You must live it, internalizing this wisdom so deeply it encodes your very character. And then ask for more.

The ninth-house truths are infinite, offering endless wisdom, ancient wisdom, and new paths of wisdom that carry new patterns of brilliance as they recombine. There's always more to learn here. Blue Sky Mind personifies Jupiter and Sagittarius inspires it, so they rule the ninth house, which provides the life arena in which this expansion can occur.

Those with Jupiter in the ninth house are particularly good at bypassing dogmatic stands and remaining receptive to Blue Sky Mind—and then shaping a specific ninth-house life arena, like news media, through the ideas of Jupiter. Marty Rosenbluth is a good example. With Jupiter in Scorpio, he read the newspapers (ninth house) every day from the age of six, to get every detail (Scorpio) of what was going on in world politics (ninth house).

In addition he has Sun in the ninth house in Scorpio very close to the midheaven, maximizing his visibility as a philosopher of considerable power. With Venus conjunct his Sun, he clearly carries a healing message. As a consequence, his insightful film on Palestine and Israel was screened at the United Nations, the only organized intersection of all nations.

Abraham Oort also has Jupiter in the ninth house, in the sign of Libra. As a scientist and author, his research has gone out into the world with no limit on how far it travels. He collaborated with a professor from the University of Lisbon on their book *Physics of Climate*, translated and published worldwide (ninth house).

Abraham's philosophy about what is ultimately true has been shaped very much by his travels (ninth house) and receptivity to new ideas, including exposure to meditation teacher Thich Nhat Hanh. He explains, "Nobody can fully live following the trainings Thich Nhat Hanh teaches but they are like the North Star to put your compass on, to strive toward; they are guidelines."

The judicial systems of every land are ruled by the ninth house, so it is not uncommon for those with planets in the ninth house to be connected to the legal profession or government positions that shape policy.

Lawyer and former judge Jerry Leonard has Saturn in Cancer in the ninth house and is outspoken about the problems with our justice system. He describes the limitations (Saturn) that human emotions (Cancer) bring into jury trials. "The jury is at all times watching the litigants. A witness might say something bad about the other side, and the jury always glances to see how that person reacts to it. You get a feel for if the jury likes the lawyer. The client never really gets to speak to the jury. They can only answer the questions. But if the jury likes the lawyer, and the lawyer at least acts like he likes his client, then they're going to receive the client better. So it's a play. You put on this little performance.

"I don't think justice is served anymore at all. I'm discouraged about it. We've become a very intolerant society where we feel better the more we put other people down."

So how can we as a society refresh the standards we look to as law? Like tracker John Stokes, we could turn to the Native Americans. With Uranus in Cancer in the ninth house, John would be a fresh interpreter of nourishing philosophies that reflect cosmic law. He does that by teaching the importance of giving thanks to all life.

He teaches every person who trains with him "The Thanksgiving Address: Greetings to the Natural World" (Ohen:ton Karihwatehkwen—Words Before All Else), based on an ancient Iroquois prayer of thanks to the Creator dating back more than a thousand years. John writes in the foreword to the published version of the address: "The Address is based on the belief that the world cannot be taken for granted, that a spiritual communication of thankfulness and acknowledgment of all living things must be given to align the minds and hearts of the people with Nature. This forms a guiding principle of culture." The end of each stanza of thanks (to the people, to the Earth Mother, to the waters, to the fish, to the plants, to the animals, to the trees, to the Sun, to the Moon) is: *Now our minds are one.*

By reintroducing this ancient concept as a living truth (Uranus) to thousands of youth, he is helping them absorb the most important principle of cosmic law: unity of all life.

Find the Ninth House at Work in Your Life

Locate individual planets you have in the ninth house below, and consider how they focus your life:

SUN IN THE NINTH HOUSE: How am I a unifier who stands at the intersection of all paths? How do I occupy the life arena of worldly wisdom?

MOON IN THE NINTH HOUSE: How can I find happiness through experiences that open my heart and mind? Do I do this through travel? Books? My profession?

MERCURY IN THE NINTH HOUSE: How can I gather information that serves the Big Picture or is universally relevant? How does this information expand me?

VENUS IN THE NINTH HOUSE: How can I be lover to the world as a unifier? What method have I chosen to deliver my grace—words, music, public speaking, teaching?

MARS IN THE NINTH HOUSE: How do I lead others into expansive ideas, sounds, stories, places?

JUPITER IN THE NINTH HOUSE: How can I be an open advocate for the truth that there are no aliens anywhere; we are all interconnected?

SATURN IN THE NINTH HOUSE: How can I commit to ongoing studies in life that require I break up my routine, travel to places I have never been before? As I do, what outdated ideas fall away?

CHIRON IN THE NINTH HOUSE: How can I become a cosmic chess piece able to connect others with their sacred path up the mountain of wisdom?

URANUS IN THE NINTH HOUSE: How can I be an innovative voice whose song or words or images travel far?

NEPTUNE IN THE NINTH HOUSE: How can I be a psychic

satellite dish, receiving guidance from every galaxy about the truths we universally share?

PLUTO IN THE NINTH HOUSE: How do I publicly promote fair play as a figurehead identity for justice?

SOUTH NODE IN THE NINTH HOUSE: How can I appreciate my larger perspectives but not get lost in big ideas?

NORTH NODE IN THE NINTH HOUSE: How am I ready to synthesize my various views into a larger life-philosophy that becomes my North Star?

If you have no planets in the ninth house, look for planets in the sign of Sagittarius, which will be energizing those planets with expansive experiences. If you have no planets in Sagittarius, look to your Jupiter, the instinct to philosophize.

To Encourage Intuitive Flow for the Ninth House

Play with the ninth house as part of your purpose if you have the Sun or other planets there.

Imagine yourself taking a trip to the Middle East led by a well-known theologian, to a great desert where you sit down to meditate with his suggestion that in ancient days there was a temple here, called the Temple of Cosmic Law. In it philosophers from all parts of the earth met, and wise men and women shared knowledge with one another. All paths of knowledge intersected here powerfully.

No sooner do you sit down in the desert than this temple materializes before you. It is surrounded by a courtyard and a great wall. The entrance has an archway over it and on the arch are these words: *I know nothing.* You wonder what that means and try to enter beneath the archway but are immediately propelled backward by an invisible force. You try again and the same thing happens.

"What's going on?" you cry out. The keeper of the gate, an old woman, steps outside and points at the words above the archway. She says, "We don't accept anyone seeking to deliver dogma. Until you believe that no matter how much you know, it is only a small part of the larger picture, you can't pass through the gate. Come back when you have no agenda, no intention of proselytizing at our main intersection. We do only heart and mind mergers here, no special interest groups."

How long does it take you to realize your inner wisdom is integrated deeply into your body and all you have to do is drop your opinions to get through the arch? What happens when you finally enter? Who do you meet? Where do they take you? How do they honor you for what you do know that you are eager to share? What suggestions do the wise ones around you make about expanding your life map?

Pass on ageless wisdom, through the flow. . . .

The Tenth House: Career

In the ninth house, you develop a cosmology, a relationship with your North Star, the worldly wisdom that guides you. In the tenth house, you create a career that embodies that cosmology. The tenth house is ruled by Capricorn (which encourages role modeling) and Saturn (commitment).

The old-fashioned name for the tenth house was the house of world teachers but in fact it merely reflects your public reputation based on what you consistently do out in the world, whether that is high-profile political work, running a grocery store, or simply sitting on the front porch and waving at the world as it goes by. Your public presence gives you an opportunity to influence more people with less effort—the forum is bigger.

How well you implement the cosmology you discovered in the ninth house reveals itself in the tenth house. Knowledge is meaningless if it isn't put to use, and the tenth house tells a great deal about how you live out your philosophy in public, day in and day out.

The tenth house is opposite the fourth and they are two halves of a whole. In the fourth house you wake in the privacy of your own bed in the morning and reinvent your personal myth, create home and family. In the tenth house you walk through a world that is not familial but requires a different set of boundaries entirely, based on what you can project of yourself out into the world, as a consistent signal.

If you were born at high noon, your Sun would appear in the natal chart at the very top in the tenth house. Likewise, the center of the wheel of your story would be public life—highly visible to others, on whatever scale suited your nature and purposes.

Children with planets in the tenth house identify heavily with their parents' professional status, public reputation, or the symbolic flag they fly from the rooftop of the house. Particularly when Saturn is involved, those experiences become grist for the mill in the larger adult life story. For example, Christian McEwen has Saturn in Sagittarius on the tenth house cusp—the midheaven—and in her adult life that has manifested through her career in writing, publishing, and teaching. But as a child, heavily influenced by her Roman Catholic upbringing with its high standards for good conduct and strong imprint of original sin, she was overwhelmed with the prospect of her own evil potential.

She says, "No wonder Buddha nature is important to me as a

concept, that one comes into the world shining, because I came into the world covered in coal dust and spent a lot of time trying, ineffectually, to wash it off. Trying to be good, trying to be better, trying to get good grades, trying to succeed, trying to be a little saint. I gave my brother a rosary when I was about ten so that he would learn to pray. I was a baby missionary and, in effect, I was trying to escape from the sense that I was a baby devil."

As an adult she has deconstructed that identity and re-created it as a teacher of grounded (Saturn) idealism (Sagittarius) through the written word.

Composer Peter Kater has Venus in Aries in the tenth house, on his midheaven. He is a self-starter (Aries) serving the arts (Venus) whose fire (Aries) goes public. The power of the tenth house is that you can naturally grow into a public role through the planets there, which gives you an opportunity to be a role model, to teach, to be the best that you can be—with an unlimited audience.

Teacher Gail Straub has Uranus in the tenth house in Gemini. She is a pioneering (Uranus) author (Gemini) and teacher who coaches people to choose work (tenth house) that draws from their true talents (Uranus), their authenticity. She says, "I think when you're an entrepreneur, in a certain way your whole life is a risk. When we started our business, the Empowerment Training Program, nobody knew the word *empowerment* the way they do now. *We did it anyway.*"

Activist Bill Monning has Neptune in the tenth house, in Libra on the midheaven. Neptune expresses where we are guided by the spirit realm, by soul itself. Bill says he feels guided when he publicly (tenth house) encourages people to advance the vision of a world where peace and justice (Libra) are attainable goals. He adds, "My dreams [Neptune] for the future involve acknowledging the very importance of dreaming. Far too often I meet people who don't know what they want. They haven't taken the time to visualize the dream."

Artist Gail Bruce has Pluto in Leo in the tenth house. She lives and works at the top of a residential building for artists in New York City. A painter herself, she also puts together art collections for clients and has photographic shoots in her studio for commercial television, magazines, and media of all kinds. She is passionate about art and the heart of the culture as it celebrates the creative life in a power center of the world.

Whether you live atop a building in New York City developing art collections or write a novel that goes out into the world from the privacy of your bedroom, the tenth-house life arena asks you: *What flag do you fly reputationally, and what work do you do that supports its image?*

Find the Tenth House at Work in Your Life

Locate individual planets you have in the tenth house below, and consider how they focus your life:

SUN IN THE TENTH HOUSE: How do I stand tall as a public symbol of something in particular? How does my professional life create a center for my life story that allows me to shine?

MOON IN THE TENTH HOUSE: How can I create a nurturing professional life? Do I feel most at home when I am working on my career?

MERCURY IN THE TENTH HOUSE: How can I be a public communicator or build a body of knowledge that goes public?

VENUS IN THE TENTH HOUSE: How can I professionalize my beauty, my grace, my gift as an artist or healer?

MARS IN THE TENTH HOUSE: How do I take the lead in creating my own career?

JUPITER IN THE TENTH HOUSE: How can I share the expansive philosophy that has placed me in a position of influence?

SATURN IN THE TENTH HOUSE: How can I commit to a career that consolidates my strengths and weaknesses into one role?

CHIRON IN THE TENTH HOUSE: How am I a bridge to the sacred through my professional work?

URANUS IN THE TENTH HOUSE: How have I trail-blazed into some new territory professionally with no role models, making it up as I go?

NEPTUNE IN THE TENTH HOUSE: How does my work symbolize a lighthouse seen from great distances, proof that inspiration is practical and valued by the many rather than the few?

PLUTO IN THE TENTH HOUSE: How can I be a powerful symbol for particular purposes in my professional life? How can I be a broker for public talent, teachers, or products?

SOUTH NODE IN THE TENTH HOUSE: How can I enjoy my roles as a public person but not rely on them as my entire identity?

NORTH NODE IN THE TENTH HOUSE: How can I accept that the world needs what I've got and release any subconscious shyness or reluctance to rise to the occasion?

If you have no planets in the tenth house, look to your Saturn, which, as ruler of the tenth house, builds the backbone of your reputation in many ways. Look for planets in Capricorn, which encourage completions of commitments that often lead to credentials and therefore magnify your influence in the world.

To Encourage Intuitive Flow for the Tenth House

Play with the tenth house as part of your purpose if you have the Sun or other planets there.

Imagine yourself picking up a newspaper and reading an article about yourself. In it, the work that you do is highlighted, as are the ways in which your character has formed around your work. Given that you are human, the article includes both praise and criticism of the role model you are. What does this article suggest about who you are as a worldly influence? How does it make you value the unique opportunity you have to reach many people at once? Who are you as a world teacher? How would you like that role to evolve and change?

Pass on wise worldly influences, through the flow....

The Eleventh House: Long-term Goals

When you throw a stone into a body of water, it creates a ripple that goes on and on. Likewise, every action and decision we make has a long-term ripple effect. The eleventh house encourages us to have foresight and to plan for the future; to throw the stone consciously with the goal of a particular ripple effect. After creating a career all your own in the tenth house, it is the natural next step to ask: *Where is it all going? What does it mean?* How can you shape the future of your culture and community, in addition to reaching personal goals and continuing to maintain your career?

The eleventh house describes the ability to answer these questions, as well as: *Where do I want to be five weeks from now? Five months from now? Five years from now? Ten years from now? Twenty? What is the vision that guides and inspires me? Where are the other people who have similar goals, and how can we cocreate the future we want?*

Networking with others becomes key to the successful navigation of the eleventh house. Just watch a flock of geese flying over great distances. It is easier to cut the wind together than alone. A product of this networking is group creativity. For example, colleges, universities, training programs, and seminars that have goals like yours may give you support for consciously creating the long-term future.

The eleventh house is the life arena in which you throw the stone into the pond and discover a long-lasting ripple effect. The eleventh house helps you plan for the long-term, for the lows and highs—especially for the high of sustained creative effort. It helps you establish a pathway of consistent dedication to your goals.

The eleventh house can be fun if you cultivate patience. It is not about instant gratification but rather lasting achievement. The eleventh house encourages you to take your creative gifts to organized groups who can act as distributors, providing an existing infrastructure to support your long-term goals. You, in turn, can support their goals with your intelligence and talents.

People with well-developed eleventh houses tend to be ahead of their time. Freethinking Aquarius rules the eleventh house. Likewise, freethinker Uranus is planetary ruler of the eleventh house but, interestingly, Saturn is also considered a coruler. Uranus is the freethinker, recognizing what is possible; Saturn is the committed implementer, capable of getting it done.

The achievements of the eleventh house are not for personal gain but for the good of all, encouraging intelligence and acuity in those people capable of foresight and steering the answers to the question, *Where are we going, long-term?*

For example, Susun Weed, with an eleventh house Sun in Aquarius, participates in a matrix of networks that help shape the future. She has taught herbal medicine, ethnobotany, pharmacognosy, psychology of healing, ecoherbalism, nutrition, and women's health issues at medical schools, hospital wellness centers, breast cancer centers, midwifery schools, naturopathic colleges, and shamanic training centers. She has also trained hundreds of apprentices and correspondence students, who spread out over the world like seeds in the wind with information on healing.

Her Sun is conjunct Venus, and so she loves sharing information freely about healing (Venus). She loves encouraging a future for healers and for health care that is authentic (Aquarian) and not owned or controlled by insurance companies. As a teacher, she made a commitment early on to accept any woman who applied to apprentice with her (Aquarius is egalitarian).

Composer Peter Kater also has Sun in the eleventh house in Gemini. He is a long-term planner around his own music goals, resulting in twenty-seven releases in seventeen years. He participates in an informal network of musicians who collaborate and record, sometimes on his label, Silver Wave Records, so he is very anchored in group creativity (eleventh house) and sound (Gemini) that have a long-term impact.

The eleventh house is like a moving train of shared vision; those who ride it well remember to move to the front of the train and become the head engineer, again and again, and to ask the question: *Is this where I want to go, long-term?*

Lawyer and former judge Jerry Leonard has Sun, Chiron, Jupiter, and Neptune tightly conjunct in Libra in the eleventh house. His instincts led him to strongly desire long-term solutions when he handed out sentences (eleventh house outcome). The eleventh house is also very concerned with equal opportunities for all (as is Aquarius). He voices those goals when he says, "Our legal system [Libra] does not look to the long haul. [It doesn't] look to solving the problem. For example, I had this guy in court who just would not pay his child support. What do you do? Put him in jail. If you put him in jail, he doesn't pay child support and he gets out, and he doesn't pay child support and you put him back in jail. So he was always there for contempt of court. So I stuck him in jail and told him he could get out when he wrote ten thousand times, 'I must support my children because I love them.'

"I didn't count, but he wrote it several thousand times. My sister-in-law was in a supermarket in Florida and she saw in the *Globe*, right beside a seven-hundred-pound man that looked like Elvis, a picture of me and it said DEADBEAT DAD BAMBOOZLES JUDGE—because he only wrote it seven thousand times. I didn't count how many times he wrote it, who's counting? But it was my effort at getting that man's attention because the standard thing was not working. Maybe this didn't work either, but I'll bet that man will never forget those words, *I must support my children because I love them*."

On some level, Jerry Leonard's sentence shaped this man's future if only by reminding him what he should strive for. Those who successfully navigate the eleventh house recognize human potential and magnify that potential, in themselves and others.

John Stokes has south node in Leo in the eleventh house, suggesting that he has an inherited skill around shaping the future of the culture he lives in. He has sixty-thousand graduates of his Tracking Project in New Mexico. He also teaches other teachers around the world. The Tracking Project is a nonprofit agency that teaches people how to enjoy nature and celebrate (Leo) all living things, long-term (eleventh house).

In the eleventh house, achievement is not motivated by personal ego, though the personal ego may be a supporting actor. The eleventh house is about deeply trusting the impact we have on one another and envisioning a better world.

Find the Eleventh House at Work in Your Life

Locate individual planets you have in the eleventh house below, and consider how they focus your life:

SUN IN THE ELEVENTH HOUSE: How do I plan a purposeful life, contemplate my goals, and watch the ripple effect move out and out, creating probable futures?

MOON IN THE ELEVENTH HOUSE: How do I gather with people who become my tribe, with whom I travel long-term? How do I care for them? How do they care for me?

MERCURY IN THE ELEVENTH HOUSE: How can I gather information about probable outcomes, long-term harvests, and possible paths, and report this information to the network I have joined that has shared goals?

VENUS IN THE ELEVENTH HOUSE: How can I be the perennial flower of possibility, enhancing the path for myself and others, creating long-term harvests that shape the future of the culture?

MARS IN THE ELEVENTH HOUSE: How can I be the lead bird as my flock flies in a particular direction, consciously planning long-term outcomes?

JUPITER IN THE ELEVENTH HOUSE: How can I achieve my goals by initiating others into the good ideas that have worked well for me? How do I see myself creating an exponential action, even a movement, that grows good things for the culture?

SATURN IN THE ELEVENTH HOUSE: How can I routinely climb into my hermit tower where I make decisions no one else can make for me and contemplate my long-term future? The long-term future of the group I work with?

CHIRON IN THE ELEVENTH HOUSE: How can I allow synchronicity to have a hand in creating my long-term path?

How can I find groups who trust the healer I am and form a tribe with me?

URANUS IN THE ELEVENTH HOUSE: How can I find people who are ahead of me on the path; who are catalysts, helping me update my goals when I need to?

NEPTUNE IN THE ELEVENTH HOUSE: How can the Muse guide me toward my future, illuminate my goals? How am I a life coach for others, cheering them on toward their unique guiding light?

PLUTO IN THE ELEVENTH HOUSE: How can I aim high as one who is able to empower people to create a meaningful future?

SOUTH NODE IN THE ELEVENTH HOUSE: How can I enjoy my ability to meet goals, without becoming trapped in constantly contemplating the future?

NORTH NODE IN THE ELEVENTH HOUSE: How can I trust that patience is necessary to live out the harvest of my goals?

If you have no planets in the eleventh house, look for planets in the sign of Aquarius. They carry the agenda of innovation, the cutting edge of your life story and evolution. If you have no planets in Aquarius, look to Uranus, the instinct to express truth. Your Uranus is the future self who walks in the front door and says: *Come on, let's go.*

To Encourage Intuitive Flow for the Eleventh House

Play with the eleventh house as part of your purpose if you have the Sun or other planets there.

Imagine that before you entered this life, a beloved teacher in spirit invited you to a final training session. The two of you climbed a mountain and gazed over a vast plain. He asked you to close your eyes and imagine the goals you have chosen for this lifetime and to love them intensely. Then he asked you to imagine the allies you will need to achieve these goals—individuals as well as group entities, organizations, schools, clubs. Then he asked you to open your eyes.

As you gazed over the expansive plain below, there were three or four shimmering visions of possible paths leading to the goals you just imagined. He asked you to gaze long at each one and to say which was the best fit. Then he asked you to bless the possibility that this path will come. He asked you to trust that there are others on this path who need you as much as you need them to achieve these goals to create a conscious future for the earth and its cultures.

Then he asked you to remember to do this at least once a year. He said, "The future shifts with every thought you think and every attitude of the heart you hold. You must be the source for the vision of where you are going. Now tell me again where you think you are going." What do you say?

Pass on foresight, through the flow....

The Twelfth House: The Spirit Call

The twelfth-house arena (the "spirit call") is where you step outside of time and merge with the Muse, infinite imagination, the source of the "I" birthed in the first house. Like the sign of Pisces, which encourages letting go, and the planet Neptune, which expresses soul, the twelfth house describes the homeland of intuition—the flow. Anything is traceable through this flow, by feel. It originates in the heart, not the head. It is connected to both your source and your destination. It offers no facts, but rather a knowing whose confidence is based upon its capacity to flow along a pathway with no falsehood in it at all.

The twelfth house can be the purest of psychic zones, a window to the archetypal realm of spirit, and dreams are its favorite medium of communication. Anything can happen in a dream. There are no boundaries. You can meet other dreamers who exist independently of your dream, people you have never met but with whom you have an indefinable agenda. "Implausible" is impossible, from within a dream. The dreamer can pass through death's door and come out the other side intact, no matter how terrifying the death.

Dreams about your daily life or family emanate from the fourth house. Group dreams about the culture emanate from the eighth house. Twelfth-house dreams seem to come from the innermost reaches of your spirit, your deepest source, the larger entity who can hold a thousand years up before the dreamer's eye and say: *See, time is nothing at all. You exist independently of time.*

The twelfth house knows that spirit always precedes and survives form. The twelfth house is where all souls live when they have no form. It is the home of the most familiar self, the eternal self who has witnessed every imaginable story. This self carries the deepest paradox of all: It is simultaneously conscious and empty.

John Cage could be describing the twelfth house when he describes the value of being empty when you create as an artist: "When you start working, everybody is in your studio. The past, your friends, enemies, the art world, and above all, your own ideas—all are there. But as you continue painting, they start leaving, one by one, and you are left completely alone. Then, if you're lucky, even you leave."

One of the biggest challenges of the twelfth house, ruled by Pisces and the planet Neptune, is understanding the difference between giving up and surrendering. Giving up is an abandonment of one's center and capacity to respond. With that abandonment comes a loss of instinct. To surrender to a circumstance, even a difficult one, is a different dance entirely. You must retain self-love and self-respect through the surrender.

Viktor E. Frankl, author of *Man's Search for Meaning* and a former prisoner of war in Nazi Germany, came to the realization in captivity that no one could control his consciousness and that freedom was more powerful than any external limitation. Frankl surrendered to his circumstance but he did not give up his center or his capacity to witness and love his life from within.

A more common example occurs in the innocence of a day at the ocean. When you are in the ocean, relaxed, feet lightly placed on the soft sand of the ocean floor, tension dissolves. The ocean water caresses you, the sun overhead warms your face as you *let go*. There is a tide that pulls you slowly out, picking your feet up and setting you down again, just a little farther out. Are you a good swimmer? Is the water reasonably calm? If so, no problem—let go. You can always swim back.

However, if you are exhausted from life problems, have had a few gin and tonics, are not a good swimmer, and are listening to your unhappy inner cynic who decided to *give up* control for the day, to "let fate have its way with me," you could be in trouble.

Giving yourself up to the wrong habit or atmosphere is usually the result of a haphazard or nonexistent relationship with inner guidance. Everybody has a guidance system, whether or not he or she has planets in the twelfth house or in the sign of Pisces (everybody has a Neptune). It becomes vitally important to have a method of picking up your guidance from the twelfth-house flow in a fully functional state so that you can implement it.

The delight of drugs or alcohol or any experience that offers psychic mobility—freedom to shift—is huge for those people with planets in the twelfth house. But they must be very careful to not let the spirit of their drug of choice kidnap them. Such kidnapping cannot occur except by choice—the choice to give up responsibility for the soul (to be soulless) and ignore what you feel (feelings communicate the state of spirit)—at precisely the moment you most need to be present for those emotions which inform you of the larger state of affairs in your sea.

Giving up responsibility for the spirit can take many forms other than alcohol or drug addiction, including that of the escape artist who uses the power of imagination to create a smoke screen behind which he or she disappears.

Usually the escape artist abandons a situation (gives up) at the precise moment that a surrender (letting go) could occur if they stayed present and surrendered the situation to compassion for all involved. (This is what people mean when they say: *Let go and let God.*) This is the twelfth step of all twelve-step programs—acknowledging a higher power. The higher power is the spirit within, the soul, as well as the place where the soul merges with universal consciousness, love that has lasted, in whatever form or face God and Goddess take.

The common denominator for all the twelfth-house affiliates—the Muse, Higher Power, God, Goddess, Source, spirit, and letting go—is imagination. Reduce the energy of the soul to a basic unit, and it is consciousness itself—the ability to imagine. The twelfth house suggests that out of the imagination of the soul, every reality is conceived. Imagination bridges soul and personality. Those with Sun in the twelfth house tend to move back and forth across the bridge fluidly. For example, artist Gail Bruce has Sun in Libra in the twelfth house. Gail says, "Of all the collaborations and partnerships I have forged, the strongest is with spirit, the source of it all" (twelfth house). She balances (Libra) the inner and the outer constantly and releases to spirit (twelfth house) what she cannot balance. She says, "I am a better artist, better at walking between worlds, when I draw energy from love—loving and being loved. That's why I am here."

Patrick Reynolds has Venus in Scorpio in the twelfth house. Venus is the instinct to love. The sign of Scorpio passionately transforms the definition of love and in the twelfth house, love answers the spirit call. "Yes, I love everything and yes, I'm a wild man," Patrick admits.

The twelfth house also rules acting, film, and the mythmakers who serve up waking dreams from out of the infinite sea of imagination. With Venus in Scorpio in the twelfth house, Patrick would have a passion for film. He starred in the 1986 movie *The Eliminators*, with themes of time travel (twelfth house) and supernatural powers (Scorpio).

Teacher Gail Straub has Saturn in Virgo in the twelfth house, and has spent more than thirty years developing a meditation practice (Virgo) that helps her balance a busy life of travel and teaching globally. Saturn's job requires that Gail pay constant attention to being steadied by spirit first—the inner life, secondary to any external measures.

She says, "Meditation is the most important tool in my life. I have a very dedicated practice—every day, a half hour. Meditation develops the compassionate witness. So instead of being seduced by my drama, I can witness it with a kind of equanimity and distance."

Saturn in the twelfth house can also be active in the world, not just through the practice of meditation. Gail says, "Meaning and wholeness come when spiritual self-care [twelfth house] is balanced with an engagement and a contribution [Saturn] to the world. One without the other leaves you rather empty."

Novelist Allan Gurganus has Pluto in Leo in the twelfth

house, which is capable of birthing creative offspring directly from the world of spirit. Allan invented the character of Lucy Marsden in his novel *Oldest Living Confederate Widow Tells All* through his Pluto, which is also conjunct Saturn (the elder). Of Lucy, Gurganus writes, "I named her *Lucia* meaning 'light.' I felt lantern-led by her in my dreams and, at every moral juncture, I consult her like the oracle she is. My tie with her remains the longest monogamous relationship of my life, and the happiest! Lucy urged me to become the seventy other people in the book. . . . Like me, she is the quintessential Gemini—mercurial, reliably unreliable, and yet a good person to choose for your life raft. She is both an archetype and one of the most specific people I've ever known."

The twelfth house is the guiding light behind your life—your source and destination.

Find the Twelfth House at Work in Your Life

Locate individual planets you have in the twelfth house below, and consider how they focus your life:

SUN IN THE TWELFTH HOUSE: How does the director's chair of my life occupy a space that acknowledges infinite possibility and that honors my Muse daily?

MOON IN THE TWELFTH HOUSE: How can I trust the value of staying emotionally tuned in to my family in spirit, listening for "voice mail" from my angels?

MERCURY IN THE TWELFTH HOUSE: What information am I able to retrieve from that timeless realm that comes spontaneously, unbidden, to my pen and paper?

VENUS IN THE TWELFTH HOUSE: How can I deliver to the

world creative or healing gifts with no ego attachment at all?

MARS IN THE TWELFTH HOUSE: How would I like to lead others to a point of inspiration that takes my breath away with its beauty?

JUPITER IN THE TWELFTH HOUSE: How can I trust the expansive permission from spirit for me to dream big?

SATURN IN THE TWELFTH HOUSE: How can I build my own door to the sanctuary of spiritual faith, needing no intermediary (such as a priest or rabbi)? How do I combine discipline with inspiration in this sanctuary?

CHIRON IN THE TWELFTH HOUSE: How can I trust my own unique bridge to the sacred, not getting caught in anyone else's definition of it?

URANUS IN THE TWELFTH HOUSE: How can I regularly step into the timeless realm so that I may be struck by the lightning of the truth about my identity behind the mask?

NEPTUNE IN THE TWELFTH HOUSE: How can I occupy a state-of-the-art dream factory that runs twenty-four hours a day?

PLUTO IN THE TWELFTH HOUSE: What high-voltage power have I discovered in the laboratory of the Muse or in the cathedral of my spirituality—or both?

SOUTH NODE IN THE TWELFTH HOUSE: How can I appreciate my tendency to live in visionary realms without living there full-time and missing opportunities to manifest the vision in real time?

NORTH NODE IN THE TWELFTH HOUSE: How am I ready to trust that there is a divine plan and my first responsibility is to begin to explore my own spiritual well-being rather than trying to finish endless tasks in the name of serving others?

If you have no planets in the twelfth house, look for your Neptune or any planet in the sign of Pisces, which rule the twelfth house. Neptune is the instinct to express soul; the energy of Pisces promotes the Muse.

To Encourage Intuitive Flow for the Twelfth House

Play with the twelfth house as part of your purpose if you have the Sun or other planets there.

Imagine yourself at the moment of death, leaving the body like a husk. Your fearful beliefs (*I am dying! This is the end!*) collide with your faith (*Spirit always precedes and survives form; this death feels familiar*). Some interesting physics begin to take over—the physics of resurrection.

Images and sensations come as you find yourself in a huge swirling circle with a light at the center. You fly into the light and merge with it but as you do you have thoughts that bounce like balls, bombarding some sort of protective barrier around identity: *Am I dead? Do I still exist?* The thoughts break a barrier, a shell remaining around you much like the sheath of afterbirth. And then there are faces—some of whom you recognize instantly, some of whom you don't—and they beam you back into existence with their love.

In a series of bursts, they stabilize you and help you cross over. Reunited with this family of souls to whom you belong, you are told, "Quickly, before the bridge that you just crossed evaporates, send a mental message back to all your loved ones there that you are fine. Tell them that every time we love one another, in a body or not, we resurrect each other. We have been sending you that message through your entire journey on Earth. Did you receive it?"

Pass on this truth, through the flow: Love lives forever....

What's Next

Now you've learned a great deal about planets, signs, and houses. In the next chapter, twelve of the twenty-nine people you've met step forward and introduce themselves to you directly. Each individual synthesizes into a whole human being with a story to tell about his or her archetypal life path. Just for fun, as you meet them up close and study their charts, ask yourself . . .

Which one used hitchhiking as an entry into the larger world?

Which one is skilled at investing money?

Which one does the FBI have a 500-page file on?

Which one can firmly fire an employee and leave him his dignity?

Which one is a wild improvisational dancer at parties?

Which one leaves notes for his or her partner that read "ILYF," and what does that mean?

Which one has a bumper sticker on his or her car that reads Visualize Whirled Peas?

Which one sees creative ideas as raindrops that fall and hit you on the head?

Clues are buried in the birthcharts and do not appear in the subjects' essays or bios. In chapter 8, you'll discover the answers as we explore "Putting It All Together to Ground Your Dreams."

CHAPTER 6

Twelve People Who Have Followed Their Best Instincts

We all recognize a true voice when we hear it and can even trace character through the sound of the voice. Tracing character, we can sometimes hear the soul itself speaking. Astrology synthesizes all three—voice, character, and soul—yet leaves the mystery of identity a luxuriously open question.

In this chapter, you will meet twelve of the twenty-nine people you met earlier, in snippets and short glances, through anecdotal example. However a paraphrase cannot capture the essence of an identity; my authoritative voice describing someone else's identity dilutes their essence still further. And so for an entire chapter, I step back as your teacher and invite these people to come forward one by one, twelve individuals with unique voices, living contemporary lives.

They are organized by Sun sign—Aries through Pisces—but they are proof of the complexity of being human and that we are bigger than astrology, yet deeply connected to a living universe. However, to enhance your ability to spot the instincts of their planets, birthcharts precede each essay, with a short outline of each planet's function. Then, in their own words, these individuals speak for themselves, with no agenda other than describing their respective life paths.

These twelve spontaneous self-portraits will give you a rich opportunity to empathize with their stories and to intuitively connect with each planet as it is channeled through them. More importantly, you can glimpse the interplay of instincts and intuition in life choices—and the resulting synthesis of a life.

Astrology points to this synthesis above all else: the larger unifying spirit an individual brings to that life script, that birthchart. Each person you meet here operates from his or her own intuitive river of life. From that flow came specific urges— instincts to act, to do. The intuitive flow suggests: *When you follow your best instincts, you follow the stars.*

I hope you enjoy these true stories of people who have followed theirs.

Bill Monning
Apr 2 1951

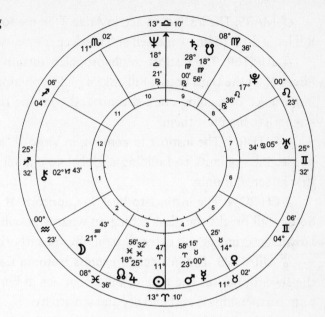

The Life Script of Bill, an Aries

☉ SUN: The instinct to shine from the center of your story; in Aries ♈ in the third house: Bill shines as an activist communicator able to make a point, a presentation, particularly to his local community.

☽ MOON: The instinct to have a home; in Aquarius ♒ in the second house: Bill is most at home as a freethinker who nurtures truth in every phase of his work.

☿ MERCURY: The instinct to communicate; in Taurus ♉ in the fourth house: Bill is a communicator about the importance of strong foundations from the root level up.

♀ VENUS: The instinct to love; in Taurus ♉ in the fifth house: Bill loves athletics that explore his physical strength and the sensuality of the earth: surfing, biking, hiking.

♂ MARS: The instinct to act; in Aries ♈ in the fourth house: Bill has a drive to know himself and his deeper intentions.

♃ JUPITER: The instinct to philosophize, to sum it all up; in Pisces ♓ in the third house: Bill enjoys philosophizing about the importance of naming one's dreams and courting the spiritual strength to manifest them.

♄ SATURN: The instinct to commit; in Virgo ♍ in the ninth house: Bill commits to building a global communications tool that honors our unity.

⚷ CHIRON: The instinct to heal; in Capricorn ♑ in the first house: Bill breaks the glass ceiling on what is possible, particularly in government and external structures of authority.

♅ URANUS: The instinct to express truth; in Cancer ♋ in the seventh house: The tone of Bill's contract in building long-term partnerships is authenticity and sensitivity.

♆ NEPTUNE: The instinct to express soul; in Libra ♎ in the tenth house: Bill expresses his spirit through his career negotiating world peace.

♇ PLUTO: The instinct to express power; in Leo ♌ in the eighth house: In crisis situations, Bill defines power as nobility of heart.

☋ SOUTH NODE OF THE MOON: The instinct to gaze at the past and recognize an inheritance; in Virgo ♍ in the ninth house: Bill was born with a gift for public service with an outreach to the entire world, based on teamwork.

☊ NORTH NODE OF THE MOON: The instinct to gaze at the future and recognize a liberating path; in Pisces ♓ in the third house: As Bill gazes at the future, he understands the importance of naming his dreams locally and cultivating a personal voice through which to communicate them.

ϒ

In His Own Words: Bill Monning
Political Activist, Lawyer, Negotiator
"The integrity of the journey to reach the goal is the goal."

All of my life, I've taken aim at specific targets. As a high school athlete, I wanted to win at every sport. As a grown man in my middle age, I am less concerned with winning and more concerned with taking good aim and moving toward every goal aware of the waves I make as I move toward it, respecting others and myself.

I learned respect for others from childhood, with excellent role models. I grew up in Los Angeles among family who also were friends. My social conscience and spirit were shaped a great deal by my parents. My father was a public servant and my mother a community volunteer. Though they never specifically asked that I dedicate myself to making the world a better place, their natures blessed that possibility, encouraged me to know I could. I chose law as a path.

The roots of that path began in high school in the '60s, and then took hold when I began to travel after high school graduation. What I saw in the former Soviet Union, Poland, East Berlin, and Western Europe led me to question intensely the role of governments, and especially our government's role in Southeast Asia. I enrolled at the University of California at Berkeley in 1969 and got involved in the antiwar movement, the Black Panthers/prison movement, and the United Farm Workers.

I learned the practical tools of organizing when I worked for a year with the United Farm Workers of America, AFL-CIO. More than a union, the farmworkers' movement incorporated the teachings of Gandhi and Dr. Martin Luther King with the "liberation theology" of the Migrant Ministry.

My desire to serve the farmworker movement played a pivotal role in my deciding to pursue a law degree. I wanted to advance the vision of a world where peace and justice were attainable goals. I continued working with the union as a student at the University of San Francisco School of Law and as a lawyer through the '70s. And I also met my future wife there—Dana Kent, who would become one of the most important allies of my life. We married in 1978.

In law school, I joined the National Lawyers Guild, an association of progressive lawyers and legal workers, with international links to global movements in Latin America, the Middle East, Africa, and Asia. As a guild member, I led delegations to Guatemala, Honduras, and El Salvador in the 1980s to document human rights violations and to negotiate the release of political prisoners. I was learning the power of focused thinking, determination, and organizing as tools—tools that can be combined and employed to move repressive regimes. It was vital to access decision makers and confront them with moral arguments backed by concerted political action.

In the U.S., I continued my work as a lawyer in California's rural areas and used the tools learned with the UFW to represent worker victims of pesticide and toxic exposure.

My personal life was a vital balance to this work; by 1984, Dana and I were blessed with two daughters. When Dana began medical school at Harvard in 1987, we moved to the East Coast. It was there in Boston that I met Dr. Bernard Lown, a cardiologist known for his ability to empower patients in their own recovery. He also founded and led the International Physicians for the Prevention of Nuclear War, the organizational recipient of the 1985 Nobel Peace Prize. In IPPNW, Dr. Lown applied the principles of individual healing to a global public health campaign in building the physicians' movement to stop nuclear weapons testing and development. I got involved and was able to work with IPPNW members in eighty nations. My skills as a negotiator, mediator, and organizational leader got a lot of exercise.

The global work with IPPNW inspired me to focus on building networks at home that might be able to change the direction of U.S. foreign policy to better address the needs of a planet in crisis. I've spent years doing that locally and nationally. I count failures as steps in a process rather than failures, including my run for Congress in 1993 and as the Democratic nominee for State Assembly in 1994. I refused to accept PAC contributions and created a contract with people that made their contributions as voters, precinct walkers, and the like the most powerful currency in the election process. I believed that to talk about fundamental campaign finance reform, candidates must be ready to practice what they preach, not just promise a future commitment to reform. That simple step was important to me, as a role model exemplifying that the integrity of the journey to reach the goal is the goal.

Currently, I teach courses at the Monterey Institute of International Studies on the art and science of negotiation and political organizing. I use practical simulation exercises to involve people in developing their own skills and tools to navigate a variety of international, cross-cultural, political, or personal negotiations.

My dreams for the future involve acknowledging the very importance of dreaming. Far too often I meet people who don't know what they want. They haven't taken the time to visualize the dream, to identify the objective of their labor. Those with a dream, with an objective, bring far more passion to the negotiating table, wherever it may be.

My dreams include the development of community and global relationships that involve people in the shaping of solutions to surmountable problems. No matter how great the challenge may seem, we can identify the problem and build consensus among those who share a moral indignation with the problem. Often, the problem originates with monolithic corporate and government structures that carry out inhumane policies while hiding behind a mask of anonymity. I believe we can create solutions that embrace the perpetrators as people within whom moral conscience can be tapped.

We are human beings first and masks second, no matter how impersonal or large the mask. I approach every negotiation with that assumption. This makes it possible to speak with respect to each person in a position of power to right a wrong. Moral conscience can be tapped in this way. And if one leader refuses to acknowledge the reality of a human rights issue, or the evil of a deliberate deception of the public, there is always another who will acknowledge it.

The goal is to search for that person and begin to talk. The worst day at the negotiating table is preferable to the alternative, which may often be war, protracted conflict, or continued exploitation and abuse. Get people to talk and get people to *listen*.

BILL MONNING serves as the president of the Pro Democracy Education Fund, Inc., a nonprofit committed to campaign reform and leadership development among low-income and disenfranchised communities. He lives with his family in Carmel, California.

Christian McEwen
Apr 21 1956

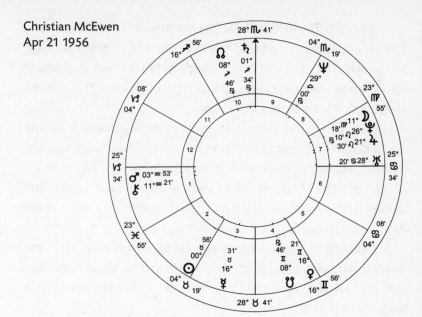

The Life Script of Christian, a Taurus

☉ SUN: The instinct to shine from the center of your story; in Taurus ♉ in the second house: Christian shines as she pays her own way in the world, doing work that matches her values and honors her love of the natural world.

☽ MOON: The instinct to have a home; in Virgo ♍ in the seventh house: Christian feels right at home in intimate relationships that improve the quality of life for both partners.

☿ MERCURY: The instinct to communicate; in Taurus ♉ in the third house: As a writer, Christian is building a steady first-person voice.

♀ VENUS: The instinct to love; in Gemini ♊ in the fourth house: Christian loves writing about family, her beginnings, her home, and women writers and their deepest thoughts about identity.

♂ MARS: The instinct to act; in Aquarius ♒ in the first house: Christian acts out her drive to be a freethinker in-person, close-up.

♃ JUPITER: The instinct to philosophize, to sum it all up; in Leo ♌ in the seventh house: Christian enjoys philosophizing about the people she loves, her intimates.

♄ SATURN: The instinct to commit; in Sagittarius ♐ in the tenth house: Christian commits to being a public voice, a teacher, unifying her many perspectives into a life philosophy she can share.

⚷ CHIRON: The instinct to heal; in Aquarius ♒ in the first house: Christian heals herself and others by speaking and writing from a free place, in person, close-up.

♅ URANUS: The instinct to express truth; in Cancer ♋ in the seventh house: Christian discovers new truths about herself in intimate relationships in which she realizes she does not have to lie in order to love.

♆ NEPTUNE: The instinct to express soul; in Libra ♎ in the eighth house: Christian expresses her spirit as she blesses her soul mates and recognizes their bond as part of a larger story of love.

♀ PLUTO: The instinct to express power; in Leo ♌ in the seventh house: Christian expresses her power in intimate relationships with equally powerful partners, with whom she collaborates creatively.

☋ SOUTH NODE OF THE MOON: The instinct to gaze at the past and recognize an inheritance; in Gemini ♊ in the fourth house: Christian was born with a strong sense of family story and a propensity toward language, letters, the life of the writer.

☊ NORTH NODE OF THE MOON: The instinct to gaze at the future and recognize a liberating path; in Sagittarius ♐ in the tenth house: As Christian gazes at her future, she recognizes the liberation of being a public teacher, unifying many perspectives into a life philosophy she can share.

☿

In Her Own Words: Christian McEwen
Writer, Editor, Tree Climber
*"There was a perfect match between my own curiosity
and strength, and the woods and fields and
hedges that were mine to explore."*

When I was small, I used to dream of living in a tree house. There'd be a wonderful swinging platform with ladders up and ladders down and a place for a table and two comfortable arm-chairs. Every morning I'd look out into layers of shimmering green leaves, with just a snatch or two of very bright blue sky. If I was hungry, I could reach out and pick a mango or a coconut or a bunch of ripe bananas. And at night I'd rock myself to sleep in my own private hammock.

In real life, I lived in London, on a street called Drayton Gardens, just off the Fulham Road. There was a plain rectangular strip of grass behind the house, and one tree—a laburnum. The long yellow blossoms made a radiant canopy, which pulsed and trembled in the slightest breeze. I was forbidden to touch the seeds, which are poisonous. But I must have sat for hours under that tree, strapped into my pram or in my child-sized chair, en-tirely surrounded by those shifting curtains of flowers.

That laburnum marks my first clear memory. Even now I can see the golden chains of winged flowers, the narrow seedpods with their hard black seeds. This was the place where I first came alive to myself, where sound and sensation first condensed into meaning: the insistent adult voice that told me, "Don't touch that!" and the gentle rustling blossoms that meant "wind" and "sun" and "home."

Laburnums flower in May; I was two, or at most just three,

when memory began. Not long afterwards, we moved to Wiltshire, to a square thatched house called Coneybury, less than a mile from Stonehenge. The next five years were the happiest of my childhood. There was a two-acre field to the side of the house, and a wood beyond, and within those boundaries I was free to go wherever I chose. I had a trail I liked to follow, with what I thought of as "sitting places" along the way: a crouched nest at the edge of the cornfield, another in the long grass between the hedge and the barbed wire, and yet another by the side of the barn. It was as if my trail made a kind of necklace, and those sitting places were the beads along its string: mini-shrines or private altars, at which I alone paid homage.

In his essay "The World Is Places," Gary Snyder writes that, "All of us carry within us a picture of the terrain that was learned roughly between the ages of six and nine. You can almost totally recall the places where you walked, played, biked, or swam." Certainly this is true for me. I remember precisely how happy I was, lying in that field with the tall corn rustling overhead, or hunched in the long grass examining a grasshopper. I never lacked for new things to investigate, from the bright-eyed forget-me-nots under the barn to the plump crimson cushions of the spindleberry, each one shaped like a tiny four-cornered hat. There was a perfect match between my own curiosity and strength, and the woods and fields and hedges that were mine to explore.

When I was eight, we moved to Scotland, and I was sent to weekly boarding school. At home, on weekends, I raced up and down like a wild thing: building houses in the rhododendrons, climbing trees. I was small then, and very light, and I used to climb up and up till I was swaying back and forth in the branches, and the trunk above me was no thicker than my thigh. It was a delicious feeling that, ecstatic, terrifying.

I climbed trees at my convent school as well, and one day an ancient nun caught sight of me. "Come down," she shouted up into the branches. "Come down, tree climber!"

The older I grew, the more I realized how many girls are ordered down from their high trees. They are told to be good, and to behave like little ladies, and all too often they capitulate. My tomboy anthology, *Jo's Girls* (named for Jo March in *Little Women* and published in 1997) was designed to redress that balance, tracking tomboys through time, from wild little girlhood on, past puberty into adult life and the full late-flowering of tom-old-ladyhood. Here were some rather different images of female possibility!

I would never have been able to complete *Jo's Girls*, or any of my other projects, without the calm and steadiness the earth has given me. I am a slow writer, and I need safety and space and time to get lost. As I've begun to take my work more seriously, I've had to learn, again and again, the power of good basic habits, in terms of managing a day, a week, a month, which then, with any luck, translates into managing my writing so it's not so frightening and all-engulfing.

I travel a lot, but when I am at home, my day is fairly structured. I get up, I have a modest breakfast, I meditate, and then I write. Only after that does the business of the day begin: a late lunch, perhaps a walk, phone calls, letters. But I give the cream of the day to the writing. Writing regularly keeps me sane, and allows me to be generous in the ways I want to be generous.

CHRISTIAN McEWEN has edited four anthologies, the latest of which is *The Alphabet of the Trees: A Guide to Nature Writing*, with Mark Statman. Christian lives in Vermont and teaches poetry at Lesley University.

Peter Kater
May 28 1958

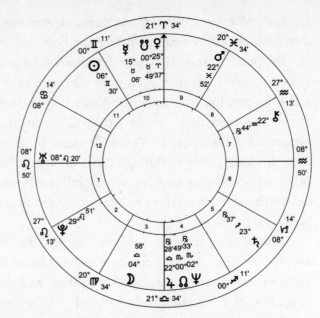

The Life Script of Peter, a Gemini

☉ SUN: The instinct to shine from the center of your story; in Gemini ♊ in the eleventh house: Peter shines as a communicator, one dedicated to deep listening. His long-term path is as a composer.

☽ MOON: The instinct to have a home; in Libra ♎ in the third house: Peter is most at home when he can listen to the life around him as an artist and explore balance, beauty, and creative collaboration.

☿ MERCURY: The instinct to communicate; in Taurus ♉ in the tenth house: As a composer, Peter translates sound and builds a body of work that is available anywhere.

♀ VENUS: The instinct to love; in Aries ♈ in the tenth house: Peter has the same heart publicly that he has privately. He flies the flag of the artist who is creating his own path, is a self-starter. He is lover to the world.

♂ MARS: The instinct to act; in Pisces ♓ in the ninth house: Peter acts on his deepest inspiration in order to touch people's spirits globally. He has more energy when he shares his full emotional range.

♃ JUPITER: The instinct to philosophize, to sum it all up; in Libra ♎ in the fourth house: Peter is developing a life philosophy around the value of privacy, the exploration of beauty, and partnerships that balance him.

♄ SATURN: The instinct to commit; in Sagittarius ♐ in the fifth house: Peter commits to working hard at playing, as he fathers his own creativity and his children.

⚷ CHIRON: The instinct to heal; in Aquarius ♒ in the seventh house: Peter heals himself by cultivating long-term partnerships which honor a mutual ability to be authentic with one another.

♅ URANUS: The instinct to express truth; in Leo ♌ in the twelfth house on the ascendant: Peter reinvents himself as he moves out into the world as artist, again and again.

♆ NEPTUNE: The instinct to express soul; in Scorpio ♏ in the fourth house: Peter's spirit is nourished by his inner and outer family, both the dark and the light of them.

♀ PLUTO: The instinct to express power; in Leo ♌ in the second house: Peter expresses his power as a producer of the arts able to earn self-respect, income, and equity, through his persistence and passion for his work.

☋ SOUTH NODE OF THE MOON: The instinct to gaze at the past and recognize inheritance; in Taurus ♉ in the tenth house: Peter was born with an ability to be a steady public figure, to hold a pose as the extroverted producer.

☊ NORTH NODE OF THE MOON: The instinct to gaze at the future and recognize a liberating path; in Scorpio ♏ in the fourth house: As Peter gazes at his future, he recognizes the value in asking the question: Who am I in my complexity? How can that complexity nourish me and my family?

♊

In His Own Words: Peter Kater

Pianist, Composer, Producer

"The creative process is all about listening."

Playing the piano was my mother's idea, soon after we moved from Munich, Germany, to New Jersey. I was five years old when she asked me if I wanted to play a musical instrument, and the fact was, I could care less. She made me think about it anyway.

At age seven, I finally said, "Okay, I want to play the trombone." She said, "What do you want to play the trombone for? That's ridiculous. If you play the piano, you can play everything." She always wanted to play the piano but her parents could never afford it and thought it was a waste of time.

So at age seven, I began piano lessons. I was terrible because I never wanted to play things the way they were actually written on the page, I wanted to play them the way I *felt* like playing them. As a result, classical music was very hard for me because it was so exact, and it wasn't what I really wanted to do. I went through three teachers in one year. Seven years of classical training followed.

Later, I began to enjoy music more when I learned improvisation from a less rigid teacher. He taught me how to take a simple melody and work with some chord changes and make it sound like a full, lush piece of music in a variety of styles. That opened up a world to me that I'd been waiting for. By my mid-teens I was playing rock and roll around New Jersey and New York and studying contemporary improvisation seriously.

When I was eighteen, my mother died a difficult death, of

cancer, which was hard in itself, a huge loss. However, she was really the only person I had in my life demanding I *be* anyone in particular. With her death, I was free of that.

On instinct, I moved to Colorado, where I knew no one at all, and dove into an exploration of music from a totally new place. While I was there, I heard a piece of music that really touched me, called "Icarus" by Ralph Towner and later popularized by Paul Winter. I learned how to play "Icarus" and to this day, I believe I'm constantly rewriting a version of that song subconsciously. There are certain things about it that gave me permission to compose from a place that had nothing to do with ambition and everything to do with my nature as a human being.

Twenty years later, I have worked intimately with some of the same musicians who performed that early version of "Icarus"—cellist David Darling and reed player Paul McCandless. I've also worked with musicians and artists from every imaginable background, to produce scores for television, film, and video, many of them award-winning. My mother would have been surprised, because she didn't believe a career in music was a wise choice, even though she wanted me to learn to play the piano.

My bestselling album is the soundtrack to *How the West Was Lost*, a Discovery Channel series depicting the destruction of the Native American cultural heritage. Many of the musical collaborations and scores I have been involved with have been partnered with a cause, or an organization like the United Nations Environment Programme or Greenpeace.

Yet, at this time in my life, I'm ready to make more music that is totally free of projections. I'm ready to return to a kind of simplicity that has no overt affiliation or message. We have projected so much onto cultures like the Native Americans and the Tibetans and even onto the earth, as environmentalists, and despite my belief in the value of those causes or cultures, I'm weary of aligning my music with anything that will immediately plug people into a notion of guilt, empathy, depth, or sympathy. I'm ready to make music from a fresher place, without the baggage.

Some of the best music I've composed is for commissioned projects, like the score for Broadway's *Redwood Curtain* or the Discovery Channel's *Our Time in Hell: The Korean War*. I get out of my own way more when I'm working on someone else's project, because it usually involves a visual I can springboard from. When I compose for that visual, my music tends to have more space and movement in it, in order for the other art form to have its space as well.

I redefine myself and my music periodically, and that refuels me more than anything else. *Doing nothing* also refuels me. I value the time that I have to do nothing over anything else. My version of doing nothing is going for a long bike ride or just hanging out. It's the most significant part of the creative process for me.

The creative process is all about listening. It's not about doing; it's about listening, and responding. You can't do that if the ego is too involved. The ego likes to identify with creativity and take the credit for it, but it's definitely not the ego that is the creator. The ego doesn't trust the value or process of doing nothing.

On the other hand, some creative people never finish anything because they're always onto the next thing. It's very important to finish something. That's where focus comes in. The ego can help out in the *doing* phase, by focusing. They go hand in hand. The completion creates an alchemical shift in you, and everything around you, in some inexplicable way. It's part of the cycle of listening, and responding fully.

Silence plays a larger role for me than for most people. Even if I'm driving in the car for long distances, I rarely put on music. I'd just rather sit there, listening. I'm aware that silence doesn't really exist, ever.

Even when I sit and meditate, my head is full of sounds, constantly. One of the meditations I do from time to time is to pick any one of those sounds or tones in my head and just follow it. It gets bigger and bigger. It becomes huge.

I cherish silence because it allows my psyche to unravel, and eventually I arrive into the moment.

PETER KATER'S first album of piano solos, *Spirit,* was released in 1983. Twenty-seven other critically acclaimed releases followed in seventeen years, ranging from solo piano to contemporary jazz, Native American collaborations, and full orchestrations. Peter lives in northern Virginia with his family.

Cindy Waszak
June 27 1955

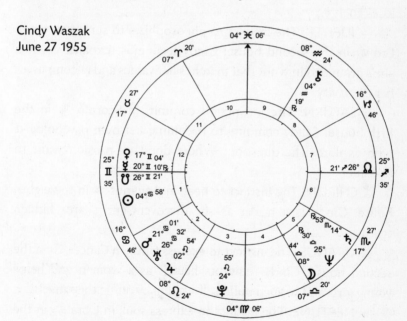

The Life Script of Cindy, a Cancer

☉ SUN: The instinct to shine from the center of your story; in Cancer ♋ in the first house: Cindy shines as an accessible advocate for women and families.

☽ MOON: The instinct to have a home; in Libra ♎ in the fifth house: Cindy feels at home in playful relationships with equals.

☿ MERCURY: The instinct to communicate; in Gemini ♊ in the twelfth house: Cindy can listen and communicate from a timeless place, without ego.

♀ VENUS: The instinct to love; in Gemini ♊ in the twelfth house: Through photography, Cindy finds an art form for her Muse's love of storytelling.

♂ MARS: The instinct to act; in Cancer ♋ in the second house: The act of owning her feelings gives Cindy energy and allows her to be more productive. When she buries her feelings she loses energy.

♃ JUPITER: The instinct to philosophize, to sum it all up; in Leo ♌ in the second house: Cindy feels most expansive when she's grounded in work that matches her values and encompasses her creativity.

♄ SATURN: The instinct to commit; in Scorpio ♏ in the fifth house: Cindy commits to becoming her own psychologist who explores the question: Where does my passion want to take me?

⚷ CHIRON: The instinct to heal; in Aquarius ♒ in the eighth house: Cindy is a healer as she discovers and shares hidden truths.

♅ URANUS: The instinct to express truth; in Cancer ♋ in the second house: Cindy reinvents herself as a woman and helps young girls and women build self-esteem by doing the same.

♆ NEPTUNE: The instinct to express soul; in Libra ♎ in the fifth house: Cindy expresses her spirit through romantic relationships, her children, and the creative life.

♇ PLUTO: The instinct to express power; in Leo ♌ in the third house: Cindy empowers herself and others as a creative communicator.

☋ SOUTH NODE OF THE MOON: The instinct to gaze at the past and recognize an inheritance; in Gemini ♊ in the first house: Cindy was born an information gatherer who can easily pass on her data in an accessible way.

☊ NORTH NODE OF THE MOON: The instinct to gaze at the future and recognize a liberating path; in Sagittarius ♐ in the seventh house: Intimacy is Cindy's liberation from merely observing life and gathering information. She is stretching toward building partnerships and a life philosophy about that shared path.

♋

In Her Own Words: Cindy Waszak
Mother, Social Scientist, and Documentary Photographer of the Human Family
"I want girls all over the world to recognize their gifts. . . ."

Over the past eighteen years I have worked for an international organization doing reproductive-health research to improve the lives of women and their families. I have traveled to Asia, Africa, the Middle East, and the Caribbean. No matter where I go, I am struck by the basic humanity we all share amid the cultural diversity.

Though trained as a research psychologist, I began shooting black-and-white photographs on my travels a few years ago, out of a desire to communicate my experiences in a different way. Photographs keep me connected to the needs of the people I am researching after I have returned home and written my reports.

My camera is certainly the most important tool in my work as photographer, but I've come to believe that taking good photographs hinges upon knowing myself. For the past few years, psychotherapy has been an important tool in learning to reconnect with myself, to accept parts of myself that I was not so happy with. This internal acceptance leads to more openness and acceptance about the world I photograph as well. I am better able to see my spiritual connection with the world.

As social scientist and documentary photographer, I love exploring communities, personal narrative, and the interrelationship of the two. Communities are composed of people with stories to tell. Their stories snowball into community identity, which in turn creates the character of the community as it extends into a larger world.

For example, a few years ago, I documented day-to-day life at a local residence for persons living with AIDS. Because I had been a volunteer there for months, I had preconceived notions about what my photographs should portray. But in the darkroom as I worked on individual photographs, my preconceptions fell away. I realized that the photographs were showing me a different story than I had anticipated and that I had to step back and let the photos tell the story. I realized, through them, how okay people are just as they are, even in ill health, their human imperfections laid bare. I learned that a medium often accused of invading people's privacy is a tool that can be used to portray personal dignity, in private moments.

I love photographing my children also. I have a twenty-three-year-old daughter and sixteen-year-old son. Motherhood has given me many insights into how a child becomes his or her own person. I enjoy watching my children integrate what I offer them into their depths. It's essential that I step back, if they are to integrate it in their own way. It is a delicate balancing act, though, knowing when to hold on and when to let go, and how to provide enough security without stifling their growth. I love my children but it is very hard work. In addition, there is the constant challenge of forgiving myself for being a less than perfect mother. Like many modern mothers, I was, and am, a working mother, and my work frequently takes me literally to the other side of the world.

Recently I was going through some old photographs of my children, and as I went through them I moved back into some old familiar guilt that I wasn't more present in their early childhood. Almost immediately, the telephone rang. It was my daughter, in tears, sick with a flu and in need of support. She no longer lives with me, but nearby. I said, "Want to come over and spend the day?" and she said, "Sure." So she did. This reminded me that mothering never ends and I always have the power of the present in which to become a better mother.

Therapy has made me a much better mother because it has allowed me to accept my own faults, which in turn makes it easier to forgive the faults of my children. I can give up the need to be so critical "for their own good."

I like the movement of my life, as I explore how to move from social science to documentary, from words and numbers to photographs. In particular I like focusing on the lives of girls as they grow into women in cultures that are changing from traditional to modern. How will the world around them influence them? How will they come to know themselves, recognize their options, and make choices in that world? How will they build self-esteem?

I believe I can help young girls with these issues, as a compassionate adult who can hold up a mirror of a young woman's potential. I'm concerned with the well-being of girls around the world, in specific and general ways. Especially in other countries, girls get left out and are virtually ignored, as if they were invisible.

Girls need someone to pay attention to them and to help them pay attention to themselves. When I was in Africa recently I was evaluating a curriculum on reproductive health that included material on self-esteem. A lot of the adult teachers did not understand the concept of self-esteem, and so I suspected that the girls didn't either, and I was right. Even though they had talked about it in the abstract, when I asked individual girls what they liked about themselves, most could not tell me. Most had never been asked to think about it.

I want girls all over the world to recognize their gifts so that they can then share those gifts with the world. It sounds so simple, but I think the results could be dramatic.

CINDY WASZAK has served as a research psychologist for Family Health International for the past twenty years. She lives in Chapel Hill, North Carolina, with her family.

Mary Bloom
Aug 15 1940

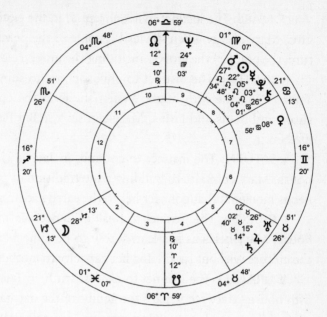

The Life Script of Mary, a Leo

☉ SUN: The instinct to shine from the center of your story; in Leo ♌ in the eighth house: Mary shines by following her joy as she works with the power of the human-animal bond.

☽ MOON: The instinct to have a home; in Capricorn ♑ in the second house: Mary feels at home doing the very best work she can do.

☿ MERCURY: The instinct to communicate; in Leo ♌ in the eighth house: Mary takes pictures as her primary form of communication and they often serve a colorful story larger than her own life.

♀ VENUS: The instinct to love; in Cancer ♋ in the seventh house: Mary loves close friendships, particularly with women who are like sisters to her.

♂ MARS: The instinct to act, in Leo ♌ in the eighth house: It gives Mary energy when she leads people to the point of the picture, the point of the story—including the unseen element.

♃ JUPITER: The instinct to philosophize, to sum it all up; in Taurus ♉ in the fifth house: When she is in the country, near sheep and fields and farms, Mary can see the Big Picture of her life better.

♄ SATURN: The instinct to commit; in Taurus ♉ in the fifth house: Mary commits to building a life tradition of play, spontaneous moments that connect her to the earth and animals.

⚷ CHIRON: The instinct to heal; in Cancer ♋ in the eighth house: Mary heals as she learns how to be a mother-at-large in the culture without sacrificing her capacity to mother herself.

♅ URANUS: The instinct to express truth; in Taurus ♉ in the fifth house: Mary recognizes the genius of the natural world and the intelligence of every living creature. Animals ground her and give her joy.

♆ NEPTUNE: The instinct to express soul; in Virgo ♍ in the ninth house: Mary expresses her deepest inspiration when she serves her community publicly.

♀ PLUTO: The instinct to express power; in Leo ♌ in the eighth house: Mary's batteries are charged through living a life of passion with a bit of risk.

☋ SOUTH NODE OF THE MOON: The instinct to gaze at the past and recognize an inheritance; in Aries ♈ in the fourth house: From birth, Mary is heavily identified with her mother and mothers everywhere.

☊ NORTH NODE OF THE MOON: The instinct to gaze at the future and recognize a liberating path; in Libra ♎ in the tenth house: As she gazes at her future, Mary recognizes her ability to bring more beauty into the world, as well as to be an influence for justice.

Ω

In Her Own Words: Mary Bloom
Photographer
*"As I took these photos, I was surrounded by death
but more alive than I had ever been before."*

I'm a photographer who explores the bond between animals and humans. My love of animals began as a child and slowly, over several decades, grew into my life work. In the 1940s and '50s, my family kept many animals in our house in New York City, and that was the beginning of my discovery of the importance of having a dog in my life.

The house was rather full. My mother, a devout Irish Catholic, invited young women who had outgrown the Catholic orphanages where they were raised to live with us. They did so until they got married or went off on their own. We had as many as twelve girls at a time, so often I felt like I lived in a boardinghouse rather than a home.

My mother was in her early forties when I was born. By the time I arrived, she had cooked thousands of meals, done enough laundry to fill the Atlantic, and washed floors until her knees were callused. She had done so many dishes, her hands were the color of beets. The mother in her was gone; a good friend was there instead.

I grew up without rules. I had chores in the house and I had schoolwork to do, but aside from that, my life was my own. I was allowed to roam the streets at all hours, ride the subway anywhere, choose my own friends, chart my own course. My mother was accused of neglecting me. The letters came from school. My long hair was often dirty and my parochial-school uniform had stains that remained for weeks. I recall her defending our lifestyle by saying that I was developing an independence and confidence that would be a tool later in life.

I never had a college education, no degrees; life experience has been my teacher. I had a difficult adolescence. My father died tragically. We moved so often after his death, I went to three different high schools. That period fortunately ended and my luck changed. One good thing happened after another. I got a well-paying job in the corporate world when I was in my early twenties. I was smart and worked hard, so it grew into a position that paid for an apartment in trendy Greenwich Village. My new skills enabled me to find work in London, which was a highlight of my life. I got married and had a loving partner. Then in my mid-thirties, I entered a restless, uneasy time in my work and in my marriage as well, and I began to question my life path. Then something wonderful fell right into my lap.

I started taking photographs of animals. This was a dramatic change from the days behind the desk. Soon after I began working with a camera, I was invited by an environmental organization to go to northern Canada to document the harp seal hunt. Baby seals were being killed for their white fur and made into coats. I was given the opportunity to photograph the slaughter, in an effort to stop it. So I went.

The journey was arduous and the sight unforgettable. Over and over, I photographed baby seal carcasses scattered across the ice. In many cases, the mother was nearby, calling her baby. It was stripped of its fur and it was dead, but she didn't have a sense of why it wasn't coming to her. She had milk, she needed to nurse, so she would lie next to this carcass and call to it.

As I took these photos, I was surrounded by death, but more alive than I had ever been before. I was energized as I realized my images could show the world the atrocity taking place for the sake of a winter coat. I could be a voice for a creature that had none.

I was able to withstand severe weather conditions on that

trip, and although I was sleeping on an uncomfortable bunk bed in a fishing trawler next to the noisy boiler room reeking of fumes, I slept soundly. I found the patience to wait out long periods of time when the ship got stuck in the ice, not moving for many hours. I was never fearful of the outcome of our journey to hostile waters where, as protesters, we were unwelcome. All because I was doing something that really mattered. At least it mattered to me. I had the responsibility to make a photo that would help prevent future killing of seals. Having that adventure and succeeding in what I intended to do, changed my life.

I returned to New York City determined to commit to photography one hundred percent. I left my marriage to live alone and concentrate on the task I now needed to fulfill. For the first time in my life, I felt really driven.

I've loved photographing animals over the years. Now it's rarely their abuse; it's more often images that illustrate the importance of animals in our lives. I also photograph events—and people, in all sorts of situations.

Photography is fulfilling but it can also be lonely. It brings me into many worlds, but then I pack up and go home, never to return. Every single day is different from the next.

One very important aspect of my life that has remained constant has been my community at the Cathedral of St. John the Divine. Located in New York City, it is the largest Gothic cathedral in the world. I have a family of friends there who have enriched my life and given me a spiritual home and inspiration for my creativity, as well.

I was introduced to my work at the cathedral in 1984 by a friend, Paul Gorman. At that time, the dean of the cathedral was the Very Reverend James Parks Morton. Jim is a visionary who molded the cathedral into an energetic arts center of great spirit.

He believed in me and saw a gift I had, long before I recognized it myself. It was that recognition, combined with his inspiration and permission, that convinced me to pursue the life of an artist. I could actually feel that growth happening.

He fertilized the creative spirit in many others as well— musicians and high-wire walkers and painters and sculptors. Jim Morton brought us all together and knighted us Artists in Residence. He combined our gifts and created a collage of art that was celebrated by the thousands of visitors and worshipers who entered that sacred space.

When I look at my roots, where I came from, and where I am now, I'm amazed. I have a wonderful life because I'm not afraid of being afraid; I'm a risk-taker. It's also because I have a strong will and good instincts. But equal in strength to my will and instincts is a faith in God.

My mother gave me that faith. When I was very young, she would tell me I was watched over by the Blessed Virgin and her angels. Planting that belief in me as a child was a wonderful gift. It gave me confidence to believe in myself and have knowledge that I'm guided. That guide loves me and protects me. That guide is God.

MARY BLOOM's photographs have appeared in *Life*, *Smithsonian*, *People*, and *The New York Times*. Since 1984, Mary has helped organize the yearly blessing of animals at the Cathedral of St. John the Divine in New York City, where she has been a photographer in residence for 15 years. She lives in the Hudson Valley.

Abraham Oort
Sep 2 1934

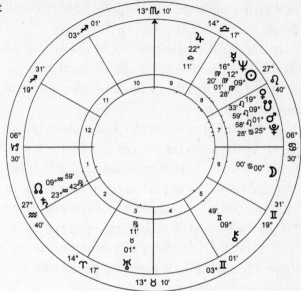

The Life Script of Abraham, a Virgo

⊙ SUN: The instinct to shine from the center of your story; in Virgo ♍ in the eighth house: Abraham shines as he studies gestalts—the ways in which a life is more than the sum of its parts. He shines as he explores energy behind the form of things.

☽ MOON: The instinct to have a home; in Cancer ♋ in the sixth house: Abraham feels at home when he is able to share ideas with his community about its purpose.

☿ MERCURY: The instinct to communicate; in Virgo ♍ in the eighth house: Abraham enjoys describing the way in which parts create a whole, whether he is discussing the variables that create the global weather or the inner wisdom and healing power of the body.

♀ VENUS: The instinct to love; in Leo ♌ in the seventh house: Grace flows from Abraham's celebration of his life partners—

from loving his wife, his children, his grandchildren, his best friends.

♂ MARS: The instinct to act; in Leo ♌ in the seventh house: Abraham has more energy, and is therefore more active, when partnered with a person who can challenge him to speak a clear yes and a clear no.

♃ JUPITER: The instinct to philosophize, to sum it all up; in Libra ♎ in the ninth house: Meeting people with different viewpoints encourages Abraham to see the Big Picture.

♄ SATURN: The instinct to commit; in Aquarius ♒ in the first house: Abraham is an accessible authority figure, a grounded free-thinker with tested ideas to whom others can look as a resource.

⚷ CHIRON: The instinct to heal; in Gemini ♊ in the fifth house: Abraham links to creativity through his healing hands as a shiatsu practitioner.

♅ URANUS: The instinct to express truth; in Taurus ♉ in the third house: Abraham pioneers a new form of communication as a craniosacral therapist whose language is grounded in touch.

♆ NEPTUNE: The instinct to express soul; in Virgo ♍ in the eighth house: Abraham's soul is in full bloom when he bridges science and spirit, the seen and unseen worlds.

♀ PLUTO: The instinct to express power; in Cancer ♋ in the seventh house: Abraham expresses his power through nurturing relationships.

☋ SOUTH NODE OF THE MOON: The instinct to gaze at the past and recognize an inheritance; in Leo ♌ in the seventh house: Abraham inherited an ability to cultivate colorful long-term partnerships.

☊ NORTH NODE OF THE MOON: The instinct to gaze at the future and recognize a liberating path; in Aquarius ♒ in the first house: Abraham is learning to establish an identity of his own, whether he has a partner or not. He grows toward honoring what is true, rather than taking sentimental refuge in the past.

♍

In His Own Words: Abraham Oort
Scientist, Sculptor, Shiatsu Therapist
"Nature is larger than the rational mind."

For about thirty years I worked at the Geophysical Fluid Dynamics Laboratory of the National Oceanic and Atmospheric Administration in Princeton, New Jersey, and taught a course in climate dynamics at the university. I studied the global system of the earth and its environment: How the atmosphere, oceans, cryosphere, biosphere (including humans), and lithosphere interact to create the present global climate and its spatial and temporal variations.

That career really began at birth, in Leiden, the Netherlands, by virtue of being the son of the well-known astronomer Jan Oort, who discovered a halo of comets surrounding the solar system, subsequently named the Oort Cloud. From my father I inherited a love for the outdoors, unspoiled nature, and venturing into new, unexplored territory. Through my mother I felt more connected with the arts.

Although not particularly gifted in science, I was slated to become a scientist. After studying physics at Leiden University, I changed to the earth sciences. My wife, Bineke, and I spent the first two years of our marriage in Cambridge, Massachusetts, where I received an M.S. in meteorology at MIT. My Ph.D. at the University of Utrecht followed in 1964. Two years later, Bineke and I decided to immigrate to the United States with our children.

Over thirty years of study and teaching in Princeton followed.

My study was of the cycles of energy, water, and angular momentum that, acting together in beautiful synergy, drive the general atmospheric circulation, create the multitude of weathers on Earth, and establish the climate. But the one-sidedness of science, in its dependence upon rationality, held me back in some sense. I felt as if some part of me had atrophied rather than expanded, with academia my primary focus for so long.

I thought often of the twelve-year-old boy I was, and his spirit before I became immersed in academics. It occurred to me that I could leave academia and pick up where I left off, as that twelve-year-old boy, at the age of sixty-three. I was also quite aware that my life as a scientist had been self-centered and driven by ambition. However the biggest blind spot of all during my career was around the family relationships with my wife and children. I did not realize how central to my happiness they were.

These realizations began to occur slowly over the late '80s and first half of the '90s and, as they did, I began to explore other things while continuing my life in science. First it was the exploration of sculpting in clay, then the study and practice of macrobiotics and shiatsu, and finally the discovery of meditation. These focuses began to call to me strongly, as I realized how much I needed them, as a balance.

I began to spend more time with my family and in 1993 I began to study Buddhist meditation with Thich Nhat Hanh, a wonderful Vietnamese Zen master, which helped this process of reclaiming my nature a great deal.

As a consequence, in 1996, I went on retreat with Thich Nhat Hanh in the south of France for two months, in Plum Village. On the Vietnamese New Year, an oracle was offered and one could ask a question to the oracle. I waited a long time for my turn to present my question. Thich Nhat Hanh (often called Thay, which means "teacher" in Vietnamese) had left the meditation hall just before it was my turn to ask a question and pull a number from a box. The number corresponds to a two-line passage in an ancient text of Vietnamese poetry, which is then read in Vietnamese, translated first literally and interpreted finally into plain English.

My question was: How could I best help people heal themselves? Just when the monks and nuns were struggling to translate the response to my question, I noticed Thay had come back and was taking over. According to Thay, the deeper meaning of the first line was that everything was possible, that there were no obstacles in my public or private life. The second line was a condition: that I let go of past suffering.

At first I was puzzled by this answer. What was my suffering? But gradually I realized my suffering was connected with my relationship with science. That realization played a major role in my decision to leave science immediately after.

Since that time, I have totally re-created my life. I continue my interests in science, but I also have many other wonderful focuses and my relationship with my wife of thirty-nine years is better than it has ever been. In 1999, Bineke and I moved to Hartland, Vermont, to begin a new phase of private and community life. There, we are closer to some of our children and grandchildren and participate in the Green Mountain Dharma Center, as well as the Mindfulness Practice Center. Both centers were founded on the teachings of Thich Nhat Hanh.

For a long time, I have considered offering a course for scientists to help develop their innate, complete humanness—a course that would support a clearer connection between the rational mind, body, heart and soul. I know how much suffering there can be in living purely as a rational being. To help others experience a greater unity, interconnectedness, and harmony on inner and outer levels would be the fulfillment of one of my dreams.

I believe that nature is one of the greatest teachers of harmony and balance. Looking back, nature has been the thread of continuity through my life. As son, husband, father, and grandfather I explore and enjoy the beauty of the natural world around us. As scientist I have studied the atmosphere and oceans. As shiatsu/acupressure practitioner and sculptor, I study the nature of the body and its energy field. As meditation student, I explore the nature of the spirit.

Nature is larger than the rational mind. I look forward to my next step, as I express that truth more fully.

ABRAHAM OORT coauthored *Physics of Climate* with the late José Pinto Peixoto of the University of Lisbon. Abraham and his wife live in Vermont.

Gail Bruce
Sep 27 1941

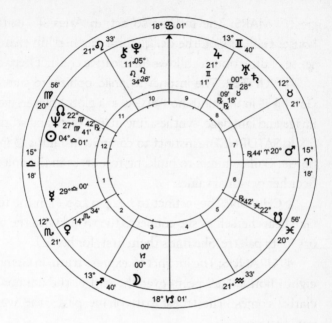

The Life Script of Gail, a Libra

⊙ SUN: The instinct to shine from the center of your story; in Libra ♎ in the twelfth house: Gail shines as she explores the balance of the inner and outer life and releases to Spirit what she cannot balance.

☽ MOON: The instinct to have a home; in Capricorn ♑ in the third house: Gail is at home as a translator of what she sees and hears, finishing what she starts.

☿ MERCURY: The instinct to communicate; in Libra ♎ in the first house: An accessible communicator, Gail negotiates collaborations with other diplomats, seasoned artists, and promoters of beauty.

♀ VENUS: The instinct to love; in Scorpio ♏ in the second house: Gail combines her creativity with her love of mystery—the energy behind the form of things.

♂ MARS: The instinct to act; in Aries ♈ in the seventh house: Gail acts on the desire for a partnership that has a clear sense of direction yet allows for creative conflict between parties.

♃ JUPITER: The instinct to philosophize, to sum it all up; in Gemini ♊ in the ninth house: Gail is a global player, working with image and language, synthesizing many voices and stories into one.

♄ SATURN: The instinct to commit; in Taurus ♉ in the eighth house: Gail commits to building resources in the culture that reflect her personal values.

⚷ CHIRON: The instinct to heal; in Leo ♌ in the tenth house: Gail heals herself as she connects the world with the missing colors in its palette. She finds them first, for herself.

♅ URANUS: The instinct to express truth; in Gemini ♊ in the eighth house: Gail peers over the cliff of the unknown and this clarity comes: The truest part of me paves the way for fresh perspectives.

♆ NEPTUNE: The instinct to express soul; in Virgo ♍ in the twelfth house: Gail sees spirit at work in the ultimate organization of the body. She sees the creator in all living things.

♇ PLUTO: The instinct to express power; in Leo ♌ in the tenth house: Gail expresses her passion through her work as artist and producer in a city that is the cultural center of the world. She understands that she is part of a larger creative impulse capable of sparking, spontaneously, a renaissance.

☋ SOUTH NODE OF THE MOON: The instinct to gaze at the past and recognize an inheritance; in Pisces ♓ in the sixth house: Gail was born with a natural sense of being a priestess, meant to serve a specific community around her.

☊ NORTH NODE OF THE MOON: The instinct to gaze at the future and recognize a liberating path; in Virgo ♍ in the twelfth house: Gail is growing toward the realization that there is an infinite amount of work to do in the community around her.

How can she serve a larger river, the infinite source from which we come, and renew herself simultaneously?

⌒

In Her Own Words: Gail Bruce
Artist, Producer, Activist
"I . . . walk in two worlds, in all aspects of my life."

I am a connector, a conduit, a producer, and an artist. I have been married over thirty years. My husband, my daughter, and my granddaughter are my life partners. We live in New York City and have a home base in New England too—in a secluded spot with an abundance of wildlife, forest, and the silence of nature around us, as counterpoint to our lives in the City.

In New York City, my husband and I have busy schedules as we work in various capacities in advertising, television production, and the film industry. But of all the collaborations and partnerships I have forged, the strongest is with Spirit, with the source of it all.

This partnership with Spirit has taken many forms. It has expressed itself most visibly through art and painting, where I have experienced not only beauty but the balance necessary to be whole. Sometimes that balance includes darkness, jagged edges, and a kind of walk-the-plank uncertainty where there are no guarantees.

Painting is an inner journey, and I came to it after a prolonged outer journey into a world that symbolized beauty: the fashion industry. In my teens and early twenties, I worked successfully for many years as a model for magazines like *Vogue* and *Glamour*. That led me to the film industry, where, after a short stint as a dreadful actress, my spirit said: *Stop. This is not where you are gifted.* After a period of soul-searching, I began to paint. I was blessed that people responded to my work, and it sold.

Always Spirit has taken me into the heart of the earth, and if one truly travels there, the culture of the people who walked before us, the Native Americans, will call to you, as it did to me.

Like most Americans, I come from mongrel stock. I am a mixed-blood who has a native heritage. No blood, just history. A great-great relative married a native woman who showed him how to grind the roots of a tree and he invented a drink called Hires Root Beer. This family legend also drew me into the world of Native Americans.

Native people honor Spirit. They honor it in their culture, songs, and ceremonies. I have been privileged to walk among these people, to learn, experience, and grow. And in the Indian way, I have tried to give back to people who have enriched me. I became a founding board member of the American Indian College Fund at the beginning of the tribal college movement. I have also helped the American Indian Higher Education Consortium (AIHEC) mastermind and launch the building of Cultural Learning Centers at thirty tribal colleges in twelve states. Built with donated materials, the first AIHEC cultural center was completed May 1999 at Sinte Gieska University on the Rosebud Sioux Reservation in South Dakota. Many more are in progress.

My involvement was hands-on as well as [that of] introducing corporations like Carrier [Corporation], a manufacturer of air-conditioners, foundations like W. K. Kellogg, and government agencies like the Department of Interior to the AIHEC Cultural Learning Centers project. The public and private sectors and many diverse cultures joined together to help preserve the beautiful and unique culture and language of our first Americans—a culture in jeopardy of being lost.

Rather than acting as museums, which serve a passive purpose with no engagement on the part of the visitor, these centers will serve as training grounds for present and future generations of all nationalities to learn, understand, and celebrate Native American culture. Most people don't know that when native people lost the war with the Europeans for their land, they were not allowed to practice their religion or speak their language openly until an act of Congress was passed in 1978. I find that astonishing, in the "land of the free and the home of the brave." This project is about continuing the healing, and sharing together, as one nation, our early history.

I was honored to be presented with a silver bracelet from a native colleague. It has two rows of turquoise stones mounted diagonally and across from each other on it, because I was told I walk in two worlds. This touched me deeply, because I do walk in two worlds, in all aspects of my life.

I occupy my partnership with Spirit, and at the same time, I occupy marriage with a feisty man, a wonderful man, my companion and lover for over thirty years. I live in Manhattan, a city of concrete and conveniences, but I am also at home in the desert or plains with the simplest accommodations.

I paint, take photographs, and produce art events that bring beauty to the larger world. I take off my paint-smeared smock and jeans, put on my business suit, and walk into corporations and garner support for the American Indian College Fund or the Cultural Learning Centers. I can do that because I speak from my heart and follow up with my head and let Spirit guide me.

In my relationship with myself, I also walk in two worlds, [those] of the body and the spirit, but I see them as one. That requires work, like all relationships, but it is joyful work—the ongoing project of unifying my life.

I've worked at my marriage, at raising my daughter, at being present for my granddaughter, and the success of these relationships is shared—they've worked at it, too. I am a better artist, better at walking between worlds, when I draw energy from love—loving and being loved.

That's why I am here.

GAIL BRUCE is an artist, producer, and philanthropist who conceived and launched RamScale Art Associates' Art Lunch, an innovative approach to marketing and presenting contemporary fine art to a broad public. She co-founded RamScale Productions with her husband, Murray Bruce, thirty years ago to produce art, stage, film, and video projects in New York City.

Marty Rosenbluth
Nov 20 1958

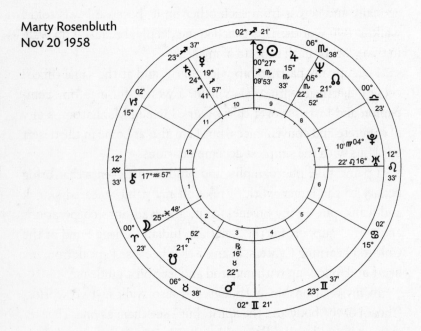

The Life Script of Marty, a Scorpio

☉ SUN: The instinct to shine from the center of your story; in Scorpio ♏ in the ninth house: Marty shines as an insightful teacher about uses and abuses of power.

☽ MOON: The instinct to have a home; in Pisces ♓ in the first house: Marty's at home nurturing other filmmakers and is accessible as one himself.

☿ MERCURY: The instinct to communicate; in Sagittarius ♐ in the tenth house: Marty uses his voice to speak publicly as a unifier.

♀ VENUS: The instinct to love; in Sagittarius ♐ in the ninth house: Marty loves being a public messenger about justice for all of humanity. Why leave anyone out?

♂ MARS: The instinct to act; in Taurus ♉ in the third house: As an activist concerned with how the media uses information, Marty counteracts propaganda by listening to local voices who not only have a point to make but also represent the values of the community.

♃ JUPITER: The instinct to philosophize, to sum it all up; in Scorpio ♏ in the ninth house: As a researcher, Marty finds the airing out of every level of information publicly is the first step in a philosophical shift.

♄ SATURN: The instinct to commit; in Sagittarius ♐ in the eleventh house: Marty commits to completing communications projects with clear conclusions, which he shares with strategists for the future.

⚷ CHIRON: The instinct to heal; in Aquarius ♒ in the first house: Marty heals himself and others by speaking from a free place, in person, close-up.

♅ URANUS: The instinct to express truth; in Leo ♌ in the seventh house: Intimate partnerships remind Marty that the heart is the real educator about what is ultimately true.

♆ NEPTUNE: The instinct to express soul; in Scorpio ♏ in the eighth house: Marty tunes into the deepest hopes and fears of the culture as an expression of his soul growth.

♀ PLUTO: The instinct to express power; in Virgo ♍ in the seventh house: Marty's partnership with his wife empowers him to function well and be of service to purposes beyond their partnership; he does the same for her.

℧ SOUTH NODE OF THE MOON: The instinct to gaze at the past and recognize an inheritance; in Aries ♈ in the second house: When Marty looks at his inheritance from the past, he sees an advocate for those who pay their own way and enjoy the harvest of their work.

☊ NORTH NODE OF THE MOON: The instinct to gaze at the future and recognize a liberating path; in Libra ♎ in the eighth house: When Marty looks at his future, he sees paradox, the life of the diplomat who can see two sides to a situation; he has more power than he had before, to negotiate change for both sides.

♏

In His Own Words: Marty Rosenbluth
Filmmaker and Political Analyst
*"Passion gives life meaning. If you don't
have passion, you're coasting. . . ."*

From 1985 to 1992 I lived in the Palestinian town of Ramallah in the West Bank. Those were pivotal years, right before and during the Palestinian uprising. For most of that time, I worked as a researcher with Palestinian human rights organizations. As an American Jew, this was slightly unusual.

Around the time of the Gulf War, I became extremely frustrated with the challenge of getting the facts out around what was happening to the Palestinians in the West Bank and Gaza. We would publish 300-page reports on human rights violations, then give journalists a 10-page summary to make it easier to digest. The reporters always wanted something shorter. I realized that if we wanted to get the word out through the media we would have to make our own media. I thought about becoming a documentary filmmaker but I'd never been to film school.

Coincidentally, shortly thereafter, I met a producer for PBS who was working on a documentary on the West Bank and Gaza. I ended up working on the film as senior researcher. It was a great way to begin a career in video and film. As far as camera work and editing went, I taught myself for the most part.

Using the skills I had just learned, I went on to make the video *Jerusalem: An Occupation Set in Stone?* in conjunction with a coalition of Palestinian, Israeli, and international human rights organizations. It has since been translated into seven languages and shown in numerous film festivals and on television throughout the world.

Every time I show the video, someone always asks, "What was it like to be Jewish and to live in the West Bank, and why did you go there in the first place?"

In response, I describe my childhood, growing up as a Jewish American in Brooklyn, New York. In 1967, at age nine, I read newspapers every single day during the Arab-Israeli war to get all the details. I was totally uncritical of Israel. I even supported the Vietnam War because it was supposed to be fighting Communism and Communists supported the Arabs.

It wasn't until I was in college that I began to discover that so much of what I had been taught simply wasn't true. I call it an "unlearning process." It was meeting Palestinians for the first time that led me to change.

Later, in 1985 when I went to live in Palestine, I became even more disillusioned with the Israelis. Intolerance is intolerance. It doesn't matter who is practicing it.

My goal became to help people shift out of old assumptions and perspectives around what was happening in Palestine. So much of what moves people politically is based on fear rather than hope, particularly those in the American Jewish community who repeat the slogan, "Never again will the Holocaust happen." What they mean is never again to *us*. I think it has to mean *never again to anybody*. To take the fear of the Holocaust and use it as a justification for abusing other people's human rights is not only wrong but is itself a violation. It's like saying, "Because of what happened to us, we have the right to do whatever we want to other people." Whereas the message should be exactly the opposite. The message should be: *Because of what happened to us, we have to make sure that nobody's human rights are ever violated*, regardless of their politics.

I am passionate about magnifying that message. Passion gives life meaning. If you don't have passion, you're coasting, and this was an issue I simply could not coast by.

To me, the greatest irony is that a lot of the torturers who are now working for the Palestinian Authority learned their torturing techniques when they themselves were tortured by the Israelis. So they learn to torture as victims, and they are now torturing other people as perpetrators. It's a vicious circle.

What we have to work toward is explaining to people on both sides that these types of things are simply not acceptable— ever. Often I think it's a question of holding up a mirror and saying, "Look at what you are doing! Look at what's happening. Aren't you doing exactly what you are protesting?" But sometimes it doesn't help.

I made the documentary *Jerusalem: An Occupation Set in Stone?* in order to hold up a mirror. I interviewed Arabs, Israelis, Palestinians, all the parties involved, especially the people who live there, who are not the press or government officials. I had no agenda other than allowing their voices to unify into a message that could say more in fifty-eight minutes than could be said in hundreds of pages of text.

The making of that video changed my life forever. Despite my love of Judaism, I love a larger justice for all of humanity more, and to make this video and tour with it and stand with it in question-and-answer sessions in which people of my own religion are calling me a traitor is not easy.

I have learned to get out of my own way. It is tempting, when you face a hostile audience, to shout back, "No, *you're* wrong." To maintain a calm, even keel in the face of that hostility has probably been the hardest lesson for me to learn, but definitely the most valuable. I just get into a groove and become very focused. It's easier to be calm because I actually understand the people who are screaming at me. I was in the exact same place they are—except possibly further to the right than most of them—when I was younger. What becomes totally clear in these dialogues is this: *Having the same human rights standards for everybody is a perfectly rational position.*

It calms me also to realize that, though I may not get to the person who is screaming most loudly at me, the person sitting two rows back may hear me very well. And so my path is simply to continue speaking the truth, to encourage change based on hope in human nature rather than fear of human nature.

MARTY ROSENBLUTH's 1995 video *Jerusalem: An Occupation Set in Stone?* won many awards, including Best Political Documentary at the Charleston Worldfest Film Festival. He is an adjunct professor at Antioch College in Ohio. He produces videos for nonprofit groups from his studio in Hillsborough, North Carolina, where he lives with his family.

Patrick Reynolds
Dec 2 1948

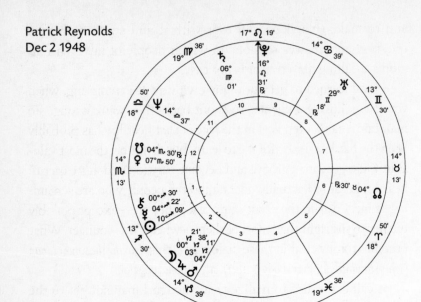

The Life Script of Patrick, a Sagittarius

☉ SUN: The instinct to shine from the center of your story; in Sagittarius ♐ in the first house: Patrick shines as he chooses to be an optimistic messenger about what is possible, up-front, in person.

☽ MOON: The instinct to have a home; in Capricorn ♑ in the second house: Patrick's home begins with self-respect; he is the executive of his own life.

☿ MERCURY: The instinct to communicate; in Sagittarius ♐ in the first house: Patrick's voice naturally reaches out to open minds, inviting them to explore the adventure of what is possible together.

♀ VENUS: The instinct to love; in Scorpio ♏ in the twelfth house: Patrick loves his discovery of power and the sacred as one path.

♂ MARS: The instinct to act; in Capricorn ♑ in the second house: Patrick is an activist around fathering youth and encouraging them to recognize their own values, and to commit to them.

♃ JUPITER: The instinct to philosophize, to sum it all up; in Capricorn ♑ in the second house: Patrick is an educator about how to build character by making conscious choices. He is a philosopher about the beauty of growing old, growing wise.

♄ SATURN: The instinct to commit; in Virgo ♍ in the tenth house: Patrick commits to building a body of knowledge designed to enhance the health of the community, whether that's his neighborhood block or the globe.

⚷ CHIRON: The instinct to heal; in Sagittarius ♐ in the first house: Patrick is a walking advertisement for a larger map of options. He helps others shift out of old wounds.

♅ URANUS: The instinct to express truth; in Gemini ♊ in the eighth house: Patrick's value to the culture is as a clear communicator who speaks the truth we all see but may not say.

♆ NEPTUNE: The instinct to express soul; in Libra ♎ in the eleventh house: Patrick dreams of a long-term future in which he brings lasting beauty and balance into the world.

♀ PLUTO: The instinct to express power; in Leo ♌ in the ninth house: Patrick expresses his power as an actor who educates people while simultaneously entertaining them, leading them to a larger perspective.

☋ SOUTH NODE OF THE MOON: The instinct to gaze at the past and recognize an inheritance; in Scorpio ♏ in the twelfth house: When he looks at his inheritance from the past, Patrick sees a search for power and a search for the sacred sometimes intersecting, sometimes not.

☊ NORTH NODE OF THE MOON: The instinct to gaze at the future and recognize a liberating path; in Taurus ♉ in the sixth house: When Patrick looks at where he is headed, he sees a search for community and work that improves the quality of life for others.

↗

In His Own Words: Patrick Reynolds
Advocate for Health, Foe of the Tobacco Industry
"[Y]ou're going to need your health in the wonderful and amazing years ahead. . . ."

I enjoy telling my life story, and I believe it has impact on the youth who hear it. My mission is to help keep them tobacco- and drug-free.

Often, the wounds we are born with, or the problems we encounter along our journey, become a part of our purpose. It often happens in ways we could never have predicted, and that is how my story begins. I was born an heir to R. J. Reynolds, one of the wealthiest men in the United States when he was alive, and father to seven children by four wives.

I grew up in privileged circumstances, financially. But I suffered deeply from being fatherless. My own father left when I was three years old, and after that I only saw him five more times, on too-brief visits to his private island off the coast of Georgia. He died when I was fifteen of emphysema caused by smoking the brands—Camel and Winston—that made him a wealthy man.

At age ten, I made a playful film of my brother Mike as a mad scientist who destroys the world. In 1969, I made another film, this one a documentary of Berkeley, California. I filmed it myself, during the period of riots over People's Park, incited by groups like the Third World Liberation Front. The 1960s were just ending, and the preceding years had seen much upheaval. Now twenty-one, I had a more unsettling and troubling vision: that our society was in decline and in trouble.

I wasn't quite sure how it would manifest, but I began to form a basic self-image as a stabilizing, positive force for good in the community. I sensed and hoped that my work would extend to the national and international level. I had developed my communication skills through my efforts in print media, theater, and film throughout high school and college. I knew I was a messenger of sorts.

But at such a young age, I was unprepared to come up with a specific role in life to play. Through my mid-twenties, I struggled as an actor/filmmaker in Hollywood. In 1985, I starred in one feature film, *Eliminators*. But it did not launch me into a successful acting career.

In 1986, I found myself in Washington, D.C., at the invitation of a businessman friend, Larry Miller. I joined his group for a private tour of the Pentagon, and got to see the human side of Washington up close. I was fascinated. Robert Packwood, the senator from Oregon, was then heading up tax reform. When he came into the room, I was quite bold, asking questions like, "Why is the U.S. so soft on Israel? Shouldn't the U.S. put strong pressure on the Israelis to make peace?"

I also asked Packwood, "I've often wondered, Senator, why the U.S. tobacco tax is so low, compared to other countries. If you're really serious about reforming taxes, why don't you raise the cigarette tax to be equal to the tax in other nations?"

He studied me and said, "You're a Reynolds, and you want to raise the cigarette tax?" I said, "Definitely. It's the right thing to do." He replied, "Well, why don't you come down to the Senate subcommittee and testify this afternoon to that effect?" And I declined, saying, "I can't do that. I'm unprepared. I'll have to talk to my family about it."

That moment was the beginning of a huge step for me. I

wasn't ready to testify yet, but his invitation to speak before a powerful congressional committee registered deeply. Soon after, I began to look into the tobacco industry's activities. I learned that cigarettes were the second most heavily promoted product in the nation, after cars, and that [tobacco companies] were spending several billion dollars a year on advertising. I learned that the industry was often protected by the same government officials whose election campaign ads were partly paid for by the tobacco industry. I learned about the efforts of the tobacco industry to suppress information linking smoking with chronic illness and death. The more I learned, the more angry I became.

At this time, I was also waking up to a long-buried grief over my father's absence from my childhood—due partly to his premature death from smoking. I connected the sadness of losing my father with my new anger toward the advertising campaigns and political manipulations of the tobacco industry. Suddenly I knew the direction in which I wanted to point my life.

If I told the truth about Big Tobacco, it would not only give expression to my anger and grief over my father, it would also give me an opportunity to educate people—a real purpose for my life. Before speaking out publicly for the first time, I had some heated discussions with my four brothers. They were worried and angry. But in time, Mike came to agree that instead of being an embarrassment, I'm someone in the family they can point to with pride.

Three months after my chance meeting with Senator Packwood, I publicly testified before a congressional subcommittee in favor of an end to all tobacco advertising. My testimony was carried by all the major news and wire services, and I was suddenly besieged with requests for news interviews and speaking engagements. I was called on by dozens of antismoking groups to testify before many state legislatures and city councils to help pass laws limiting smoking, banning vending machines, limiting youth access, and raising cigarette taxes. Long before the lawsuits against the tobacco companies had any success, I joined other advocates to encourage legal action. I became increasingly dedicated to the cause of fighting tobacco, and in 1989 founded the Foundation for a Smokefree America. Since that time, I've had a full calendar of speaking and advocacy work.

These days my heart and passion are in our efforts to prevent youth from becoming addicted. I am doing more live assemblies to middle and high school students. I educate them about tobacco advertising, how to say no to peer pressure, and I offer a new perception of film stars who smoke in movies and TV. In my live talks and new video, I also revive the lost practice of initiation into adulthood. The core of this is to let teens know that at times life is going to be difficult, even painful. "When the tough moments come," I counsel them, "don't alter your dark feeling like so many adults do with cigarettes, food, alcohol, drugs, TV, or turning up the stereo. Stay with your thoughts, but don't isolate. Talk to your parents, the school counselor, or a trusted teacher—and solve the problem. Don't run away from it. Welcome to the world of adults."

In 1998, I learned that recent studies have shown that among teens today, there's widespread fear and anxiety about the future. Many believe that their outlook is bleak. According to a 1999 Yankelovich Partners study, 50 percent of children ages nine to seventeen were worried they won't live very long.

From 1988 to 1998, there was an astounding 73 percent increase in teen smoking. Like other advocates, I believed this was largely due to ad campaigns [featuring] Joe Camel and the Marlboro Man, and to a substantial increase of smoking by stars in movies and on TV; but I also formed the idea that many teens, out of this new pessimism, might be saying, "Why not smoke? Why not use drugs? There's no future for me anyway." From this, I concluded that if I could inspire them to have more faith in the future, that would help motivate many young people to hold on to their health.

In this section of my presentation, I take young people through four basic steps. First, I encourage them to develop the habit of talking about their feelings to others, and not isolating. Second, I train them to think positive. Third, I ask them to reevaluate their notion of wealth. I ask, "What is real wealth?" Fourth, I share my own strong faith in the future. I tell them, "Because the future's looking so great, you're going to need your health in the wonderful and amazing years ahead in this twenty-first century. So don't start smoking, don't use drugs, and don't drink alcohol— because I have faith and a vision that the future looks incredible!"

I am devoted to my work of opening young eyes. It energizes me as well as them. It's work I will continue to do. Our children are the future.

PATRICK REYNOLDS's testimony before Congress helped bring about the current airline smoking ban. In 1989, he founded The Foundation for a Smokefree America. Patrick lives in Los Angeles, California, and travels internationally, speaking primarily to youth audiences.

Gail Straub
Jan 14 1949

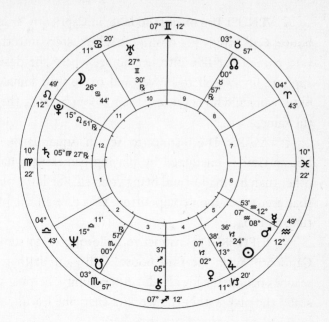

The Life Script of Gail, a Capricorn

☉ SUN: The instinct to shine from the center of your story; in Capricorn ♑ in the fifth house: Gail shines as she plays teacher and is taught by the spirit of play. Living a conscious creative life sparks the center of her story.

☽ MOON: The instinct to have a home; in Cancer ♋ in the eleventh house: Gail creates home with a husband who has a strongly developed feminine side and the same vision of the future she does, one that honors self-care. She also creates home through a women's group that has met regularly for decades.

☿ MERCURY: The instinct to communicate; in Aquarius, ♒ in the sixth house: Gail speaks well to groups who are interested in entrepreneurship. She encourages groups and individuals to choose work that best suits their talents rather than redesigning their talents to do the work.

♀ VENUS: The instinct to love; in Capricorn ♑ in the fourth house: Gail brings her desire for self-mastery into the most private part of her life, into her home, where she designs elegant support for herself to flower and to be fully female. She loves older women who never lose their bloom because they have done the same.

♂ MARS: The instinct to act; in Aquarius ♒ in the fifth house: Gail is energized by playing games that have no rules other than having fun and being yourself. She loves playing games that aren't based on competition, that give all the players equal time and space.

♃ JUPITER: The instinct to philosophize, to sum it all up; in Capricorn ♑ in the fifth house: Gail gains faith in life as she teaches people the joy of self-responsibility, helping them understand the play within the work of that. She learns as much from her students as they learn from her.

♄ SATURN: The instinct to commit; in Virgo ♍ in the twelfth house: Gail must pay constant attention to the inner life, as balance to the outer. As she does, she restores her body and health.

⚷ CHIRON: The instinct to heal; in Sagittarius ♐ in the third house: Gail heals herself and others as she acknowledges what is disconnected in her life story from her best maps of possibility and voices what is broken, allowing it to speak, to be heard, and then to heal.

♅ URANUS: The instinct to express truth; in Gemini ♊ in the tenth house: Gail lives a life as an entrepreneurial communicator afoot in the world, a pioneer teacher.

♆ NEPTUNE: The instinct to express soul; in Libra ♎ in the second house: Gail is inspired to create a rhythm of work that balances her rather than loads her down; as she grows lighter through her work, her ability to express compassion grows deeper and stronger.

♀ PLUTO: The instinct to express power; in Leo ♌ in the twelfth house: Gail's passion is to introduce others to spirituality as powerful play, the sacred as a sense of humor—an energy that can move mountains of resistance, once the resistance has served its purpose.

☋ SOUTH NODE OF THE MOON: The instinct to gaze at the past and recognize an inheritance; in Scorpio ♏ in the second house: When Gail looks at her inheritance from the past, she sees a hard worker who built an external harvest through passionate overdrive.

☊ NORTH NODE OF THE MOON: The instinct to gaze at the future and recognize a liberating path; in Taurus ♉ in the eighth house: When Gail looks at her future, she sees a slower pace for herself, shared wealth with others, a wealth earned as she shapes the dream of the culture, educating others about manifestation. She shares her secrets.

♑

In Her Own Words: Gail Straub

Student of Reality, Teacher of Grace

"[T]houghts sow seeds . . . our beliefs empower us—or limit us."

My work requires that I travel a lot, which pleases me; I love travel. Sometimes someone sitting next to me on a plane or bus will ask, "What do you do?"

I answer, "I am a teacher." I don't say more than that, unless they ask for more. I could be a first-grade teacher, I could be a university professor, but those four words—*I am a teacher*—sum up my life path.

Teaching is part of my family tradition. I grew up in the '50s and '60s among a family of teachers. I started tutoring children when I was only twelve. I loved teaching, and these particular children introduced me to a second joy: cross-cultural experiences. I was a tall white girl living in a middle-class neighborhood, and they were African-Americans living in the inner city of Wilmington, Delaware. I helped them learn more easily, and they introduced me to the larger human family in its diversity. It made me want more.

After college, I joined the Peace Corps, went to Africa, and taught English as a second language. I also spent as much time playing with my students as teaching them. A very important thing happened there that gave me a glimpse of the tradition I would ultimately serve. My supervisor watched me practice-teach one day, and afterward she took me aside and said simply, "You have the makings of a master teacher." I felt my inexperience before such praise, but I also recognized the tradition of teaching as mine and [as] a gift I was to develop.

However, at the age of twenty-three, my life education was just beginning. I physically embraced life with all the passion of youth. I lived in Paris for a year studying Marxism; I explored consciousness movements at every turn. I was hungry to know the world, to be a cultural ambassador, as soon as possible. I did just that, all over Europe, South America, and the United States in the '60's and '70s.

But I needed to learn focus. My body had taught me a great deal of focus. I learned to breath deeply and stretch before I ran. I trained in my youth as a massage therapist, and again the body taught me focus, but it also became a laboratory in which I could explore the interface between mind and body. As I began to explore the mind more, I realized that whatever we place our mental, emotional, and spiritual attention on grows. I became a full-time student of the principles of manifestation.

In 1980, while I was teaching a workshop, I met David

Gershon and we fell madly in love. We both had an idea of "empowerment," which is now a buzzword but in the early '80s it wasn't. We both felt that our work and education [were] about empowerment—empowering people to manifest their visions. Shortly after we met, we got married and began to develop our business—Empowerment Training Programs, which has become our life's work. We launched the first workshop in 1981. Our empowerment work combined my love of teaching with my love of cross-cultural adventures. We took the training to Europe, Asia, Russia, and China. I got to know the planet—and many cultures—pretty well.

In some countries, like China and Russia, the premise of our teaching was radically new: that thoughts sow seeds, that our beliefs empower us—or limit us. Many people recognized and claimed an inner creative source for the first time. They let go of Big Brother—the government—as creator of their lives. As a consequence, an enormous amount of human creativity was unleashed, as brilliant and spontaneous as sunlight.

In all of our work, David and I helped people identify and transform limiting beliefs in order to manifest a vision. We did our best to be role models ourselves. For example, in 1986, in partnership with UNICEF, we organized a run around the planet in the name of world peace. "The First Earth Run" involved millions of people with one vision: to carry a torch around the earth, to unify all people. That experience tested our principles of manifestation in every imaginable way.

By the early '90s, I found myself ready to explore a new focus as a teacher. Within my inner life, I have always accepted the reality of grace. Grace is an extension of the sacred—spirit moving through each of us. Grace likes to be invited into a situation. I wanted to supplement my teachings on manifesting one's dreams and visions with an exploration of grace, and to invite grace into as many situations as possible, including the biggest trouble spots on the planet and in the community—the areas of suffering that most need grace.

The result was a training I called Grace, which combined spiritual growth and social responsibility. Since 1992, I've worked with committed students who wanted to explore with me. I saw myself less as a teacher and more of an architect of gatherings that called in grace, and then directed that grace toward particular people or places on the planet who needed it. This satisfied the mother I am—to the planet, to people, to myself—more than I can say. My book *The Rhythm of Compassion* describes that exploration of grace, as my students and I asked the question: *How can I take care of myself while also connecting to society?*

Our answers have made my faith in the human heart deeper than ever, in its capacity to create a more conscious global community.

That faith inspires the teacher I am, and the cross-cultural ambassador. That faith gives me the joy to begin again, to say to life each day: "Come! Play with me! Give me the next adventure!"

GAIL STRAUB is author of *The Rhythm of Compassion: Caring for Self, Connecting with Society* and coauthor, with her husband David Gershon, of *Empowerment: The Art of Creating Your Life as You Want It*. Gail and her husband live in upstate New York.

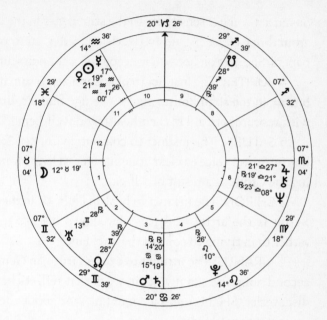

Susun Weed
Feb 8 1946

The Life Script of Susun, an Aquarius

☉ SUN: The instinct to shine from the center of your story; in Aquarius ♒ in the eleventh house: Susun lives a life designed to awaken herself and her tribe to create conscious futures.

☽ MOON: The instinct to have a home; in Taurus ♉ in the first house: Susun is most at home living close to the earth. She introduces herself to others as an herbalist who teaches the healing properties of plants.

☿ MERCURY: The instinct to communicate; in Aquarius ♒ in the eleventh house: Susun speaks easily to people who are interested in thinking for themselves as pioneers of the future.

♀ VENUS: The instinct to love; in Aquarius ♒ in the eleventh house: Susun loves encouraging a future for other entrepreneurial healers.

♂ MARS: The instinct to act; in Cancer ♋ in the third house:

Susun acts on her sensitivity to the stimulants in the environment around her by saying no to television, radio, stereos, and newspapers. She acts on her yes by becoming a connoisseur of essence.

♃ JUPITER: The instinct to philosophize, to sum it all up; in Libra ♎ in the sixth house: She is a bridge builder, linking people with resources to aid in their health and well-being.

♄ SATURN: The instinct to commit; in Cancer ♋ in the third house: Susun voices a clear commitment to living long, to becoming the Crone as a result of self-care.

⚷ CHIRON: The instinct to heal; in Libra ♎ in the sixth house: Susun is the artful healer as she allows disease to inform her rather than trying to control the imbalance.

♅ URANUS: The instinct to express truth; in Gemini ♊ in the second house: Susun invests in work that reflects her pioneering discoveries. She becomes a communicator about these discoveries and gets paid for it.

♆ NEPTUNE: The instinct to express soul; in Libra ♎ in the sixth house: Susun is partnered with intuition in her immediate work environment.

♇ PLUTO: The instinct to express power; in Leo ♌ in the fourth house: Susun empowers women to claim the full and rich cast of characters within them, including what they or society may regard as taboo.

☋ SOUTH NODE OF THE MOON: The instinct to gaze at the past and recognize an inheritance; in Sagittarius ♐ in the eighth house: Susun recognizes an ancient resonance within her around the unity of all life; she was born knowing the song celebrating that unity.

☊ NORTH NODE OF THE MOON: The instinct to gaze at the future and recognize a liberating path; in Gemini ♊ in the second house: Susun is becoming a clear communicator of specific, grounded perceptions. She earns a living as she does.

≈≈

In Her Own Words: Susun S. Weed
Pioneer, Publisher, Pagan
*"Making my dreams real means jumping
into the icy waters of life. . . ."*

My first commitment to joy occurred when I was eleven. I was riding the city bus home from my daily swim at the Y, full of enthusiasm, thrilled to be alive, tingling in all parts of my body, eager to savor every moment of life. As I gazed at the adults around me, I was struck by how gloomy, dull, and dead they seemed. "Whatever's gotten into them, I hereby promise it won't get into me," I swore to myself.

Joy is a choice. I made it then, and I have continued to make it throughout my life. For me, choosing joy is not about looking on the bright side, nor [about] positive thinking. Pain is inevitable, but joy can turn lemons into lemonade.

Electrical circuits require both positive and negative currents. No negativity, no light. Choosing joy means enjoying and nourishing all parts of myself with compassion. This, of course, helps me enjoy all parts of life.

In 1986, at the age of forty, I created a ceremony wherein I dedicated the next twenty years of my life to illuminating the Wise Woman Tradition. I have been called a backward pioneer because I have reclaimed the oldest ways of healing—herbs and shamanic skills, women's ways of nourishing and relating—and made them accessible and workable for today. I have helped change how we think about health care in America as we enter the twenty-first century. Herbal medicine is regaining its place as a simple, safe form of primary care.

My ally and most profound teacher has always been nature. Even as a child in the fifties in Dallas, I found a tiny bit of wild woods to roam. Since 1968 I have lived in the Catskill Mountains of the Hudson River valley, where I grow most of my own food and herbs, heat with wood, and milk the goats twice a day. No radio, no recorded music, no TV, no newspapers intrude on my day or interrupt my thoughts. I listen to nature, to the plants, to the wisdom of the animals and my own body.

My home is also my teaching center, where I help women become bitches, witches, dykes, and sluts (and herbalists and goddesses). From March to November, I open my home to students, apprentices, and visiting teachers. Nourishing wholeness through story, ceremony, and wild foods, the Wise Woman Way, we reweave the healing cloak of the ancients with classes on herbal medicine, spirit healing, sacred sex, chanting, moon lodges, priestess trainings, and "Green Witch" intensives. Women from around the planet come to the Wise Woman Center to study with me. But to me, their teacher is really nature, also known as the Great Goddess. Apprentices are mentored by a goddess archetype and allied with a plant of their choosing in addition to [spending] time with me.

I do my best to offer the apprentices the kinds of situations that helped me hear the plants talking and that opened my heart to nature—shamanic trances, drumming, chanting, walking in the woods at night barefoot, sleeping outside alone, and goatherding (which requires being alone in the woods all day)—everything but psychoactive plants!

While the Wise Woman Center is a dream made real, my other big project, Ash Tree Publishing, just happened. I didn't intend to be a writer, or a publisher. When a friend did a reading for me in 1979 and told me I would write many books, I laughed. It was so far from my plans. Writing grew naturally from my commitment to spread the Wise Woman Tradition. It seemed natural to publish it myself so I wouldn't have to edit it to suit someone else. Now Ash Tree has published not only my four books but seven titles by other women.

Running a workshop center and a publishing company from my home (where I also homestead and train apprentices) may seem like a lot, but I also personally mentor more than 300 correspondence students and teach in Europe as well as throughout America. I demand a lot from life. I want to wake up joyous and eager. I want the energy to work twelve to sixteen hours a day and enjoy every minute. I want to feel superb in my body. I want to go to sleep easily. And I don't want to do dream work, the last refuge of the Puritan work ethic. Sleeping is my time off, not time to do more work.

Actually, I find I have fewer dreams these days. As I live my dreams during the day, my night dreams don't have to compensate. When I do have dreams, they are clear and to the point, reminders or alerts to coming events. Living my dreams is one of the results of choosing joy. Living my dreams means being whole and real every moment. Making my dreams real means jumping into the icy waters of life; it means not flinching from the blazing fire of life. (Anything less makes you a lukewarm drink, said one of my Wise Woman teachers.) Living my dreams means being the possible human, means embodying the power I have as a woman and sharing that power with all other women. Living my dreams means embodying the wisdom of nature and speaking with the voice of the goddess. Living my dreams means embracing change while caring tenderly for the part of of me that hates change. Living my dreams means growing up to be a joyous old woman.

SUSUN S. WEED rediscovered the Wise Woman Tradition: healing by nourishing. She authored these books: *Wise Woman Herbal for the Childbearing Year, Healing Wise, Menopausal Years the Wise Woman Way,* and *Breast Cancer? Breast Health! The Wise Woman*

Way. Susun is editor-in-chief of Ash Tree Publishing and director of the Wise Woman Center in Woodstock, New York.

Marie Runyon
Mar 20 1915

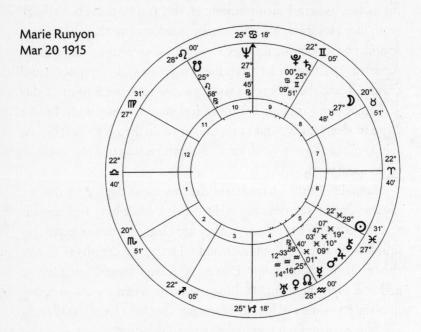

The Life Script of Marie, a Pisces

☉ SUN: The instinct to shine from the center of your story; in Pisces ♓ in the sixth house: Marie shines through trusting in a divine plan. She steps into the flow of that every day. That flow takes her into the spirit of her community and allows her to inspire them as well.

☽ MOON: The instinct to have a home; in Taurus ♉ in the eighth house: Marie is happiest when she knows she is working for everyone to have a home. She raises funds and builds cultural resources to make that possible.

☿ MERCURY: The instinct to communicate; in Pisces ♓ in the

fifth house: Marie talks to dogs as if they were people and enjoys a telepathy with them. With people, Marie's communication style often includes humor, no matter how serious she is about any topic or circumstance.

♀ VENUS: The instinct to love; in Aquarius ♒ in the fourth house: Marie loves forming family in any way she chooses. She is loved, in turn, by free spirits who recognize her style of loving as egalitarian, not based on whom you know or positions of privilege in the world.

♂ MARS: The instinct to act; in Pisces ♓ in the fifth house: Marie refuels by losing herself in play, by arousing the child within. She is an activist guardian of the vulnerable and innocent. "Abuse of any living creature really bugs me, and I'll put up a fight to stop it," she says..

♃ JUPITER: The instinct to philosophize, to sum it all up; in Pisces ♓ in the fifth house: Marie explores compassion for all living creatures as a path and life philosophy.

♄ SATURN: The instinct to commit; in Gemini ♊ in the ninth house: Marie is committed to making public any information of impact. She is committed to fighting discrimination—the doors that are closed due to closed minds.

⚷ CHIRON: The instinct to heal; in Pisces ♓ in the fifth house: Marie heals as she lets go of who she thinks she is and relaxes. She stops thinking, she gets out of her own way, and she steps into the flow.

♅ URANUS: The instinct to express truth; in Aquarius ♒ in the fourth house: Marie routinely reinvents herself based on the latest truth she has recognized about her own nature and what she needs next to thrive.

♆ NEPTUNE: The instinct to express soul; in Cancer ♋ in the tenth house: Marie is an influence in the world as a guiding light of inspiration around the family of humanity.

♀ PLUTO: The instinct to express power, in Cancer ♋ in the ninth house: Her passion is to be a role model who cares about public policy affecting families.

☋ SOUTH NODE OF THE MOON: The instinct to gaze at the past and recognize an inheritance; in Leo ♌ in the tenth house: When Marie gazes into the faces of her ancestors, she sees the faces of leaders who led with a flourish.

☊ NORTH NODE OF THE MOON: The instinct to gaze at the future and recognize a liberating path; in Aquarius ♒ in the fourth house: Marie has pioneered her way into an entirely new definition of home and family, even into a different culture from the one she was born into. This has helped her discover herself.

♓
In Her Own Words: Marie Runyon
Carrier of Compassion
"There can be no greater reward in life than seeing a group of formerly homeless . . . human beings move into a renovated . . . building with heat and hot water at all times."

There I was, minding my own business one spring night in 1974 in Harlem, when a member of our mostly African American collective called and said he would like to drop in for a few minutes with something important to say. He came, and said he and others in the collective thought I should run for the New York State Assembly against the incumbent, whom all of us knew to be no damn good. I told him he was out of his mind, that we were enemies of the establishment, not participants. The next week all of the collective came to see me and finally convinced me— though [I was] white and southern-born—that I should run to represent Harlem in the state assembly. I ran, and won by twenty-six votes.

During my stint in the legislature, I spent most of my time on housing, prisons, ex-prisoners, and racism, and irritating the Albany leadership by not doing what they told me to do. I was defeated for reelection by 100 votes, but my work wasn't remotely finished.

And when did my work begin? Behind much of my life work is this memory of the south, in 1923: I am eight years old, in the car with my father. He gives a ride to a black hitchhiker (which most whites would not), but makes him stand on the running board of our 1921 Nash. That didn't seem reasonable to me, since there was plenty of room inside.

Ever since, discrimination against anyone because of the color of his skin has bugged me, and I've been moved to act. That activism became the major focus of my life after I left the south. I moved to New York City and settled in Harlem and came to know and love it.

After my defeat in the legislature in 1976—though I had no money and no connections—I decided to rebuild Harlem, tackling the housing problem, and established the not-for-profit Harlem Restoration Project [HRP]. Our collective and other groups had generated much publicity in high places about how much of Harlem had to live in rat holes, and how hideous it was that there were so many solid buildings crying for renovation. Our plan to employ ex-offenders to do the work was a lead balloon for bureaucrats who controlled funds. We were determined to succeed without them and got moving.

By 1998, [the] HRP had renovated many buildings and owned sixteen—all affordable to the community—working almost exclusively with minorities and those with very little money.

HRP succeeded despite all odds because of commitment, determination, and not giving a damn who was offended or vowed to block the program. HRP also succeeded because we had our priorities in order. We had no interest in power or publicity, we were just interested in trying to provide one of life's necessities for some of our most vulnerable and deprived people of color.

Who helped to make it happen? An occasional politician or bureaucrat who thought we were doing the right thing and helped, very privately. A few in the religious community. Some of the wealthy people whom I had gotten to know in earlier days as donors to far-out causes helped too. The friends I'd made in prisons became invaluable in running the program. A growing number of community people decided that they, too, would stand up and demand help for those who could not—or dared not—speak for themselves.

But the most important allies were those countless community members who became the recipients of our efforts. With a roof over their heads, they improved themselves and therefore bettered the community. There can be no greater reward in life than seeing a group of formerly homeless or horribly housed human beings move into a renovated, or new, safe, comfortable building, with heat and hot water at all times.

In 1998, I left HRP. I'm still part of a number of groups and activities, fighting racism, police brutality, bureaucratic nonsense, rotten landlords, and inhumane prison conditions. And I'm still getting arrested when a statement is to be made. I must.

When I look back at a lifetime of activism, what I remember as important are things like getting Choo Choo's head bandaged after he had been beaten by the prison guards, or James's teeth fixed—possible only because I was an elected official and the prison hierarchy had to listen more to my complaints than if I were a mere angry enemy of the establishment.

So that ride with my father when I was eight years old, living in the south and witnessing total segregration and hate, shaped me, led me to a lifetime of doing what I could to turn the tide, to remind people: "God hath made of one blood all nations of men." It led me here, to Harlem, to over fifty years of community.

Harlem is home.

MARIE RUNYON has lived in Harlem since 1947. For more than fifty years, she has worked to right racial and criminal injustice through such organizations as the ACLU and SANE. She has been arrested more than twenty times for her participation in demonstrations for countless causes, including the student rebellion at Columbia University in 1968.

The twelve people you've just met could be called practical mystics, though they themselves might never use such a label. What is a practical mystic? Practical mystics merge timeless inspiration with discipline in time. They commit to a purpose beyond personal ambition which, if fulfilled, will inspire others to be their best selves. This doesn't mean that they are perfect people but rather that they recognize that they have talents to cultivate, like good gardeners. Like all of us, they need support. More than half of the twelve people you've just met have worked with me for years, each integrating what they've learned in sessions into the deeper fabric of their life.

Marie Runyon describes the impact of our first session this way: "In 1994, I was in a great deal of turmoil with my professional life and in despair. I made an appointment with Elizabeth. As a consequence of what I learned in that first reading about my life blueprint and the deeper meaning of my challenges, I let go of the despair—and am I ever glad I did. Astrology has made it easier for me to follow my purpose but more importantly to understand that my purpose has many forms, not just the work at Harlem Restoration Project. I left HRP and now I've taken up abolishing the death penalty, among other things.

"I've continued to get readings yearly to hear more about the shifts in emphasis in how I am to grow over time. Astrology validates my inner sense of direction but sharpens [that sense]."

Gail Bruce explains that she frequently uses astrology before hiring people, to validate her own hunches about their compatibility with the role she needs filled. Cindy Waszak has used astrology to understand her children and their different natures and what they are going through at any particular time.

Peter Kater describes the way he uses astrology to understand his relationships and life this way: "I understand that I have free will on how to manifest my astrological grid and that there is a difference between my astrological patterning and my soul. I came to this more clearly when I married a woman with a twin sister born seconds after she was. They have different tastes, beliefs, aspirations, and attitudes, although it's obvious that they are both Scorpios with many similarities. It's also obvious that their souls are different. Their choices have created who they are, but in both cases their birthcharts *affirm* who they are; they share the same grid or map. The details of how they've lived it out is just different. Astrology helps me understand my partner's life questions, however she chooses to answer them, and I have more compassion and patience as a consequence. Astrology is a map that helps determine where I am in relationship to her and the rest of the universe and that is a very helpful tool."

Christian McEwen uses astrology similarly and describes our first session and its impact this way: "When I got my first reading in the late 1980s, I was amazed because it was like being given a map of the territory that I'd been stumbling over, unknowing, the entire previous part of my life. Suddenly I understood, 'Oh, this is where the hill is, this is where the forest is, this is where true north is.' I wasn't expecting that. It really was more useful to me than any other set of explanations I had been given by school, by therapists, by religion, by whatever else. There was an amazing level of precision about it that really was my inner landscape. It has been supremely helpful to take the astrological mirror on board for life—to trust that in my inner landscape I have the Himalayas over here, and a dark jungle over there, and not to blame myself for inhabiting such a complex landscape. It's affirming to know that that complexity shows up in my chart, and my task is to walk through it with some clarity, some courage, some latitude and flexibility.

"After that first reading, I played the tape of the reading over and over, and in a sense then lived in that landscape ever afterward. I did not need to run back to Elizabeth's lap for another reading in six months, though I did get updates from time to time. I've found it very important at crucial junctures to see what is happening from the perspective of the astrological landscape and see what is on the horizon in terms of possibilities."

Empowered by astrology, Christian and others you've just met have trusted their relationships and the shape of their lives more deeply. Each person you have met has identified a dream and the necessary tools and training to ground it. Allies have been important in all of their stories, as well. Time, tools, and allies are key ingredients for you, as a practical mystic, and in chapter 8, we'll explore your specific relationship with them to synthesize what you've learned.

But before we do that, I'd like to give you one more foundational tool in understanding astrology: aspects.

CHAPTER 7

The Aspects: Basic Syntax in the Language of Astrology

Aspects are the angles between planets in your chart, which create the harmony (often called harmonics). Some planetary aspects are difficult and create issues that require concentration and creativity to resolve. Others are more graceful and imply ease. There are many interesting foundational aspects but for the purposes of this book we need only to recognize and master four: *the conjunction, the opposition, the square,* and *the trine.*

Remember, the symbol for degrees looks like this °, and the symbol for minutes looks like an apostrophe '. There are thirty degrees in a sign, sixty minutes in a degree, and sixty seconds in a minute. So you may see a planet in your chart identified like this: 8° ♏ 40'38", which means it is at eight degrees, forty minutes and thirty-eight seconds of Scorpio. Most birthcharts show only degrees and minutes, and in discussing aspects, most astrologers further round off minutes to the degree. (In other words, if you see a planet that is 8° Scorpio 29', you would round it to 8° Scorpio. If it is 8° Scorpio 31', you would round it to 9° Scorpio. If it is 8° Scorpio 30' and 31", you would round it to 9° Scorpio.)

☌ A **conjunction** refers to a fusion between the energies of two planets when there are 0 to 8 degrees of separation between them. Obviously the two planets have not physically fused and do not occupy the same space, but by virtue of being on the same celestial longitude, the *energies* of the two planets have merged.

These degrees of separation are called orbs. For example, if the orb between Saturn and the Sun in a birthchart is seven degrees, the two are said to be in a conjunction with a seven-degree orb. Count anything up to 8 degrees of separation as a conjunction. Many astrologers use a smaller orb of 5 to 6 degrees when one of the outer planets is involved (Uranus, Neptune, or Pluto).

□ A **square** reflects 90 degrees of separation between two planets. Squares are building blocks. Look at a table leg to comprehend quickly a square aspect. The table would not stand up without one or more legs at a ninety-degree angle to the top. Planetary squares suggest certain issues or tasks that can cause breakdown and difficulty if you don't pay attention to them— similar to the collapse of a card table. Squares can also create breakthrough rather than breakdown, producing a new level of discrimination, skill, and creativity. You can't miss a square's teaching over time.

Count three signs over to spot a square. In other words, if you're looking at a planet at 4° Leo, count three signs back (Cancer, Gemini, *Taurus*) and three signs forward (Virgo, Libra, and *Scorpio*). Planets around 4° Taurus and Scorpio (give or take eight degrees) square the planet at 4° Leo.

△ A **trine** refers to 120 degrees between planets. Trines create unimpeded flow—sweet and deep support. Think of two trapeze artists who have rehearsed and mastered the moment of connection and exchange. Trines always occur in the same element (fire, earth, water, or air), which is the equivalent of speaking the same language; there is great compatibility. Count four signs over (in both directions) to spot trines.

☊ An **opposition** refers to 180 degrees of separation between two planets. Oppositions broaden you as you must import and export the qualities of the planet on either end of the seesaw toward the other; there is a cross-pollination as a result. "We're married but we don't live together" summarizes the situation of the two planets in the opposition. To get together requires conscious intention to swap seed. Count six signs over if you are not yet able to spot oppositions immediately.

In the discussion of aspects below, you may want to cross-reference with the chart of the person mentioned, to visually anchor your understanding of the aspect.

A Look at Conjunctions ☌

Take a look at your chart and make a list of any conjunctions you see there, using an orb no larger than 8 degrees (unless it is a Sun/Moon conjunction, in which case it should be 9 degrees). Keep in mind that conjunctions represent a fusion of instincts and can involve more than two planets. Think of conjunctions as carefully prepared mixtures of instincts for you to cultivate and explore for a specialized mission. Due to their potency, we will spend more time exploring examples of these than any other aspect. Here are some examples:

Marty Rosenbluth has a Sun/Venus conjunction, with his Sun ☉ at 27° Scorpio ♏ 53' and Venus ♀ at 0° Sagittarius ♐ 09'. (See page 242 to reference the chart.) A conjunction is determined by the size of the degree of separation, or the size of the orb between two planets—not whether they are in the same sign or house. The point is that when they are within eight degrees of each other their functions are fused.

Though these two planets technically are in the ninth house, they are very close to the midheaven and are therefore charging Marty's public reputation and influence with connotations. What kinds of connotations?

Scorpio Sun learns to choose change, to transform, as it deepens in life experience. Marty does that publicly as a philosopher and political analyst. He says, "If I didn't believe in change, I certainly couldn't be where I am now. Obviously I believe change is possible because I went from being a right-wing Zionist, totally uncritical of Israel, to working full-time for Palestinian human rights." He has become a philosopher of political change.

Having Venus conjunct his Sun helps Marty speak about such volatile topics as the Israeli-Palestinian conflict without losing his equilibrium. He says, "I have learned to get out of my own way. It is tempting, when you face a hostile audience, to shout back, 'No, *you're* wrong.' To maintain a calm, even keel in the face of that hostility has probably been the hardest lesson for me to learn, but definitely the most valuable."

Notice that Venus is ruler of Marty's north node in Libra— what he is growing toward. Venus asks him to personally embody the characteristics of the diplomat, which supports him toward a Libran skill: the ability to see two sides to a situation.

Mary Bloom has a Sun/Mars conjunction in Leo in the eighth house. (See page 225.) Her Sun ⊙ is at 22° Leo ♌ 48' and her Mars ♂ is at 27° Leo ♌ 34'. Round her Sun to 23° Leo and her Mars to 28° Leo, and we have a conjunction with five degrees of separation. How does this translate?

We already know that the eighth house has a great deal to do with the dream of the culture. Mary shines with her Leo Sun there, as she plays out her love of animals in an archetypal way. What's more, with Mars fused with her Sun, she is a powerful advocate for animals—an activist against animal abuse and the abuse of people in powerless positions.

Mars is also the instinct of courage; Mary shot all the photos for the book *Everyday Heroes, Extraordinary Dogs Among Us*, which features dogs performing heroic deeds in crisis situations.

The eighth-house theme of unknown variables (what is unseen) as well as archetypal story comes up in a major way every year for Mary when she organizes the celebration of the animals, St. Francis Day, at the Cathedral of St. John the Divine in New York City. Mary is well aware she does not have control over every outcome and question: *Will the elephant swing his trunk the wrong way and knock an old lady down? Will the animals keep silent at the moment of prayer? Will it rain, ruining the outdoor fair afterward?*

But with Mars conjunct her Sun, she directs the event, wearing a headset and appearing everywhere at once. If she leads well, the event is more likely to go well with minimum chaos.

Abraham Oort has a Sun/Neptune/Mercury conjunction in Virgo in the eighth house (see page 231); because Mercury travels so close to the Sun it is common for it to be conjunct the Sun in a birthchart. As a climatologist much of what Abraham studied were the unseen (eighth house) variables that create climate, and with Mercury in Virgo, he would excel at gathering accurate data. Neptune rules the ocean, and so Abraham naturally worked with the ocean and its role in creating climate.

Also, with Neptune conjunct the Sun, Abraham would naturally turn the definition of reality—mind, nature, spirit—round and round, discovering the sacred there. He says, "Nature is larger than the rational mind."

With Sun conjunct Neptune, Abraham's central life journey must include the conscious owning of his spiritual needs. When he went to see the oracle (Neptune) in the south of France at Thich Nhat Hanh's retreat, it all came clear for him: *Everything is possible, but you must let go of past suffering, specifically the suffering of living purely as a rational being* (Virgo can be the ultimate rationalist with its propensity for order and specifics). With that shift, Abraham's life expanded into a broader expression of his soul and with it, he became a better channel for the gifts of Neptune. With Mercury involved, he develops descriptive skills about the process.

Abraham says, "My experience is that when I let go of ideas of how the day or future should look, and I let it evolve naturally, miracles start to happen that are unexpected, very different from what I might have planned, and usually much more interesting and challenging."

When a planet is conjunct your Sun, it will fuse with your central life path. When a planet is conjunct your Moon, it will fuse with the nurturer you are, with your homing instinct. For example, Patrick Reynolds has Moon conjunct Jupiter and Mars in a tight conjunction of four degrees in Capricorn in the second house (see page 248). He says, "I'm a very big believer [Jupiter] in mentors [Capricorn] and mentoring. I play big brother to a young fellow who I found in my driveway looking up at the tree above, wondering if there was a wounded bird in there. I said, 'I'm Patrick and I live here. If you want to come by and knock on my door, do it.' And he did. The next day, knock, knock, and this kid came into my life. He's now twenty-two and I still see him one or two nights a week. We're good friends, and I've seen him gradually becoming a man."

In Patrick, the nurturer (Moon) and the philosopher (Jupiter) merged to become the benevolent father figure (Capricorn) for this young man—a stabilizing force in his life. Subsequently Patrick's self-esteem also goes up, as does his confidence in his ability to role model, to heal his own father issues. He has more energy (Mars) when he plays this role as father figure.

As a frequent speaker in public schools, Patrick not only helps children parent themselves but helps them understand how to be proactive (Mars) in getting their parents to stop smoking.

And what happens when Saturn, organized endurance, is conjunct radical Uranus? Gail Bruce has expressed her Saturn conjunct Uranus in the eighth house (see page 237) in a clear way. The eighth house is where cultural power is defined. Gail is a pioneer (Uranus) communicator (Gemini) who updates (Uranus) ancient information (Saturn) from earth-based cultures (Taurus)—specifically Native American culture, making it fresh and accessible again for contemporary culture (eighth house) to learn from.

Gail says, "In 1990 Congress passed into law the Native American Graves and Repatriation Act stating that all sacred items were to be returned to the Tribal Nations. One of the excuses used for the lack of attention to this act of Congress is 'there is no place on the reservations to house repatriated material culture.' So we are building places—Cultural Learning Centers—at thirty tribal colleges on reservations in twelve states. These centers grew out of the need for native people to reconnect with their culture and language and have a place to house their material culture for study and celebration."

Conjunctions serve as superpotent storytellers about the blueprint you are working from in your birthchart, the details of which you are to flesh out in your own way. Even conjunctions to the nodes are informative.

My grandmother had Sun in Leo conjunct the south node in Leo, suggesting that her primary identity was deeply merged with an inherited pattern, whether through past lives, genes, or ancestral memory. With south node in Leo, that past was grand, creative, celebrative—and possibly privileged, identified with the aristocratic class.

All of her life my grandmother made fun of the society she belonged to, suggesting a certain boredom with it. But she also had no problem drawing on that identity to get her way. She thought nothing of breaking into a grocery store line rather than going to the end. When she had to stop driving in her eighties, she persuaded the police in our village to drive her to the next town over (on the ruse of having to run an urgent errand), and they delivered her to my aunt's house with the siren wailing.

To Encourage Intuitive Flow for Your Conjunctions ☌

Identify the conjunctions in your birthchart and then walk each one through the following exercise.

Imagine that before you entered this life, you made out a list of strong and varied instincts you hoped to pursue for a lifetime. Each instinct became a little light floating around your head, round and round, as you sat in meditation. A few of them began to dodge in and out of one another and then linked, in tandem, and continued to move around you. Contemplate the beauty of this, the gift of these hybrid instincts. Celebrate your recognition that you have somehow had a hand in attracting a blueprint to yourself, a perfectly prepared package of possibility for what you long to express.

Where are the mergers in this blueprint that you are expressing?

Pass on purposeful mergers, through the flow....

A Look at Squares ☐

Look at any table in the room you occupy right now and marvel at its functionality. Consider the thoughtfulness of its construction, the vertical legs as they meet the horizontal top at that perfect ninety-degree angle that makes it steady. The carpenter who made the table probably was very conscious about his task as he worked. Maybe he even needed that table right away for a particular purpose.

Sometimes we must develop very sophisticated methods of combining talents to maximize our creative gifts to the world. To do this, we need to be like the carpenter building a table—aware of variables, present with our tools, our full attention, and a substantial fund of patience.

Square aspects in the birthchart reflect a combining of talents that may seem discordant but in fact are simply different. Squares are always about learning to live your life more fully and richly. However, this calls for patience, as you are learning a new skill that requires two steps backward to go one step forward. Even a skilled carpenter may have had to overcome an obstacle or solved a problem to get that table built. He had to pay attention; he didn't try to have a party or watch TV at the same time.

Within a square, you may have a blind spot, much like the ninety-degree angle you experience when driving a car and looking in the rearview mirror to see if another car is passing. There is a blind spot at ninety degrees that the mirror misses entirely. So squares reflect an opportunity and a blind spot, both of which become informative when you consciously look to see what is there and then integrate it into the journey.

For example, Cindy Waszak's Sun ☉ at 4° Cancer ♋ 58' in the first house squares her Moon ☽ in the fifth house at 8° Libra ♎ 44' (see page 219). She spends her lifetime integrating the role of nurturer (Cancer) with the role of partnering (Libra). If she plays the role of the mother in her most intimate partnerships, a power imbalance ensues. Libra wants intimacy with an equal and Cindy's heart will not be happy if she cannot experience this. Her home base (Moon) will be off-balance, emotionally. On the other hand, if Cindy plays the role of partner with her children, behaving as friendly equal, she sabotages her mother role with them.

Obviously it is appropriate at times for her to mother her partner, or to be a friendly equal to her children. But when is it inappropriate? When will there be a conflict within her identity as a consequence of playing the wrong role at the wrong time?

Successful navigation of squares (which takes practice and paying attention) results in dynamic and highly creative break-throughs, which then become the equivalent of the table ready for a variety of purposes.

I take special care coaching people with any planet square the Sun—especially Saturn. Saturn can be extremely productive, yet challenging. Saturn is the prayer that was upon your lips when you were born, your vow to make your best effort here and work to convert a weakness into one of your greatest strengths. The Sun is in charge of convincing you that this is the only life you're ever going to have, so you'd better take it seriously. Put that seri-ous driver (the Sun) behind the wheel of a car, and then put Sat-urn in the blind spot at 90 degrees. What is the result? You must cultivate a method of communicating with Saturn and linking Saturn very consciously to your Sun. You must have clear proto-col within yourself for what allows you to work well, without concern for speed.

Squares are like speed bumps. Squares are the cautious ques-tion: *Can I do this if I take my time and navigate carefully?* The quickest way to get into trouble with a square is to ignore the symbolic as-signment it contains, to ignore the blind spot. Even the most con-scious person with a square aspect in his chart (and squares are common) tends to second-guess himself a little around the in-stincts involved.

For example, Marie Runyon has a Pluto/Saturn conjunction in the house of worldly wisdom (ninth house) squaring her Sun in her workplace (sixth house) (see page 266). Her Saturn ♄ at 25° Gemini ♊ 51' is conjunct Pluto ♀ at 0° Cancer ♋ 9'. Marie expresses the Pluto passion through recycling abandoned buildings in Harlem to provide homes for people who need them (Cancer). Her authority (Saturn) is reflected in her statement: "I organize people and projects and yell at the powerful a lot. I've inspired other people to get moving."

Marie's control room, her Sun ☉, is at 29° Pisces ♓ 22' in the sixth house, her work space. She really shines as a hands-on worker who inspires her community. In addition to the hands-on work, she also studies the Big Picture and voices her findings publicly through her Saturn/Pluto.

Marie expresses her square by second-guessing her public voice in this way: "I've never felt very smart. No question about it. I was always a little reluctant to speak up at demonstrations, lest I shouldn't say the smart thing, the bright thing, and missed the heart of the matter. Of course I learned (Saturn) to speak up (Gemini) anyway. You have to. I'm a doer, yes, but brilliant, no." Even so, Marie has earned a reputation by owning that square. In the seventies, a newspaper headline about Marie read: "The Lady Is a Fighting Lion." What if she had played small and been so concerned about a lack of brilliance that she never went public as a voice? Would Harlem Restoration Project exist in that case? Probably not.

Keep in mind that the house position of the square aspect outlines the life arenas in which the conscious effort must be made, and it isn't always about complex service to others; it can be about something quite simple, such as learning to relax. For example, Mary Bloom's Sun ☉ at 22° Leo ♌ 48' is squared within an eight-degree aspect by three planets—Saturn, Jupiter and Uranus—in Taurus in the fifth house. (See page 225.)

In order to discover her own joy (fifth house), her own private playground, Mary must not work nonstop in the eighth-house realm. Her fifth-house planets represent the constant reminder of that need, but it is an inconvenient need for the speed demon she can be. (Remember, she has a Sun/Mars conjunction.)

Like a speed bump, Mary's fifth-house Taurus planets are embodied in the form of a canary, a rabbit, and three dogs who continually remind her: *Slow down! Play with us. Enjoy life.* Creatively resolving her eighth-house Sun square her fifth-house planets is a life challenge for her and enriches her story.

Squares create a restlessness that becomes an energizing force demanding you experiment again and again to get the combination of instincts into a functional form; to build that table leg and attach it to a tabletop for an important task that you grow into slowly.

To Encourage Intuitive Flow for Squares □

Make a list of the squares in your birthchart and then walk each one through the following exercise.

Imagine that one planet in the square is a Japanese traveler moving through an international airport on a trip around the world, and as this traveler goes through customs, the customs officer demands to check the luggage in a separate room. A delay in the journey occurs. During the delay, while the luggage is searched, the Japanese traveler meets a French traveler (the other planet involved in the square) who is also on a trip around the world and has also been delayed by the customs officer. The Japanese traveler knows a smattering of French and the French traveler only a smattering of Japanese but the two talk and come up with a collaborative plan around traveling together on occasion through the next leg of the journey.

Each has something to offer the other—ideas about hotels, a

nice beach, and even a possible business collaboration, combining purposes in some way that would never have occurred without this unexpected delay that came from left field. As the two travelers discuss their home territory (the life arena, the house position) and their general interests and purposes (the signs they occupy), how do they understand each other or require second translations? What creative collaboration do they come up with? *Pass on dynamic breakthroughs, through the flow....*

A Look at Trines △

Unimpeded flow occurs with trines. Two trapeze artists who have rehearsed and mastered the moment of connection and exchange offer an image of a trine. Trines always occur in the same element (fire, earth, water, or air), which is the equivalent of speaking the same language in some regard; there is great compatibility between the two planets. The two planets in a trine create such a sense of ease and grace that you may be tempted to take the talent for granted. Instead, try to work the trine; treat it as an opportunity to accomplish with style what others might not be able to accomplish at all. You not only have no obstacles here, you have great flow. It's fine to lie in the hammock and meditate upon your good fortune and consider actualizing it tomorrow, but it's even better to get up today and take advantage of that ease to accomplish a great deal. Trines are lubrication for the squares in your chart. In fact, look at every planet you have in a square to see if it is in a trine with some other planet, which will provide easy support for the square aspect.

Gail Bruce has Sun trine her Saturn/Uranus conjunction in the eighth house. (See page 237.) As a Libra, Gail creates partnerships very intuitively, having answered the twelfth-house spirit call. She has a stream of guidance flowing through her like a channel to the ocean itself.

With her twelfth-house Sun trining her eighth-house Saturn/Uranus, Gail easily links visions that are timeless and eternal with contemporary cultural dreams. She has been a major organizing force behind the building of the Cultural Learning Centers at Native American tribal colleges. She seems to be speaking directly from the twelfth-house vision when she says, "The nations I work with aren't interested in having cradleboards or baskets returned to them; they want their sacred items like medicine bundles returned because they are an intricate part of their religion. Important members of the tribe look after these bundles; if these bundles are lost, that part of their culture and religion is also lost. If you are a Pipe Carrier, for example, which is an important position in the Sioux Nation, it is your job to look after that pipe and pray over it every morning and every evening. The Pipe Carrier looks after it, cleans it, takes care of it, because it is used to call down spirit, and that is sacred."

Gail's twelfth-house Sun wants, above all else, to call down spirit, to honor the sacred. With Saturn/Uranus trine her Sun, she wants the pipe to take form, not as a museum piece but as a living spiritual force, relevant for future generations of Native Americans in contemporary culture. Planets in the twelfth house are deeply wedded to super powers on the spiritual plane. It's as if you are a conduit for the ocean of love to resend its signal through you. Any planet trine that twelfth-house planet is the instant, easy delivery point for the signal, into real time and space and form.

For example, Cindy Waszak has Venus in Gemini in the twelfth house trine her fifth house Neptune in the fifth house in Libra. (See page 219.) Both the twelfth house and Neptune easily work through the (timeless) medium of photography, and in fact

Cindy's Venus in Gemini has chosen that medium of communication for her muse. As Venus trines her Neptune in the fifth house, Cindy has a delivery chute for those pictures through spontaneous moments of beauty, particularly between lovers. For life, she has been hired by spirit to be on call as artist (Venus) capturing images (Gemini) of spiritual partnership (Neptune in Libra) that occur spontaneously. (Note that her north node is in the seventh-house partnership—and consider the trine a promoter of her growth toward partnership.) Her first win in a photography competition was of an African refugee couple holding hands naturally, but with obvious tenderness, and gazing directly into the eye of the camera with the dignity of their love.

Peter Kater has what's called a grand trine, with a planet at each end of a triangle of fire signs (Sagittarius, Aries, and Leo), setting up a three-way resonance of easy linkage and communication. (See page 214.) Grand trines imply talent that is not only obvious to the individual but to others as well. Peter links his Saturn in the fifth house, where he explores "doing nothing" as the first step in the creative process, with his Venus in Aries on the midheaven (sharing his music publicly as his own art director) with his Pluto in Leo in the second house (his confidence that his creativity is worth mining and developing as an asset). One of his early CDs, a perennial seller, is titled *Pursuit of Happiness* and reflects the optimism of this trine and the inherent happiness in it.

Trines involving only two planets can be a constant source of optimism to draw from, the perennial talent you can easily develop.

To Encourage Intuitive Flow for Trines △

Identify a trine in your chart and imagine the two planets involved are the two friends below.

You are in good health and spirits on a bike ride with a like-minded and familiar friend. You each enjoy your individual strength and spirit as you cruise along an empty country road for hours, the air crisp, the sun warm, the temperature perfect. You are hardly pedaling and yet able to go very fast, effortlessly. On a break, you share snacks and a drink and talk, exchanging life stories with pleasure, fueling each other and enjoying the flow of events as good fortune and somehow inevitable—the grace of how life should always be when there are no obstacles and you are at your best. You think about the ways in which this friend enriches your life and vice versa. What do the two of you talk about?

Pass on the gift of effortless ease, through the flow....

A Look at Oppositions ☍

An opposition refers to 180 degrees of separation between two planets. In opposite signs, the planets are two halves of a whole and deeply attracted to each other but radically different. In childhood and young adulthood, oppositions can be frustrating, as we all have a tendency to settle into one end of the seesaw and feel stymied about expressing the other as well. This frequently gets played out through projection onto someone else, but with more life experience, we develop the skills to embody both ends of the seesaw, energetically promoting dual purposes that are two halves of a whole. An old-fashioned well with a hand pump offers a great illustration of an opposition. In order to gain enough pressure in the pump to bring the water to the surface you must exert a lot of effort at the beginning, called priming the pump. Once the pump is primed, the water flows easily, against the force of gravity to the opposite end of its point of origination.

Likewise, once you work at claiming two opposed planets, a flow between the two ensues.

Bill Monning's chart is loaded with oppositions. (See page 203.) His Aries Sun (the human rights activist) opposes his Neptune; there is a cross-pollination of his Aries goals and a Neptunian dream of tapping moral conscience; he presumes higher vision is present in all people, be they ally or enemy. He presumes that his central role (the Sun) is to act on that conviction.

He says, "Far too often I meet people who don't know what they want. They haven't taken the time to visualize the dream, to identify the objective of their labor. Those with a dream, with an objective, bring far more passion to the negotiating table."

Bill also has Saturn opposing Jupiter, producing a powerful exchange of faith—faith through testing (Saturn) and faith that flows freely (Jupiter). His Saturn is in Virgo, which promotes efficiency, and his Jupiter in Pisces promotes empathy. Virgo loves pure form; Pisces loves pure spirit.

Bill's Saturn in Virgo in the ninth house brings a deep commitment to educating himself and others about the Big Picture, including global governments. He has committed to using his law degree (Saturn) to do international human rights work in an organized and efficient (Virgo) fashion.

Bill's global work took off through his involvement with the International (ninth house) Physicians (Virgo) for the Prevention (Saturn) of Nuclear War for many years. He says, "The global work with IPPNW inspired me to focus on building networks at home that might be able to change the direction of U.S. foreign policy to better address the needs of a planet in crisis."

The local orientation shows up through Jupiter in the third house. Bill has a local radio show that allows him to share his faith, to spread the word of what is possible, and to be empathetic locally. He takes particular interest in the health of the ocean—the California coastline policies around clean water (Pisces).

Bill also has a Pluto/Moon opposition. Through his eighth-house Pluto in Leo, he wants to be a powerful (Pluto) player (Leo) in the larger political process, shaping our definition of power and the dream of the culture. Through his second-house Moon in Aquarius he refuses to accept PAC money; he wants to control his own base (second house) and be owned by no special interest groups (Aquarius) if elected to public office. He has been stretching to resolve this question for a lifetime.

Abraham Oort has Saturn opposing Venus, with Saturn in the first house in Aquarius and Venus in the seventh house in Leo. (See page 231.) His marriage is reflected a great deal through his Venus in the seventh. Abraham says, "Of primary importance for me is that my partner is willing to be open to my feedback. Even if the situation is bad at a certain time, as long as there is openness and room for change, I am encouraged to pursue the relationship."

His first-house Saturn symbolizes both Abraham's capacity for self-containment outside the relationship as well as his desire for unsentimental feedback, from anyone—including his wife. This calls for conscious effort to mirror both ends of the opposition.

Children cannot make the conscious effort called for by an opposition aspect; two states of consciousness cannot be held simultaneously by the individual. However, circumstances—and the memories of those circumstances—can set the stage or remind us of the need for developing both awarenesses represented by the opposition.

For example, Gail Straub has a Sun/Moon opposition, with Sun in the fifth house in Capricorn and Moon in Cancer in the eleventh house. (See page 255.) Her instinct to shine, to thrive, is at maximum separation—180 degrees—from her homing instinct, her instinct to seek nourishment (literally, to nurse). As an infant she was allergic to her mother's milk and nearly died until they switched her to goat's milk. As an adult, Gail has had to consciously incorporate self-care and nurturance into her lifestyle lest she forever be climbing the quite ambitious Capricorn mountain.

Christian McEwen has her Sun in Taurus in the second house opposing her Neptune in late degrees of Libra, in the eighth house. (See page 209.) She needs both the anchor of good grounding (both Taurus and the second house) through a routine and stable life rhythm *and* the spiritual adventure of Neptune in the eighth house, where she can call her muse to her. When loved ones die, the eighth house can be an access point for contact with them. Christian describes the ways in which she has reached out to her dead and been reassured they are energetically there and still involved in her life.

"Once when I was younger and living in New York I was lost and baffled and I went to bed one night crying and said to my [deceased] uncle Rory, 'You've got to help me. This is too hard. Here I am in America and I'm just not getting a chance to live my life.' The next morning I called the Teachers & Writers Collaborative, which I had called many times before, but this time the man at the other end of the phone heard my name and he said, 'Are you any relation to *Rory* McEwen?' The man had known Rory in London. He asked me over and they found a way to bend the rules to employ me. That changed my life."

Through her Sun/Neptune opposition, Christian is learning that she is partnered with mysterious forces and that the more she stretches into those partnerships, the more productive and meaningful her life will be.

Her eighth-house Neptune in Libra is also encouraging her to maintain flexibility as a bridge between different types of cultural values (eighth house) while remembering her own (second house). "There has been so much moving back and forth between worlds in my life and classes of people," says Christian. "I look at my photograph album and I see a picture of an upper-class wedding in London with tuxedos and roses in buttonholes and the next minute there's a photo of me doing a handstand at a construction site on the Lower East Side of Manhattan when I worked as a gofer."

Every opposition calls for a stretch. You have to first consciously send the call out and then, somehow, be in two places at once, embody two instincts simultaneously. Discovering the right context in which to do this comes with life experience and experimentation. The dynamic of an opposition is the cross-pollination. Opposites attract and merge and change each other. That is the fertility of an opposition.

To Encourage Intuitive Flow for Your Oppositions ☍

Identify any opposing planets you see in your chart and initiate an intuitive dialogue with them through the following exercise.

Imagine that these two planets are pen pals, one on one side of the earth and one on the other. They exchange letters (thoughts) a few times a month. The two correspondents represent radically different instincts and orientations yet are somehow two halves of a whole. What is in the content of their letters? When they decide to plan a vacation together, they decide on a vacation with a purpose—a shared project. Where do they go and what is the purpose?

Pass on cross-pollination, through the flow....

Now you have encountered every foundational piece of the language of astrology. Next, let's play with putting it all together through the reality of your life first and astrology second.

CHAPTER 8

Putting It All Together to Ground Your Dreams

To explore your birthchart is to gaze into a cosmic mirror that deepens with your growth, revealing new secrets all along the way. As you have explored your own astrological mirror, my hope is that you have also deepened your trust in the unknown, recognizing that we are all perpetually in a state of becoming, and there is always mystery behind the magic of creation. To trust this mystery and its purpose may be the purest form of prayer.

The synchronous connection between your life and the planets is bigger than the chicken-or-egg question—i.e, *Do the planets create our instincts or do we somehow have a hand in creating the planets?* In intuitive astrology, psyche and external events (and planets) are deeply wedded. They both spring from the same spirit; they cannot be separated. The resulting synchronicity is an affirmation of a living universe. Somehow, your birthchart reflects your partnership with this synchronicity, and simultaneously affirms your best instincts as *yours*. You will expand that affirmation of partnership with a living universe and self-responsibility for the rest of your life.

This last round of exercises is designed to act on that affirmation in a way that will help you in the immediate present, by allowing the reality of your life story to take the lead. For example, if I were to sit down with you and ask, "What are your dreams? How do you plan to manifest them? What good things would you like to grow in the garden of your life?" you would have specific answers. You can now use your astrological knowledge to support those answers, that reality.

This final chapter is an excellent opportunity to get a new notebook or journal with large pages. Draw images and jot down ideas to update the blueprint of your dreams, using your birthchart like a cosmic database—a wellspring of creativity, encouraging you to grow good things.

Identify Your Dream

You have a dream. You have the ability to step into the flow in order to remember the inspiration that is part of you. Take some time now to articulate your dream in your journal. Think of the dream as a natural organic extension of your life. Play with images or words or feelings. Consider this phrase: *Nothing satisfies like satisfaction.* What dream would satisfy you, if it came true?

Look for support in identifying your dream through:

* Your Neptune
* Any planet in the sign of Pisces
* Any planet in the twelfth house

This is where you are getting voice mail from the Muse twenty-four hours a day, which you, in turn, pass on to others. Given what you have learned so far about planets, signs, and houses, what does the guidance suggest is your gift? Don't presume that the dream has to be grand or spiritual or "sweet." It can be as mundane as being the best builder of garden fences in your county. What matters is that you are inspired and feel led to express this inspiration—this dream—as achievable.

Example: Marty Rosenbluth has a dream of a powerful peace achieved by shedding a strong light on perpetrator-victim dynamics. He gets guidance about how to do that and then becomes a guide to others around it. He says, "Often I think it's a question of simply reflecting back to people what they are doing so that they can see the pattern. A lot of the torturers who work for the Palestinian authorities learned their torturing techniques when they themselves were tortured by the Israelis. So they learn to torture as victims and they are now torturing other people as perpetrators. You have to explain to people that these types of things are simply not acceptable ever—no matter the justification."

Marty's astrological mirror reveals his Neptune (strong light, Muse) in Scorpio in the eighth house (detective exploring unseen energy and dynamics that define power) as supporter of this dream.

Identify Spiritual Support for Your Dream

Most of us not only acknowledge the value of naming our dreams but the reality of support from the spiritual realm. How do you access spiritual support for your dream and ask for blessing? This access can be in the form of prayers to God, Allah, Buddha, or the Goddess, or it can be conversations with your deceased grandmother. What is important is to realize, when you actively ask for spiritual support, guidance, or blessing for this dream, that you are flipping a large switch to *on.* The intuitive flow will increase.

Where do you go for spiritual support? What is the source of the sacred in your life that carries a contagious and generous light? Be creative as you jot your answers down. It's fine to include simple examples such as "a walk in the park" or "exchanging a few words with the kind lady at the cash register who always smiles at me." But also go to higher-powered sources. If you aren't religious or spiritual, think of the most loving person you ever encountered—and the blessing of that encounter—and honor it as ongoing spiritual support. Consider it active now.

Again, you can look for spiritual support for your dream through Neptune, planets in Pisces, or the twelfth house.

Example: Marie Runyon gets spiritual support every day through prayer, and every Sunday at St. Mary's Episcopal church in New York City. She says, "I pray for the buildings at Harlem Restoration. I pray for the drug dealers to get a new look on life." She's fond of the book *Jesus CEO*. "It's about how Jesus used his principles to organize people, to get things done." The book also talks about the ways in which Jesus consciously worked with a higher power. "He got organized, but then he let go and let God take over." Marie turns it over to God but she doesn't stop organizing to protest injustices or to bring about positive changes for Harlem.

Her astrological mirror reveals five planets in Pisces supporting her dream. Jesus Christ is affiliated with Pisces as unconditional love and universal compassion (as is the Buddha). With Saturn conjunct Pluto in the ninth house square her Sun in Pisces, Marie is restless to do more than pray. The tension of the square demands she be politically active as well (ninth house). She has been so politically active that the FBI has a 500-page file on her.

Identify Your Talent for Making the Dream Real

Now that you've identified the dream and asked for spiritual support, the next step is to identify your talent, your creativity. Your creativity is your love affair with life, finding form and expression without delay. You don't have to be a Picasso to have creative flow. Where is your talent? Where are you drawn to capture grace or beauty and ground it? Take a few moments to outline your answer. Are you gifted at intimacy? At some aspect of your professional life? At making art? At making music? Support for your talent comes from any planet but particularly:

- **VENUS.** Your Venus signifies where you fall in love with life. Venus births talent and creativity as a natural extension of your love affair with life.

- **PLANETS IN THE FIFTH HOUSE OR THE SIGN OF LEO.** Consider that their desire to celebrate life and explore spontaneous creativity produces talent.

- **URANUS.** Your Uranus, as your truth compass, also expresses your brilliance, a talent no one else can duplicate.

Example: Abraham Oort discovered a talent as a sculptor relatively late in life, which gave him great joy and encouraged him to take risks in other areas. His astrological mirror shows up through Uranus in Taurus in the third house. Taurus can be physical, literally the clay in one's hands. The third house represents tangible exploration of one's capacity to see, including through touch. Abraham's Uranus brought a stroke of brilliance to the process and, with it trine his Sun, sculpting somehow enhances his larger role as visionary scientist—and vice versa.

Example: Peter Kater has never had a lack of creative ideas, which is a talent in itself. He says, "I have always had the image of creative ideas trickling down from somewhere—from source, the ethers or heaven—like raindrops, and if you happen to be walking outside at the right time, and you get hit with one of these drops on the head, you get an idea. And so at any given time in the creative process, there may be a few hundred people with the same idea. It's their responsibility to act on it, once they have the initial inspirational opening and direction. If they don't act on it, then someone else will, and there's the manifestation. That's why movements happen: Concepts surface all at once in different places.

"You don't need to get stuck in, *Oh, I lost that creative idea because someone else has manifested it*, because there are an infinite number of ideas being served up. You just need to be in present time to follow the one being served up—to be able to respond to whatever idea comes along and inspires you—without delay."

Peter's astrological mirror reveals Saturn in Sagittarius in the fifth house, which supports his ability to be creative (fifth house) and to understand that if you take care of the details, the unified whole (Sagittarius) will naturally occur. Saturn asks Peter to become masterful at building a form for his creative idea before the moment of inspiration (fifth house) has passed.

By virtue of his Saturn trining his Venus and his Pluto, not only will Peter build the form but he will want to share it with a mass audience (Venus in tenth house) and infuse the project with his passion (Pluto).

Engage Your Will

How do you want to take aim toward your dream? Some people work from a list. Other people do therapy and emerge with an agenda for steering their lives.

You've just identified a dream, the support for it, and the talent that can serve as medium for the dream. Take a moment now to engage your will. There is no substitute for taking aim and following through. Remember that energy follows intention. The strength and clarity of your intention becomes the equivalent of a bow in an arrow. Your own energy (and support from elsewhere) will support that clear aim. Remember that your will is really a tool for self-mastery—for controlling yourself, not for controlling others, though setting a boundary with others can be an exercise in self-control.

Align your will with the dream you have just identified. How can you ritualize this to make it easier to remember and return to? By going for a run every day and imagining that every step takes you closer to manifesting the dream? How can you make a priority list, breaking the dream down into steps that are achievable? Support for the will comes from:

* **MARS.** Your Mars knows what you want and what will energize you. Your Mars has a clear *yes*, and a clear *no*, about your path. It is in charge of you surviving, and thriving, in part through manifesting your dream. Mars informs you when you are on the right path by giving you energy gain *(yes)*. If you are on the wrong path, you have energy drain *(no)*.

* **PLANETS IN THE FIRST HOUSE OR THE SIGN OF ARIES.** They can inform you about how to lead your own life, where you are gifted at finding a clear *yes* and a clear *no*.

Example: Gail Bruce has a photography studio in New York City. As studio director, she has to clarify the goal of the day and lead her team efficiently.

The first time I met her, I went to her studio to give her a reading. I arrived a little early and sat down to wait in a foyer, where I couldn't help but overhear the conversation in the next room. Gail was firing an assistant who was chronically late. She made sure the man understood why she was firing him—that he could not hold up an entire crew over and over and that she had given him more than one second chance. She made sure he knew she valued his work. She made sure she left him his dignity. And she made sure he understood she would not rehire him. It was nonnegotiable. Her voice throughout was even, respectful, and firm. This was my first impression of Gail Bruce.

Her astrological mirror reveals Mars in Aries in the seventh house (house of partners and collaborators). With Mars in the sign it rules, Gail is to the point. With her Libran Sun, she leads from her center rather than waiting until she is off-center. The employee was not in alignment with Gail's direction or the goal, but her anger was clean. She did not insult him or escalate the issues involved. She conserved her energy for the real work around which she had taken aim—her project.

Dedicate Your Discipline to the Task, Invest LOTS of Time

You've identified a dream, called spiritual support to it, identified your talent, and aligned your will. Now dedicate your discipline to the long-term timetable called for, to make the dream real. Rome wasn't built in a day.

In your journal, explore the theme of sowing seeds, reaping what you sow, and the joyful responsibility of tending the seeds all along the way as you manifest your dream. Support for your discipline and time-management skills comes from:

* SATURN. Saturn is the instinct to commit, and to commit time—to put in hours, weeks, months, years. If you befriend Saturn, everything else in your life story will fall into place. What sign is your Saturn in? What house? Remember, Saturn is about building inner authority through real experience. Make a list of the ways in which Saturn the Teacher can help you get organized to ground the dream you identified previously.

* PLANETS IN TAURUS, VIRGO, OR CAPICORN (OR THEIR CORRESPONDING HOUSES—SECOND, SIXTH, AND TENTH). Planets in these signs and houses are all builders, with slightly different agendas. Each of them is skilled at committing and at investing time. Taurus wants to build work that expresses strong personal values. Virgo wants to build lifestyles or products that are of service and improve the quality of life for others. Capricorn wants to build teaching tools or traditions.

In the second house, you put in time and discipline by investing in a character trait and developing it—and possibly getting paid for it. You can't skip over the fieldwork. In the sixth house, you put in time and discipline to craft a skill and serve the community. In the tenth house, you put in time and discipline through your career and profession. Planets in these signs and houses are bulldozers, helping to lay the ground for your dreams.

Dedicating your discipline to a task isn't always easy, even when you're inspired. Discipline comes more easily for some people when they commit to a degree program, training, or a job that demands the cultivation of particular skills.

Example: Cindy Waszak's discipline as an educator about reproductive health hinged on her training—an undergraduate degree and then a Ph.D., which took her six years to complete—a major time investment. The result is that she is in a position to fulfill her dream of helping young girls everywhere realize not only reproductive responsibility but also self-esteem.

Cindy's astrological mirror reveals Mars in Cancer, which led her to invest (second house) in her capacity to care as her livelihood (second house). Mars trines her Saturn in the fifth house in Scorpio, which encourages her to get the training necessary to be an educator (Saturn) about birth control and fertility (Scorpio) to youth (fifth house)—in her case, frequently, young girls.

Example: Marty Rosenbluth finishes projects through sheer endurance. He has a bumper sticker on the back of his car that reads Visualize Whirled Peas, mocking the folly of visualization with no follow-through. He says, "Learning to finish what I start has probably been one of the hardest things in my life. I'm almost classic ADD [attention deficit disorder]. It's really difficult for me to complete tasks but very important. I tend to drag projects out way beyond where they need to be, so that's been a really key lesson, very hard. The video I did on Jerusalem took almost two years to complete. It's a matter of just forcing myself to be disciplined. There are so many distractions."

His astrological mirror reveals Marty has Saturn conjunct Mercury in the eleventh house, in Sagittarius. He takes responsibility as a philosopher with a message (Mercury) that affects the future of the culture (eleventh house). His responsibility (Saturn) is not only to himself but to the network of people (eleventh house) who hope for the same future he does. That network supports him to stay focused as he speaks for them too, through his work.

Invest in Your Dream in the Present

Build a reserve of self-confidence around your dream by getting experience in the field *now*. See how your own nature converges around the roll-up-your-sleeves work involved in this dream.

For example, you can get experience apprenticing with someone who has already mastered a similar dream to see how the day-to-day life goes. You'll find out how strong your spark of inspiration is around this focus and can begin psychologically investing in it, building confidence through doing rather than just thinking about it.

Let's say you already have a dream well under way—a half-finished novel, a painting series, a class for children that you want to expand in some way. To follow through, it is vital you not drain your enthusiasm, energy reserves, or financial reserves. We all need a "bounce account"—resiliency both psychologically and financially. Guarding your reserves will support your entire life but also give you a sense of a well-maintained dream in progress. Support for building confidence in the dream in the present comes from:

* **SATURN.** Consider Saturn your walking stick for life— a walking stick of discipline that needs exercise daily. Saturn builds the backbone of your dreams—not to mention your life story and its details. Saturn always knows precisely what you are doing and what you are not. Saturn can help you build confidence if you keep a daily log of how much time you spend on the dream, day by day. A brief log read over at the end of every month helps you identify the natural rhythm of productivity around the dream and develop more confidence in it.

* **VENUS, THE SECOND HOUSE, AND TAURUS.** Venus is always dependable for leading you to a steady relationship with the dream because you feel good when you play out Venus behaviors. Venus naturally builds resources and reserves too, out of sheer enthusiasm.

The second house and Taurus encourage you to take the time to digest your learning experience so that it becomes solid beneath you, reality-based. You are getting to know yourself as one who can ground this dream. Are you going to write a novel on caffeine in five sleepless weeks? Probably not. You need a rhythm that will carry you through to the end. You want it to be a positive enough experience that you'll want to do it again. That way your psychological investment, not to mention your inspiration, remains strong.

Example: Gail Straub is articulate about the importance of having "the silo," a reserve of stored energy, just as you would store up grain for the winter. In her Empowerment Training Programs, she and her husband teach that a reserve of energy, including financial energy, creates a resiliency that allows for ups and downs. We want not only to survive but to thrive. Options are power, and you have no options if you are always in a survival mode. How can you possibly manifest a dream if it takes all your energy each day just to survive?

Gail's astrological mirror reveals south node in the second house, implying that she came into this life skilled at doing the fieldwork that results in a harvest and that she knows quite a bit about the value of stored energy—a reserve of psychological, spiritual, and financial energy that will carry you through if there is a downturn or setback or you need a rest. Living her own dream has been more possible given Gail's understanding of this.

Example: Marty Rosenbluth got his training as a videographer through a barter with a PBS producer; he never went to film school. While living in Jerusalem, Marty was approached by a man from WGBH Boston who not only needed a steady guide around town but a translator. Marty was fluent in Arabic and had an abundance of human rights contacts on both sides of the conflict. He swapped his language skills and contacts in exchange for learning documentary filmmaking from a working professional.

His astrological mirror reveals Saturn conjunct Mercury, which suggests that Marty could excel as a communications specialist or translator. With Sagittarius in the eleventh house, he would easily make contacts in networks of people who shared his philosophical outlook. Like Gail, Marty has south node in the second house, which helps him value fieldwork and develop confidence through doing.

Identify Tangible Financial Resources

You've identified a dream, blessed it, funded discipline for it, cultivated confidence through hands-on experience around it. Now how are you going to pay for it? A common challenge for dreamers is literally financing the dream. It becomes critical to have a positive attitude about money and clarity about how to make money and build a financial base. How do you intend to finance your dream(s)? If you have already begun to do so, how is that a natural extension of the good things you grow? Are you comfortable having a day job, possibly for years or decades, to finance your dream, so that the dream is not burdened with the pressure to pay your bills?

Be cautious about asking someone else to fund a dream for

you that you yourself cannot, in part or in full, finance. Dreams often mature best as *we* mature in our ability to pay our own way through the stages of imagination, cultivation, fruition, and harvest. If someone funds your good idea before you finance the basic grounding of that dream or idea, how skilled will you be at defining its form on the road to completion? Investing your own money or energy in the foundation proves to the Muse behind the dream that you are committed. In addition, the foundation matches your values and sets the tone for everything that follows.

Take a moment to jot down your thoughts about where your money comes from, how you feel about it, and, if you want or need more money, how that might occur as a natural extension of your life. Support for your funding comes through:

- **THE SECOND HOUSE OR THE SIGN OF TAURUS,** with their capacity to build self-esteem. Both are builders of good work habits around the dream. Through either, you are willing to invest in your own ideas, put shoulder to the wheel, and manifest some version of that dream, even if it is in miniature to the ideal. The second house helps you develop a track record, starting with precisely where you are.

- **VENUS.** As ruler of the second house and the sign of Taurus, Venus is a potent focalizer of all of the qualities mentioned above. Venus rules your reproductive power in addition to your talent. It can reflect your golden goose—the talent that pays its own way rather well.

- **SATURN.** Employ your Saturnian discipline as bookkeeper, no matter what sign or house Saturn is in. Know how much it costs to maintain your lifestyle. Can you afford to be who you think you are? It takes little time to keep financial records and the tally at the end of the month is a stepping-stone to sound decision making.

* **MARS.** Mars knows intention is everything. If you intend to make money, set financial goals.

* **THE EIGHTH HOUSE OR THE SIGN OF SCORPIO.** These reflect collective resources and hidden sources of energy, which you can tap into to finance your dream. Grant money, for example, comes from the eighth house.

Example: Susun Weed has maximized her financial muscle in order to manifest her dreams in a nontraditional and shrewd way. "What is the biggest building in any city?" she asks. "It's the insurance company. When you buy insurance, you are basically betting that you're going to get sick. You win the bet by getting sick. I don't want to make that kind of a bet, because I don't want to win by getting sick."

Instead, Susun invests her money, including money that would have gone for health insurance, into PAX World Funds, **the first mutual** fund to adopt broad, socially responsible standards for its investments, pioneering the idea of a mutual fund with a conscience.

"I put my money where my mouth is, ten years ago, and PAX has done very well, double-digit returns. They all said we were fools for doing social investment. Who's laughing up whose sleeve now? This is why I say to people, 'Why are you letting the insurance companies jerk you around? Take the money you'd invest in insurance and invest in what you think makes the earth healthy, and then not only is the earth healthy, but you have that money in case you have a medical problem. Create your own medical insurance fund.'"

Her astrological mirror reveals south node in the eighth house, suggesting that Susun came into this life experienced in the ways of collective investment, whether through money or the group dream of the culture. She understands the role of belief and the resultant return. The insurance industry is based on fear of the unknown and the return to the investor is pricey protection. Her shift to a different belief and relationship with collective investment has netted a higher return. In addition, she has the golden goose Venus conjunct her Sun in the eleventh house in Aquarius, suggesting that she can do quite well every time she consciously makes a plan for the long-term future (eleventh house) based on her truth (Aquarius).

Prioritize Self-Care—Have a Home!

We aren't robots. Each of us sprang from a womb that was a safe place for us until we were ready to be born. We still need a womb, even after birth—a place where we can remove the mask, take off the armor, and be nourished and renewed. You have to incubate yourself as you incubate a dream. What is your self-care technique? Take a moment to describe your nest and the circle of people who mean *home* to you, who nourish you. Well-nourished, you can manifest your dream. Look for support from:

* **THE MOON.** What does your Moon suggest about the best nest for you to live in, to be nourished by? Don't get confused if it isn't warm and fuzzy. It may be a laboratory at the hospital (a sixth-house Virgo Moon could produce that sort of home).

* **PLANETS IN CANCER OR THE FOURTH HOUSE.** These planets will tell you a bit about where your homing instinct will take you to be nourished and then in turn

to nourish others, even if it isn't a home with a white picket fence. They may also tell you about other people you create family with.

Example: Gail Straub. She says repeatedly in her workshops and books, "If you take really good care of yourself, you can carry a larger vision." Her home is elegantly simple and beautiful, with precisely what she needs, nothing more, nothing less. It is her womb space to return to after long trips and teaching workshops, to renew herself with her husband.

Her astrological mirror reveals that Gail has Venus in the fourth house, in Capricorn. Her Venus in the fourth house places self-care and self-love as a top priority (Capricorn). She chose a home surrounded by mountains (Capricorn) with beautiful (Venus) views. A busy teacher in the world, at home Gail has privacy and belongs to herself.

Identify Your Power, Your Passion

What brings up your passion most quickly? Passion is not tame. It can be conscious and empower, but it also requires accepting the wild, untamable aspect of your nature that bypasses the brain. It is where you feel compelled to go—and by virtue of going there, you are renewed.

Like the primal nature of the universe, power is always a bit mysterious, but as your passion point, it must be called on to fertilize your dream.

Support comes from:

* **PLUTO.** Pluto is the battery pack within you capable of charging your dream with life force.

* **PLANETS IN THE EIGHTH HOUSE OR SCORPIO.** What kind of power are those planets courting? Think of them as deep reservoirs of energy capable of penetrating the thickest mystery.

Example: I am renewed every time I write in my journal. Since I was able to write, I have kept it (and it has kept me) as my most dependable source of power. It touches what is untamable in me and has nothing to do with "writing," love of literature, good English or bad. Its functions are two: to let out and to let in.

The journal is the letting out, the recording of events, impressions of my own reactivity racing through my fingertips in a longing to tell the tale and find beneath it the unexpressed emotion.

Everything beneath my conscious mind arrives when I "let in." The letting in involves an unknown and compelling element that pulls me to it and wants me to play with what I find to give names to emotions, insights, and experiences as an explorer in invisible worlds that have a story to tell too. Everything good I have ever grown first flew through my fingers as a passionate possibility, onto the pages of my journal.

My astrological mirror reveals that I have Pluto in Leo in the third house. The third house has a dual function of communicating and listening (letting in and letting out). In Leo, the heart both listens and speaks. Pluto has been my battery pack for a lifelong diary, creative writing, videography, more than a thousand client files detailing astrological histories, and a ten-year audiotape collection of poignant messages left on my answering machine. Pluto in the third house says: *Listen to the story, love it (Leo), and take it deeper.*

Identify Your Voice

Each of us uses a different voice for different functions. Which voice would best support your dream? What experiences do you need to strengthen your voice in order to support the dream? Take a moment to write about your voices; specifically, which ones clarify your dream or enhance it. What voices do you find yourself relying upon again and again?

For support look to:

* **MERCURY.** Your Mercury is your twenty-four-hour-a-day reporter, gathering information and building a database from it as well as retranslating it.
* **PLANETS IN GEMINI** (personal voice) or Sagittarius (universal voice) or the third house (open your eyes) or the ninth house (worldly wisdom).

Example: Christian McEwen's internalized childhood voice ("I was born into original sin") was heavily colored by the Roman Catholic Church. She began to deconstruct this identity as she made forays outside her family and social class. As an adolescent turned anonymous hitchhiker on the roads of Northern Europe, Christian discovered her pleasure in listening to the stories of strangers, which in turn broadened her own story. The voice of the traveler became an integral part of her literary voice.

Her astrological mirror reveals that Christian has Saturn in Sagittarius on the midheaven, in the tenth house. Sagittarius is the philosopher within her; Saturn is the crystallization of her authority. To a teenager, the tenth house is the larger world, her own influence on the open highway. Christian's early hitchhiking escapades and deepened love of story helped her cultivate a literary voice. As an adult writer, she is a transatlantic teacher mentoring students in both the U.S. and the U.K., encouraging them to identify the larger picture of which they are a part.

Allow for Plenty of Imperfection as Part of the Process

Do you trust imperfection? Perfection is an ideal that is a finished and complete state. We are always in process; therefore, imperfection abounds. Many people abandon their dreams before they ever begin to manifest them because anything less than perfection is unacceptable. They don't allow for the mess of life—flat tires, headaches, and completely unexpected downturns. In addition, many people never acknowledge they have a shadow side (we all do) and presume perfection of themselves. Learning to raise a humorous eyebrow when you spot your shadow side and to trust it as a helpful informant about self-sabotage is key in manifesting your dream.

Take a moment to write in your journal now about your relationship with imperfection. What is "enough" for you, as you seek to embody a particular standard? Where are you afraid of beginning, lest you feel overwhelmed by the imperfections that follow? What attitudes do you bring to breakdowns (of equipment, of projects, of relationships)? How able are you to fund tenderness toward imperfect situations? How able are you to ask for help when you need it?

The truth is that struggles with perfectionism or control issues can come from anywhere, but to help you begin to explore this common challenge, look to:

* **CHIRON.** Chiron is fond of identifying imperfection. It reminds us that sometimes problem solving is best done

by allowing for the imperfect circumstance to simply be what it is. Your dream can still manifest and may reroute itself as a consequence of the block or imperfection.

* **SATURN AND THE SIGN OF CAPRICORN.** Saturn can forbid you to begin a project, lest you not do it perfectly, or you may fall into a trap of constant striving, which creates an addiction to perfection, a fixation on external form. The Muse grows faint under these conditions. The Muse, your dream, never asked for perfection.

* **PLUTO.** This planet can be challenging for perfectionists because it can be messy and unpredictable; Pluto power has surges—ups and downs. It can be a vortex of unknowns, producing uncontrollable circumstances of varying degrees. These events can be quite mundane but nevertheless troublesome for anyone counting on constant order.

Example: Marty Rosenbluth says, "Much of the work I do is heavily dependent on technical pieces of equipment and I am just not a technical person. I have constant software glitches that are completely unexplainable. It drives me crazy, absolutely bananas. I hate it, because it's more than a tool, it's a vehicle for getting where I want to go—it's something I need in order to do what I do. I live with it but even something as basic as E-mail can be such a technical mystery. Why isn't it working?"

Marty's astrological mirror reveals Pluto in the seventh house in Virgo, which rules tools and systems that allow us to do our work. Marty is quite partnered (seventh house) with his video-editing equipment; it is there, rather than through his wife, that he encounters what he cannot control.

Example: Gail Straub describes her struggles with perfection in her book *The Rhythm of Compassion*: "My sister was born only fifteen months after I came into the world and so I formed the belief that to get love, especially my father's love, I needed to distinguish myself by being the best at everything I did. Love was equated with doing, performing and overachieving. I perfected this mask in high school and continued relying on it until my mid-thirties, when I entered rigorous spiritual counseling. On the outside, I was successful, hopping around the globe and saving the world, but on the inside there was an emptiness nothing could ever fill. I was blessed to find a gifted counselor who helped me dismantle the mask of perfection I presented to the world."

Gail's astrological mirror reveals Sun in Capricorn, which led her to the search for perfection and self-mastery in the first place but also supports her in remembering to ask for help. The healthy Capricorn is the teacher who can be taught.

Example: Susun Weed says about perfection, "One of the statements I find myself making a lot, especially to the apprentices, is that they are not here to learn how to steal anybody's pain or change anybody's problems. Pain is inevitable. Be alive, you will experience pain. Suffering, however, is optional. If you were to lean over and slap me, that would hurt, but I would not suffer until I made up the story about why you slapped me. So health is wholeness. The healer doesn't come in and control the energy, the healer doesn't steal the pain, the healer doesn't change the problem, because the person who wants help is really saying, *I bet you can't love me the way I am. I bet I can get you to want me to be different.* How outrageous to be able to say: *You are perfect exactly as you are. With your cancer you are perfect; with your diabetes you are perfect.*"

Susun's astrological mirror reveals Chiron in the sixth house in Libra, supporting her to relate to others as perfect as they are, in her work (sixth house) as a healer.

Example: When Cindy Waszak documented daily life at a

hospice center for people dying of AIDS, she had preconceived ideas about what her photographs should portray. But in the darkroom, "I realized that the photographs were showing me a different story than I had anticipated.... I realized, through them, how okay people are just as they are, even in ill health, their human imperfections laid bare."

Cindy's astrological mirror reveals Chiron in the eighth house in Aquarius. The eighth house is the house of death and rebirth. With Chiron there, Cindy is learning how to be present and comfortable with the truth (Aquarius) of what she sees.

Up the Joy Level

It is always easier to stay inspired around your dream and its manifestation when there is a significant amount of joy and love in your life. What do you do for fun? How does the love in your life give you joy? List the specific ways you experience joy. (Through your children? Your dog? Playing the guitar?)

Support for bringing more joy into your life comes from:

* LEO OR THE FIFTH HOUSE. Both swing wide the door to reminding you that joy will find a way (to manifest the dream).
* VENUS (the lover) and Mars (the energizer).

Example: Gail Straub not only loves to dance, she loves to dance wildly. Her joy in her body and capacity for foolish fun is obvious to anyone who sees her move across the dance floor.

Gail's astrological mirror reveals Mars in the fifth house in Aquarius. Aquarius can be free-form, Mars is sheer energy—her life force exploding on the dance floor in fifth-house fun.

Example: Marty Rosenbluth and his wife, Liz, had a baby, Solomon, in 1999. Marty fell so deeply in love with his son that he let go of his round-the-clock activist role in the political arena. "All I wanted to do was lie on the sofa and let Sol crawl on me. I didn't care who owed me money, I didn't care how far behind I was on my projects. It was total bliss." Sol helps Marty relax. When Marty does return to his work, he has more energy and better perspective.

His astrological mirror reveals Uranus in Leo in the seventh house. Marty is pioneering into a partnership with his creativity, and his child is a catalyst to the creative heart in an unmistakable way.

Example: Bill Monning's joy is deeply related to his love for his wife, Dana. He says, "Dana and I leave notes for each other that we sign ILYF, which is 'I love you forever.'"

Bill's astrological mirror reveals Venus in the fifth house in Taurus. Venus is love and Taurus is a stabilizer, creating a steady rhythm of romance in the moment (fifth house).

Linking to Community, Honoring Allies

One day when I was around sixteen years old, there was a knock at the door. I opened it and it was Mrs. Emry, an elderly entrepreneurial businesswoman and architect in our small town. She was different from most of the other people in town. She had several college degrees (including a law degree) and was fiercely independent and rather eccentric. Her car was covered in dents from front to back. She hated parallel parking.

She had met me as a child, but we had never had a long conversation until the previous day at my father's furniture store (he rented the building from her). I'd enjoyed the conversation immensely. She was a breath of fresh air and very observant.

"Are you here to see Daddy?" I asked.

"No, no," she said. "I'm here to see you."

I was surprised and it showed.

"I don't quite know why I'm doing this," she said. "But I wanted to give you a little money to put into a savings account for something special. I enjoyed talking with you yesterday, and I think you have good ideas. You're a dreamer, like me." She paused. "I don't think you'll stay in this town. I'm a dreamer, and it didn't kill me to live here, but I've been lonely for good company. You were good company yesterday. Anyway, here's a little money to tuck away, and I don't ever want to hear about what you did with it. You do as you please."

And she left. I was stunned. It was fifty dollars.

I went upstairs and cried and didn't know why. I loved my life. I loved my parents and grandparents. I loved my little town. But some part of me had been lonely all of my life *because I had never been seen in full.*

Mrs. Emry took that away. She saw something in me that was my best self, lying latent, some coiled power that would not, on its own, become that best self. I had to choose. I didn't know what I was supposed to choose, but I knew that fifty dollars was about precisely that. I also knew that what she really meant, when she said, "I don't think you'll stay in this town," was that the community I belonged to had a lot of people very much like me in it. *They definitely weren't here.* I was on a slightly different wavelength from everyone in my world, though I understood and loved their world.

I have replayed that conversation with Mrs. Emry a thousand times since 1968, usually thinking about community. Each dream I have worked for and manifested has somehow played a role in creating a new community for me. With whom do I want to share the harvest of my dreams? Knowing the answer to that question becomes fuel toward manifesting the dream. Who are my allies? Mrs. Emry was a very powerful ally. How can I play the same role she played for me, with others—seeing them in full? Who am I as an ally to others?

As your astrologer ally seeking to mirror back to you who you are in full, I ask you again:

What is your dream? With whom do you want to share it? Who is your community? Your community is the recipient of your dream but also your support. It is the rare person who manifests a dream without help. Allies become important, whether as mentors ahead of you on the path or as muscle power at a key moment when you are pushing a big rock up a hill.

Take a few moments to write about that in your journal and define community broadly. They don't have to all live in one place. Take a moment to identify your allies, past and present. What role does each play? Those who merely witness your dream serve a purpose, through their faith in you. Count those people too.

Look for support in identifying allies and community *from any part of your birthchart.* The community that benefits from your talent can be anyone or any group of people who share your interests. People bond together naturally around shared interests, which could be any of the planets, signs, or houses.

Even the south and north nodes can be informative indicators of community—old community (an inherited tendency to affiliate with one group versus another) and new community (stretching toward new affiliations that are good for the soul).

Example: Marie Runyon is a guiding light in Harlem, and the community takes care of her in return, even on tough blocks. Young men drinking on stoops speak to her, children call her by name. One night the street was nearly empty and Marie was walking briskly down the sidewalk when she heard someone run to catch up to her and she whirled to face him. The man said,

"Marie, are you all right? You were hurrying and I thought maybe somebody was after you." Community takes care of its own.

Marie's astrological mirror reveals a sixth-house Sun in Pisces. Sixth house rules community. Marie is a guiding light for her community, and they light her way as well.

Example: Patrick Reynolds says, "In the early 1990s, I became much less concerned with what people could do for me, career-wise, or what their status was in the world or how much money they had. I was concerned with who loves me. I made a conscious choice: I'm going to go where the love is. In the end, I think what's important is having loving relationships with people around you."

Patrick's astrological mirror reveals Neptune in Libra in the eleventh house. The light of loving relationships (Neptune in Libra) calls Patrick toward an optimal future (eleventh house).

Example: Gail Straub has been meeting with the same women's group for more than twenty years. "We spend weekends together, being funny and decadent and drinking wine and going dancing, but really being the most unbelievable support for one another. We're just this little pod that forms about four times a year," says Gail.

Her astrological mirror reveals Moon in the eleventh house in Cancer; Gail's happiness hinges on a network of friends who can nurture her and vice versa. They are her community and key allies.

Example: Mary Bloom's community is the Cathedral of St. John the Divine in New York City. She says, "The dean of the cathedral, Jim Morton, started the artists-in-residence program there to honor people who took their art and made the world a better place with their gift. His idea was that you can't just have the gift. You have to have this desire to use your gift to heal the earth. After a series of projects I did for them, they unexpectedly and officially made me part of the cathedral family one Christmas. I remember sitting at a service, and hearing, 'We have a new artist-in-residence—Mary Bloom,' and I almost fell out of my chair. It meant so much to me.

"Jim Morton fertilized the creative spirit in many others as well, people like musician Paul Winter, high-wire walker Philippe Petit, and many others. He knighted us Artists in Residence, and created a collage of art that was celebrated by thousands of visitors and worshipers who entered that sacred space. It was that recognition, combined with his inspiration and permission, that convinced me to pursue the life of an artist."

Mary's astrological mirror reveals north node in Libra in the tenth house, suggesting the importance of learning to see herself as an artist (Libra) who is an influence in the larger world (tenth house). The cathedral ritualized that for Mary in a concrete and unforgettable way.

The Community Within You— Worthy of All Your Effort

What is my dream? How can I best cultivate the discipline to manifest this dream? Who are my allies? Who is my community? You can bring these life questions, as well as others, to your birthchart again and again. Your questions won't be magically answered, but the symbols are wise guides who, with time, will tell you all you need to know, reminding you of limitless inner resources. The key word here is *inner*.

Many of the people you have come to know through this book use astrology to validate their inner resources, recognize their choices, *and then align those choices with a specific skill: intuition.* They either use astrology on their own or seek support from a skilled astrologer like me.

The day I overheard Gail Bruce fire her employee with such grace, she was in a transit in which her Mars—her will—was being tested repeatedly for a year, in order to clarify her intentions. When I told her this in the session that followed that day, it validated both her experience and her own intuition about navigating this time in her life as consciously as possible. It helped her value the challenges that were coming her way as an opportunity rather than an inconvenience.

Likewise, when Christian McEwen conceived her idea for an anthology of tomboy tales and began developing it, we discussed strategies for the challenges of such a task, using her astrological mirror as guide. With her choices clarified through the session, she brought her own intuitive wisdom to those choices and manifested a beautiful book, step-by-step.

My hope is that this book has given you a foundational primer in understanding your birthchart so that you can explore your dreams as well as your strategies for manifesting them.

The planets in your chart mirror a sacred community within you, a careful system of checks and balances, cohesive and whole. Even if you live in isolation, this inner community sends a signal out into the world, inviting that world to meet you, symbolically.

The sacred is the emotional force that connects the parts to the whole. Consider the quality of that signal, your invitation, when it originates from intuitive flow and moves out into the world. To strengthen that quality, and to celebrate the completion of this book, let's do one more intuitive exercise.

Prepare: Set aside at least ten minutes to sit in a quiet room where you will not be disturbed. Sit comfortably and breathe deeply for a few moments.

Imagine: You are the Sun at the center of your life story, unifying every detail that has arisen through your studies in this book. You don't need to remember them all. Think of them as little lights that fly to the center and become a steady flame. Relax there and enjoy your certainty that you are here to celebrate your center, the precious chord only you can play.

Invite: After a few minutes, ask yourself the following series of questions. Invite the sea of intuition to come near you again, *to engage with you.* Ask each question, then wait for a *yes* or a *no.* If you get a *no,* just move on to the next question.

> *Can I imagine a flow of life that is infinite?*
> *Do I believe that this flow is benevolent?*
> *Do I believe that this flow moves through me?*
> *As I feel this flow, does it accept me, just as I am?*
> *Does stepping into this flow benefit not only me but all life?*
> *Will this flow support me to grow good things?*
> *Will this flow lead me to the community that is mine?*
> *Will we, together, grow more good things?*

Pass on all good things, through the flow.

Resources Guide

Birthcharts

Birthcharts are available by phone:
Astrolabe (800) 843–6682
ASI (212) 949–7211.
Prices are generally under ten dollars.

Free birthcharts are available from the Internet:
http://www.astro.com and http://www.astrology.com

Birthcharts are available by mail:
Send birth information and five dollars to Wild Rose Consulting,
P.O. Box 449, Rhinebeck, NY 12572.

See http://www.intuitiveastrology.com/tools.html for more listings, astrological reports, and contact information for every resource (authors, artists, books, or organizations) mentioned in this book.

Recommended Reading on Astrology

Chiron: Rainbow Bridge Between the Inner and Outer Planets by Barbara Hand Clow (Llewellyn Publications, 1987).

The Complete Idiot's Guide to Astrology by Madeline Gerwick-Brodeur and Lisa Lenard (Simon & Schuster Macmillan Co., 1997).

The Inner Sky—The Dynamic New Astrology for Everyone by Steven Forrest (ACS Publications, San Diego, Ca.).

Living in Time by Palden Jenkins. Available online at no charge: http://www.isleofavalon.co.uk/time.html

Making the Gods Work for You: The Astrological Language of the Psyche by Caroline W. Casey (Harmony Books, 1998).

The Mountain Astrologer. This bi-monthly magazine is rich with information for both beginners and experts: Visit www.Mountain Astrologer.com or call (800) 287-4828.

The Night Sky—The Science and Anthropology of the Stars and Planets by Richard Grossinger (Jeremy Tarcher Publishers, 1988).

Glossary

AIR Gemini, Libra, and Aquarius constitute the air signs. They are communicative and intelligent, reflecting the light of mind. Air is one of four fundamental substances—the other three being earth, fire, and water. *See* **elements**.

ARCHETYPE Human experiences or character qualities that run universally through every culture. For example, the archetypes of the Teacher, the Master, and Father Time emerge from the sign of Capricorn. Archetypes unify the personal and universal and therefore charge a story with meaning as a timeless myth, distinguishing it from a cultural trend that deteriorates to a cliché.

ARIES The first sign of the tropical zodiac, Aries begins around March 20 and ends around April 19. (The exact dates of each sign can vary slightly from year to year; always consult an ephemeris for accuracy.) A cardinal fire sign, Aries is proactive, an excellent leader, and ruled by Mars, the planetary instinct of action.

ASCENDANT The ascendant describes how you "dawn" on the rest of the world and offer a first impression. Also called the *rising sign*, the cusp of the first house is the ascendant and represents the eastern point of the horizon line; appearing at the far left of the chart.

ASPECTS Aspects are the angles between planets, which create the harmony (often called harmonics). Some are difficult, requiring concentration and therefore creativity. Others are more graceful and imply ease.

AQUARIUS The Sun transits this eleventh sign of the tropical zodiac from around January 21 to February 18. A fixed air sign, Aquarius is ruled by the planet Uranus and is affiliated with the eleventh house. Aquarius encourages evolution through truth and therefore liberation.

BIRTHCHART A picture of the sky at the moment of birth, reflecting precise planetary locations, zodiac signs, and house positions.

CANCER The Sun transits this fourth sign of the tropical zodiac from around June 21 to July 22. A cardinal water sign, Cancer's ruling planet is the Moon. An extremely sensitive sign, Cancer enjoys creating a safe place in which new life can grow. For that reason it is often considered to be the archetypal mother.

CAPRICORN The Sun transits this tenth sign of the tropical zodiac from about December 21 to January 20. A cardinal earth sign, Capricorn's ruling planet is Saturn. Capricorn fuels the teacher and explores self-mastery, structure, architecture, history, and tradition. Capricorn is often considered to be the archetypal father.

CARDINAL Cardinal is one of the three qualities, or modes, of the zodiac. The Cardinal signs are Aries, Cancer, Libra, and Capricorn. They initiate the beginning of a new season and therefore represent peak energies. *See* **qualities**.

CHIRON Discovered in 1977, Chiron is a planetoid, having characteristics of both a planet and an asteroid. Chiron symbolizes the healer capable of shifting out of wounding assumptions and partial insight. The centaur is associated with Chiron—the unity of horse and human, rather than the horseman (ego) owning the horse (the body) in an act of separation. Chiron can pinpoint where the connection needs to be made, can find the missing link, and can raise the vibration as it accesses wisdom and the sacred through synchronicity. Located between Saturn and Uranus, Chiron has an orbit of 50.7 years.

CONJUNCTION When there are 0 to 8 degrees of separation between two planets, they are in a conjunction, as they are on the exact same celestial longitude.

CONSTELLATIONS Often called the fixed stars because they do not move visibly in relation to one another, the constellations occupy the Milky Way galaxy (of which our solar system is a part) and have been given names based upon images they seem to project. Constellations helped ancient cultures track the Sun, Moon, and other planets against a background that never changed. The signs of the tropical zodiac and the constellations share the same names but have no relation to one another otherwise. *See* **signs**.

CUSP Cusp is used in two contexts in astrology—for houses and for signs. The entrance to each of the twelve houses is called the cusp. Likewise, as the zodiac signs change from one to the other in thirty-degree increments, the thirtieth degree becomes zero degrees of the next sign. When a person is born with his or her Sun at the twenty-ninth degree of a sign or zero degrees of a sign, the person is said to be on the cusp. In that case, the person possesses characteristics of both signs.

DESCENDANT The entrance (or cusp) to the seventh house, the descendant is on the western horizon line of the birthchart. The descendant symbolizes the way you seek your missing half; it describes the qualities of the "other," who is permanent partner. *See* **birthchart.**

DEGREES There are thirty degrees in each of the twelve signs. Each degree can be divided into sixty minutes. Each minute can be further divided into sixty seconds. A chart position that reads 5° ♐ 37'2" means that a planet is at 5 degrees of Sagittarius, 37 minutes, 20 seconds.

EARTH Taurus, Virgo, and Capricorn make up the earth signs. They are practical builders, interested in stabilizing and grounding the individuals who channel their energies. *See* **elements.**

ELEMENTS Ptolemy (second century A.D.) applied the theory of the four elements to astrology, assigning to each element three signs that together made up the triangle of that element (*see* **trine**). The four elements—fire, water, air, and earth—describe four necessary elements for life. *See* **fire, water, air,** and **earth.**

EQUINOX Equinoxes occur during the two moments of the year when the Sun crosses the equator and day and night are of equal length all over the earth, on or near March 21 (the spring, or vernal, equinox) and on or near September 22 (the fall, or autumnal, equinox).

EVOLUTIONARY ASTROLOGY Often called choice-centered astrology, evolutionary astrology recognizes that free will plays a major role in the outcome of any life, regardless of astrological influences.

FALL EQUINOX (the autumnal equinox) The fall equinox refers to one of two moments during the year when the Sun crosses the equator and day and night are of equal length all over the earth, on or near September 22. *See also* **spring equinox.**

FIRE Aries, Leo, and Sagittarius consitute the fire signs. They have the quality of action, spontaneity and quickness, energy, and enthusiasm. *See* **elements.**

FIXED One of three qualities, also called modes or quadruplicities, which provide a classification system of the signs. The other two qualities are mutable and cardinal. The fixed signs of the tropical zodiac are Taurus, Leo, Scorpio, and Aquarius. These signs are stabile and at times stubborn, capable of endurance, persistence, and magnetism. *See* **qualities**.

GEMINI The third sign of the tropical zodiac. The Sun transits Gemini from about May 21 to about June 21. Gemini is a mutable air sign and describes the dual nature of listening and communicating, translating what you see and hear.

GEOCENTRIC POSITION (from the Greek *gaia*, "Earth," and *kentron*, "center") The position of planets described from the viewpoint of Earth, rather than the Sun (which would be the *heliocentric position*).

HOUSES The twelve houses are the life arenas, the "where" of astrology. (See chapter 5.)

INTERCEPTION Sometimes one sign is enclosed in a house, bracketed by the previous sign on the cusp of the house, and the next sign on the cusp of the following house. Intercepted signs require somewhat more attention to develop. Imagine a store with no sign out front, or even at the back door, announcing: *the store is here.* Planets in intercepted signs behave similarly. They function well, but other people may be less likely to pick up on these parts of your character.

LEO The fifth sign of the tropical zodiac. The Sun transits Leo from about July 23 to about August 22. Leo is a fixed fire sign and celebrates life, art, creativity, animals, and nobility of heart (chapter 4).

LIBRA The seventh sign of the tropical zodiac. The Sun transits Libra from about September 22 to about October 23. A cardinal air sign, Libra explores balance, beauty, justice, and relationship (chapter 4).

MUTABLE Mutable signs of the tropical zodiac are: Gemini, Virgo, Sagittarius and Pisces. These signs are flexible and adaptable, capable of changing quickly, mutating. See **qualities**.

MIDHEAVEN The cusp of the tenth house is the midheaven and is at the uppermost point of the chart. Just as the Sun is directly overhead at noon, the midheaven correlates to the noon hour. Therefore, people born at noon have their Suns at this point in the chart.

MINUTES A minute comprises sixty seconds. There are sixty minutes in one degree and thirty degrees in a sign.

NATAL The natal position refers to where planets were when you were born.

NODES The south and north nodes of the Moon are calculated by looking at where the Moon's orbit around Earth intersects Earth's orbit around the Sun. The south and north nodes are always opposite signs (at a 180-degree distance from each other). See also **north node, south node**.

NORTH NODE The north node of the Moon symbolizes what you are growing toward that is a liberation from the past and the cutting edge of your future path. It is sometimes called "the head of the dragon." When ordering a chart, be sure to request the true north node rather than a mean node, as it is more accurate. See **nodes**.

OPPOSITION One hundred eighty degrees of separation between two planets represent an opposition. Oppositions broaden you, as you must import and export the qualities of the planet on either end of the seesaw toward the other.

ORB An orb is the distance involved between two planets or points, described in degrees and minutes. For example if the orb between transiting Saturn and transiting Jupiter is seven degrees, they are said to be in a conjunction with a seven-degree orb.

PISCES The twelfth sign of the zodiac. The Sun transits Pisces from about February 18 to about March 20. A mutable water sign, Pisces encourages letting go, unmasking in order to reach the soul itself (chapter 4).

PLANETS Mercury, Venus, Mars, Earth, Jupiter, Saturn, Uranus, Neptune, and Pluto. (See chapter 2.) Astrology also refers to the Sun and Moon as planets, though of course they're not. They're also known as the two "lights."

PREDICTIVE ASTROLOGY Predictive astrology presumes events are fated and therefore predictions can be made about what precisely will happen.

QUALITIES Characteristics associated with the signs of the tropical zodiac—cardinal, fixed, and mutable. There is a rhythm to our seasons, which peak, stabilize, then change. The cycle repeats itself four times over the course of a year. Cardinal is the peaking quality, fixed is the stabilized, and mutable is the changing (which precedes a new peak).

RISING SIGN See ascendant.

RULERSHIP Signs of the zodiac are said to be ruled by planets that carry an instinct that matches the agenda of the sign. (See chapter 4.)

SAGITTARIUS The ninth sign of the tropical zodiac. The Sun transits Sagittarius from about November 22 to about December 20. A fire and mutable sign, Sagittarius explores unity in an extroverted way. Sagittarius's nature is expansive as it explores the larger map that unifies us all.

SCORPIO The eighth sign of the tropical zodiac. Scorpio begins around October 23 and ends around November 22. A water and fixed sign, Scorpio excels at penetrating beyond the surface of a matter to discover the subtext. Like its ruling planet Pluto, Scorpio has profound depth, powerfully integrating the dark and the light.

SIGNS The tropical zodiac is the system of signs most widely used by contemporary astrologers. It is based on the seasons and actual Earth orbit rather than on the constellations. The earth follows a path called the ecliptic as it journeys around the Sun every year. The path of the ecliptic is divided by twelve, forming the zodiac signs.

The signs, or tropical zodiac, are shaped by the turning points in the earth's seasons called the solstices and equinoxes, which, in astrology, stand at the beginnings of the signs Aries and Libra (the equinoxes) and Capricorn and Cancer (the solstices). Earth's seasons are caused by the annual seasonal tilting of its north and south poles toward the Sun.

The zodiac signs are not the same as the starry constellations (called the sidereal zodiac). They possess the same names because much of the astrology we now know was written down two thousand years ago, in Latin, when the signs and constellations with those (Latin) names were synchronized. The signs and constellations kept their names as time went on, but they are quite different, and that difference is the source of most of the confusion around astrology today. The tropical and sidereal zodiacs move out of synch with each other by one degree every 72 years and by one sign every 2,160 years. Thus, the signs and constellations are now roughly one sign apart.

SOUTH NODE The south node of the Moon represents what you have inherited from your ancientness, your ancestors, or both. It is sometimes called "the tail of the dragon." *See* **nodes**.

SPRING EQUINOX (the vernal equinox). The spring equinox, also called the vernal point, is the beginning of the tropical zodiac (0 degrees of Aries), when the Sun enters the first day of spring in the northern hemisphere. It is one of the two points where the ecliptic intersects the celestial equator. *See also* **fall equinox**.

SQUARE Ninety degrees of separation between two planets.

SUMMER SOLSTICE Summer solstice occurs around June 20 of each year as the Sun enters the cardinal sign of Cancer. The Sun is farthest north from the celestial equator June 20, creating the longest day of the year in the Northern Hemisphere.

TAPROOT A term coined by the author to describe the imum coeli (i.c.) of the birthchart, which is the fourth-house cusp. It symbolizes the deepest point of nurturance.

TAURUS The second sign of the tropical zodiac. The Sun transits Taurus from about April 20 to about May 21. An earth and fixed sign, Taurus encourages patient productivity. Ruled by Venus, Taurus has a deep appreciation of the beauty and wealth of the earth.

TRANSIT A transiting planet is a planet in motion, in orbit around the Sun (as opposed to a *natal* planet, the one-time position of a planet in a birthchart). Astrologers use the term *transiting* to mean any planet in motion and consider it significant, as the transiting planet aspects natal planets in the birthchart, or aspects other transiting planets.

TRINE One hundred twenty degrees between planets creates a trine, which enjoys unimpeded flow. Two trapeze artists who have rehearsed and mastered the moment of connection and exchange offer an image of a trine. Trines are always in the same element (fire, earth, water, or air), which is something like speaking the same language; there is great compatibility.

TROPICAL ZODIAC SIGNS *See* **signs**.

VIRGO The Sun transits this sixth sign of the tropical zodiac from around August 23 to September 22. A mutable earth sign, Virgo's ruling planets are Mercury and Chiron. Virgo explores the finest of functions and wishes to be of use, always.

WATER Cancer, Scorpio, and Pisces make up the water signs. They are psychic, sensitive, and know through feeling. *See* **elements**.

WINTER SOLSTICE The winter solstice occurs around December 21, signifying entry into the sign of Capricorn and the longest night of the year. It is one of two moments during the year when the Sun is farthest from the celestial equator (in this case, south of the equator) in the Northern Hemisphere. The other solstice occurs June 20, the longest day of the year.

Acknowledgments

I would like to thank the people who trusted me with their life stories and patiently endured my questions, calls, and many correspondences to produce this book: Mary Bloom, Gail Bruce, Peter Kater, Christian McEwen, Bill Monning, Abraham Oort, Patrick Reynolds, Marty Rosenbluth, Marie Runyon, Gail Straub, Cindy Waszak, and Susun Weed.

I'd also like to thank Ananda Apfelbaum, Judith Berger, Quita Brodhead, Miriam Cooper, Mildred Council, Allan Gurganus, James Kullander, Jerry Leonard, John Mickelson, Kary Mullis, Stuart Quimby, Giovanni Sollima, John Stokes, John and Jim Thornton, Gioia Timpanelli, and Ellen Wingard for their contributions to the book.

Thanks are due to many others who agreed to be interviewed and whose life stories fueled the spirit of the book but are not included in the final text due to space constraints.

I'd like to thank everyone at Ballantine Books, as well as the readers who traveled with me through twenty-four months of writing: Elizabeth Beerman, Philippe Bodin, Janis Brock, Catherine Cloud, Walker Hammon, Gina Mandel, Mary Phelps, Lorraine Reid, Mary Ruth, and Maria Marmo Skinner.

Thanks for technical advice from astrologers Amanda Owen

and Palden Jenkins. Thank you to astrologer Steven Forrest for introducing me to astrology as the eloquent language it is. Thanks to Astrolabe for permission to use its charts and fonts.

Thanks to the many clients who supported Wild Rose Consulting between 1985 and 2003 and who, in essence, paid for my astrological research time as they hired me, one by one, to cross-reference the hows and whys of their deeper stories and cultivate symbolic voice.

Thank you to these people, who I heard say it first: Eleanor Johnson ("Become who you always intended to be"); Dr. Gene Faulcon ("Keep a Blue Sky Mind as you write that book and you'll be fine"); Patricia Sun ("The truth that is so big it is written on our inner parts"); Palden Jenkins ("You places yer bets and gets yer outcomes"); Joanna Macy ("The heart that breaks wide open can contain the entire world"); and Seth of the Jane Roberts series ("In spontaneity there is a discipline that utterly escapes you and an order beyond any that you know").

Thanks to the Virginia Center for Creative Arts, Ragdale Foundation, Mary Agnes Pierce Campbell, Molly Quarrier, and my agent, Caroline Carney, for being irreplaceable supports for my creative life between 1998 and 2003.

Thanks to my mother, Sarah West Campbell, whose ear for story trained mine; my sister, Kack, whose long laugh unites the worlds; and my father, Walker Aylett Campbell, Jr., whose spirit somehow seeded this book and supported it to the end.

Barbara Docktor

About the Author

ELIZABETH ROSE CAMPBELL graduated from the University of North Carolina at Chapel Hill with a degree in journalism in 1975. Though she initially worked as a writer for a literary magazine, *The Sun: A Magazine of Ideas*, Elizabeth was quickly drawn to the human potential movement and became a program coordinator for the Omega Institute for Holistic Studies in 1982. Based on earlier astrological studies with Steve Forrest, she began giving informal astrological consultations to Omega staff and faculty. Elizabeth became the first astrologer invited to offer consultations to participants at their Wellness Center. Her unique blend of intuition and the age-old science attracted a strong word-of-mouth following and led to the opening of her astrological firm Wild Rose Consulting in 1985. She has advised celebrities, CEOs, painters, diplomats, athletes, teachers, writers, housewives, activists, and more, helping thousands to unlock their creative potential.

Visit the author's Web site at intuitiveastrology.com.